WILLIAM GRANT STILL

AND THE FUSION OF CULTURES IN AMERICAN MUSIC

Second Edition
Revised for the 100th Anniversary
of William Grant Still
Judith Anne Still, Managing Editor
Celeste Anne Headlee & Lisa M. Headlee-Huffman,
Assistant Editors

Robert Bartlett Haas, Editor (First Edition)

Thematic Catalog of Works
Celeste Anne Headlee, Editor

Contributors
Verna Arvey
Donald Dorr
Howard Hanson
Louis & Annette Kaufman
Rev. Charles White McGehee
Jean Matthew
Miriam Matthews
Carolyn L. Quin
Anne Key Simpson
Paul Harold Slattery
William Grant Still
Grant D. Venerable, II

With Introductions By
Howard Hanson and Frederick Hall

The Master-Player Library
Flagstaff, AZ 1995

The Master-Player Library
P. O. Box 3044
Flagstaff, AZ 86003-3044
U.S.A.

Second Edition, Revised
Composer's 1995 Centennial Celebration Printing

ISBN 1-877873-05-5 (ppbk)
ISBN 1-877873-01-2 (hdbk)

WILLIAM GRANT STILL'S
CENTENNIAL YEAR: 1995

*"A triumph 100 years
in the making!"*

For the issuance of this 100th anniversary edition,
we lovingly and gratefully acknowledge
the untiring encouragement of
Joan Palevsky,
our friend and scholarly advisor.

DEDICATION

By William Grant Still
1975

For my father and mother:

WILLIAM GRANT STILL, SR.
1871-1895

CARRIE LENA FAMBRO STILL SHEPPERSON
1872-1927

"We all rise together,
Or not at all. "
-- William Grant Still

TABLE OF CONTENTS

William Grant Still's place in music history as the dean of America's Negro composers is assured. It is a proud distinction, but it is not enough. For Still is, above all, an American composer, interpreting the spiritual values of his own land through his own brand of personal genius.

He has been able to do this because he is not only a creator but a warm, human being with a deep affection and compassion for people. It is natural that his music should be forthright, direct, and without artifice. Whether in the poignant, emotion-filled slow movement of the *Afro-American Symphony*, or the hard-driving chants and dances from his great ballet, *Sahdji,* it is always people-music. His music does what, I believe, most if us feel music should do, it communicates.

I have known William Grant Still as a close friend and have admired him as a colleague for almost a half-century. I have had the privilege of conducting most of his major works, many of them for the first time. I recall the excitement of conducting the Scherzo from his *Afro-American Symphony* in Berlin with the Berlin Philharmonic Orchestra in the early thirties and the vociferous demand of that conservative audience that we repeat it--which we did! All of which tends to prove that music which has its roots deep in the human heart is the most personal, the most national, and also, the most universal.

Howard Hanson

i

One writer has said that music is one of God's choicest gifts to mankind, and that American Negro Music is one of the nation's richest gifts to the civilization of our time. For many decades the only voice that the American Negro had was his music. William Grant Still, Dean of American Composers, has made this voice to be heard and respected throughout the world. His genius is one of a rare and peculiar kind. Everything that he touches he adorns, whether his is a simple melodic line, or a massive structure of operatic or symphonic architecture.

Still writes in every medium of musical expression with a power that is undergirded by a spirit of great humility and honest dedication. It is such a spirit that causes him to rise above the technical and creative skills of musical composition, over which he has complete mastery, and give forth utterances that "lift a race from wood and stone to Christ." What he has done and is doing for American Negro Music is inestimable.

In writing for entertainment, he displays a dignity so necessary to the honest evaluation of music in this category; in religious writing he shows a depth of consecration; in larger forms, instrumental and vocal, he creates a new freshness without destroying the strength or beauty of the old.

American Negro Music owes Still an eternal debt of gratitude; the voice of the world is ready to exclaim, in clarion effulgence, "Hats off, gentlemen, a genius."

Frederick Hall

ii

AN APPRECIATION FOR NOW

When Miss Mary D. Hudgins, writing in the *Arkansas Gazette*, called William Grant Still "the Dean of American Negro Composers," she thought this might be overly dramatic.   Now we know her characterization was quite right.

No other Negro composer (in fact few other composers after the Romantic era) has set such a consistent musical path for himself and followed it. Those who preceded him had their work to do but did not achieve his breadth: Burleigh's accompaniments for Spirituals made them more effective; Dett wrote some choral works in larger scale utilizing folk sources; Clarence White dealt with folk materials, too, but not always--and when he moved away from them, he managed to produce only pleasant salon-pieces.

Therefore, William Grant Still knew he too had work to do. His first course was to take up the Negroid idiom and elevate it to symphonic form--not the folk themes but the idiom. Then he branched out to use in his music all the ethnic strains which combine in his own background. Thus he reached a distinctive personal idiom which has traced out the fusion of musical cultures in America.

In the earlier part of his life Still was not acquainted with the Negro idiom at all. He had to learn it as he learned other things. Someone is always trying to find out what Spirituals he used in the *Afro-American Symphony*. None. Only themes he has created himself. And, although at one time he did something with this Negro idiom, he used it as he used everything else, then left it behind, shutting out nothing new. Still went into popular music to learn what he could, but never let it control him. The European and American *avant-gardists* tried to claim him, but he is an independent thinker, not a musical faddist. He has always spoken for himself. He doesn't disclaim the right of others to do what they want, but for him the consistent path was devoted craftsmanship, form, melody, beautiful sounds--and the exploration of the racial strains which fuse in his own background.   Father: Scotch, Negro and Choctaw Indian. Mother: Negro, Indian, Spanish and Irish. On his own (on occasion) he has added the Creole idiom of French Louisiana and the Hebraic as he learned it through his commission undertaken for the Park Avenue Synagogue.

Then, of course, there is the part of Still that combines all of this--the "American" Still. And the part which floats above to touch only on universals, where the idiom is William Grant Still alone with his God and on his very personal inward adventure with music.

Because of Still's encompassing perspective and personal security, the "Black" music movement, the "soul music" tradition, hasn't diverted him. He sees it as limiting and essentially racist. The militants claim he is writing "Eur-American", not "Afro-American" music, but this is not an historically accurate statement. Hale Smith, Ulysses Kay, Arthur Cunningham, Olly Wilson, and others, Black composers, *avant-garde* to a greater or lesser degree, all recognize Still as a pioneer who has increased the stature of Negro music. And some, like Smith and Kay, have not hesitated to say openly that their way was made easier because of William Grant Still.

Although the music of William Grant Still is steadily played in this country, there is an enormous body of his work which hasn't yet been heard and which awaits a conductor who does for Still what Sir Thomas Beecham did for Delius. Other conductors may someday discover their reputations rest on what they didn't play rather than on what they played.

Meanwhile, this book is an invitation to all men of good will everywhere, to understand and appreciate the musical legacy of William Grant Still, "Dean of American Negro Composers" and citizen of the universe.

Robert Bartlett Haas

CELEBRATING WILLIAM GRANT STILL'S
CENTENNIAL YEAR

May 11, 1995 is the 100th anniversary of the birth of the "Dean Of Afro-American Composers," and much has changed since *William Grant Still And The Fusion Of Cultures In American Music* was first released. When the book was originally published, William Grant Still was nearing the end of his life and experiencing a disappointing lack of interest in his music. He was finding it difficult to get his works performed, published, or recorded. This book was written with the specific goal of introducing the American public to the composer and his music. Since his death on December 3, 1978, his works have been slowly coming back to the forefront. In fact, his compositions are now receiving well over 6,000 presentations a year, mainly due to the efforts of the composer's daughter, Judith Anne Still, who revived William Grant Still Music in 1983 and has been running it successfully ever since.

Orders for music have been received from all over the world, ranging from Bogota to the Azores to Tanzania. Many other exciting things have been happening: *In One Lifetime*, a biography of William Grant Still by his wife, Verna Arvey, was published in 1984 by the University of Arkansas Press; a major PBS documentary, narrated by Alex Haley, was aired, also in 1984; and, of his works, the *Sunday Symphony*, *Wailing Woman*, *Minette Fontaine*, *Path Of Glory*, *Those Who Wait*, and *Los Alnados de España* have been premiered. More than two dozen Still recordings have been issued, and two of them are on their way to being best-sellers. The world premiere of Still's last great opera, *Mota*, will occur in 1996 at NCA&T State University.

To reflect the changing landscape, this edition of the book has been completely revised and updated, and is now the most definitive resource about the life and works of William Grant Still available. It includes the first *complete* listing of his works, from his early days in New York to his last years in California. It is augmented by articles of old friends and new friends of the family. Hopefully, *William Grant Still And The Fusion Of Cultures In American Music* will help to put the life and achievements of Dr. Still into historical perspective and will aid in shaping a future appreciation of his work.

Celeste Anne Headlee

v

I

THE STORY OF
WILLIAM GRANT STILL

THE STORY OF WILLIAM GRANT STILL

William Grant Still was born in Woodville, Mississippi, May 11, 1895, the son of William Grant and Carrie Lena (Fambro) Still. Both parents were teachers with a college education. "His father taught music at the Agricultural and Mechanical College of Alabama and died when his son, William, was but 3 months old."[1] Having relatives in Arkansas, the young widow Still brought her tiny son to Little Rock and accepted a teaching job in that community, a position she was to hold until her death in 1927. During the next few years, the musical background of young William was to be enriched through the influence of his maternal grandmother. Verna Arvey comments on this exposure to the music of Still's people:

> While his grandmother worked about their house, she sang hymns and spirituals. "Little David, Play On Yo' Harp" was one of her favorites. Thus he grew up with the songs of his people, and grew to love the old hymns, which he plays today with the addition of such exquisite harmonies that they assume unsuspected beauty. A communal habit of the childhood days was that of serenading. It was pleasant to be awakened from slumber by such sweet sounds. He has always deplored the passing of that custom.[2]

The next enriching factor to enter the life of young William Still was his stepfather, Charles B. Shepperson. Hudgins describes this second marriage of Mrs. Still.

> When her son was yet a small boy she married Charles B. Shepperson, a railway postal clerk, possessed by a deep love of music, particularly opera. Fortunately his salary permitted him to buy a phonograph, and thus enrich the lives of members of his family with a constant stream of the best Red Seal records.[3]

The relationship between William and his stepfather was a positive and rewarding experience. Mr. Shepperson enhanced the boy's musical background by taking the family to the best musical shows, by singing

---

[1] Mary D. Hudgins, "An Outstanding Arkansas Composer, William Grant Still," *Arkansas Historical Quarterly*, Winter 1965, p. 309. In actual fact, Still was six months old.

[2] Verna Arvey, *Studies of Contemporary American Composers: William Grant Still* (New York: J. Fischer & Brothers, 1939), p. 9.

[3] Hudgins, *loc. cit.*

duets at home, and by discussing with his son the plays and concerts they had attended. The activities mentioned made a significant and highly beneficial contribution to the early life of the composer.

Verna Arvey describes the influence of the composer's mother:

His mother's determination, good sense, talent and high moral character influenced his life strongly. She was the sort of vital personality who could command attention merely by entering a room. Her students adored her, and learned more from her than from anyone else; so did her young son, for he too was in her classes at school. Here she was stricter with him than anyone else, for she did not want to be accused of favoritism.[4]

At the age of sixteen, William Grant Still was graduated from high school; he was the valedictorian and first honor bearer of his class.[5]

Experiences at Wilberforce University. By the age of sixteen, William Still's primary interest was music; he aspired to be a musician and a serious composer. His mother, although she understood his yearnings, felt that there was no future for a musician, especially a Negro musician; she openly opposed a career in music. Accordingly, the young man was enrolled at Wilberforce University to work toward a Bachelor of Science degree and a career in medicine. Though his heart was not in accord, William respected his mother's wishes; he maintained a slightly above average scholastic record.[6] While at Wilberforce, the aspiring young musician was able to continue his musical pursuits. His first step was to organize a string quartet in which he played the violin; this led to his first experiments with writing arrangements. He learned to play the oboe and the clarinet and became a member of the college band, which lead to further experiments in the field of orchestration. This important experience is described by Verna Arvey:

In his capacity as bandleader, he had to learn to play different instruments such as a piccolo and saxophone so that he could teach them to other players. The intimate knowledge of all instruments gained in this fashion has meant much to him in later years, and to his career as an orchestrator.[7]

Some of the teachers at Wilberforce encouraged his musical efforts

---

[4] Arvey, *op.cit.*, p. 10.
[5] For detailed coverage of Mr. Still's early life consult "My Arkansas Boyhood" by William Grant Still (see Bibliography) and Verna Arvey's booklet, *op. cit.*
[6] Arvey, *loc. cit.*
[7] *Ibid*, p. 11.

and it was here that the first recital of Still's compositions was given. This recital included songs and a few band numbers. The recognition accorded him as a result of this successful concert reinforced the young man's desire to devote his life to music. Hudgins comments on this concert and subsequent happenings:

> On one occasion the band offered an entire program of his compositions. But this wasn't enough to satisfy young Still. He quit college and went to work as a professional musician. After several years with commercial units, including that of W. C. Handy, he felt sufficiently financially secure to go back to the classroom.[8]

The unsettled years. Following the years at Wilberforce there came lean, unsettled years; these were years filled with an assortment of experiences that included an unsatisfactory marriage, playing the oboe and 'cello with various orchestras, starving, freezing, working at odd jobs for little money, and a hitch in the U. S. Navy in 1918. Returning home from the Navy, Mr. Still renewed his association with W. C. Handy who had by this time moved his firm to New York City. Verna Arvey comments on this:

> W. C. Handy, father of the Blues, offered him his first job in New York City as an arranger, and as a musician on the road, traveling through large and small Southern towns with Handy's Band.[9]

The field of popular music satisfied him for a while, but Still's desire to write meaningful, serious music remained with him.

Extended formal training. During the lean years Mr. Still had received a legacy from his father. This legacy was used for further formal training at Oberlin College in Ohio. William first studied theory and the violin. His teachers at Oberlin were so impressed by his talent and his sincerity that a special scholarship was established which would enable him to study composition with Dr. George W. Andrews.[10]

A few years later Still was playing with Eubie Blake's orchestra for the very popular show *Shuffle Along* which was on an extended road trip. Verna Arvey reports on the happenings in Boston:

> While *Shuffle Along* was playing in Boston, Still became aware that he

---

[8] Hudgins, *op. cit.*, pp. 310-311.

[9] Arvey, *op. cit.*, p. 12.

[10] *Ibid.*

could now afford to pay for musical instruction, and filed his application at the New England Conservatory of Music. When he returned for his answer, he was told that George W. Chadwick would teach him free of charge. He protested that he could afford to pay, but generous Chadwick refused to take his money.[11]

After four months of training with Mr. Chadwick, Still returned to New York to accept the position of recording director of the Black Swan Phonograph Company. Through a stroke of good fortune, he learned that Edgar Varèse was offering a scholarship in composition to a talented young Negro composer. Still applied for the scholarship, was accepted, and spent the next two years (1923-1925) in the study of composition with the French ultra-modernist.[12] Thus came about Still's introduction to Edgar Varèse and the Modern idiom. Still's attitude toward his instructors is reported by Verna Arvey:

> When I was groping blindly in my efforts to compose, it was Varese who pointed out to me the way to individual expression and who gave me the opportunity to hear my music played. I shall never forget his kindness, nor that of George W. Chadwick and the instructors at Oberlin.[13]

Hudgins reports on the influence of Varese: "At first Varese made a deep impression on Still, and so inspired, he produced deliberate dissonances. But he soon returned to the more melodic forms of composition."[14]

A career as an arranger. Mr. Still was much in demand as an orchestrator and arranger. Had he chosen to do so, he could have adopted this as his life's work. At various times he worked for Earl Carroll, Artie Shaw, Sophie Tucker, Don Voorhees, and Paul Whiteman.[15] One of the best selling records of all time, Artie Shaw's *Frenesi,* was arranged by Still. As an arranger and conductor he worked for both CBS and Mutual networks. He was given credit by many for the popularity of the "Deep River Hour," which featured Willard Robison on the NBC network. In later years, on the west coast, he sometimes worked as an arranger for moving pictures.

Famous "firsts" for William Grant Still. Hudgins submits the

---

[11] *Ibid.*, pp. 12-13.

[12] Madeleine Goss, *Modern Music Makers: Contemporary American Composers* (New York: E.P. Dutton and Co., 1952), p. 210.

[13] Arvey, *op. cit.*, p. 13.

[14] Hudgins, *op cit.*, p. 311.

[15] *Ibid.*, p. 309.

5

following impressive list:

Dr. Still's "firsts" are legion. In 1931, his *Afro-American Symphony* was heralded as the first major piece of music written by a Negro to be played before an American audience. Five years later he was the first Negro to conduct an important orchestra, when he picked up the baton to direct the Los Angeles Philharmonic in the Hollywood Bowl in an evening of his own compositions. In 1955, through conducting the New Orleans Philharmonic at Southern University, he became the first Negro to conduct a major all-white orchestra in the deep south.[16]

Special awards. In 1928 William Grant Still was the recipient of the second Harmon Award. This award is granted annually by the Harmon Foundation for the most significant contribution during the year to Negro culture in the United States.[17] Mr. Still was also the recipient of a 1934 Guggenheim Fellowship which was twice renewed for periods of six months each.[18] He was commissioned to prepare specific compositions for the League of Composers, Cleveland Orchestra, American Accordionists' Association, New York World's Fair (the theme music for the fair of 1939-40), and the United States Military Academy band at West Point.[19]

Honorary degrees. Nine institutions of higher learning have awarded honorary degrees to Mr. Still as listed:

Wilberforce University	Master of Music	1936
Howard University	Doctor of Music	1941
Oberlin College	Doctor of Music	1947
Bates College	Doctor of Letters	1954[20]
University of Arkansas	Doctor of Law	1971
Pepperdine University	Doctor of Fine Arts	1973
New England Conservatory of Music	Doctor of Music	1973
Peabody Institute of Music	Doctor of Music	1974
University of Southern California	Doctor of Laws	1975

---

[16] *Ibid.*, p. 312. Correction: Still conducted two of his own pieces at the Hollywood Bowl in 1936. Also, the Los Angeles Philharmonic was already a "major" orchestra.

[17] Arvey, *op. cit.*, p. 17.

[18] *Ibid.*, p. 47.

[19] Hudgins, *loc. cit.*

[20] John Tasker Howard, *Our American Music* (3rd ed.; New York: Thomas Y. Crowell Co., 1947), p. 466.

The citation which accompanied the Bates College honorary Doctor of Letters degree read:

> Some men have improved race relations through court instruments; others have written flaming books, or moving plays. William Grant Still's contribution has been as a dedicated man who strongly believes that if a Negro's creativeness is of first quality, he will be ranked among the leaders in inter-racial influence. In this endeavor he used the method he knew best--music.[21]

The latter years of Mr. Still. The composer moved to the west coast in 1934 and married Verna Arvey in 1939. This marriage produced two children, Duncan and Judith. Both of the children are college graduates, are married and are launching successful careers of their own. For a period of 14 years (1939 through 1953) William Grant Still continued to work at a man-killing pace. He would put in a work day of from twelve to sixteen hours. Although his commercial work would have been considered more than a full-time occupation, he refused to set aside his most important work, his composition. Eventually, the long hours took their toll and his eyes started to show the strain. In recent years, Mr. Still has accepted a less demanding schedule. However, he still finds time for new compositions plus the continued process of revising and editing older works.

Paul Harold Slattery

---

[21] Hudgins, *op. cit.*, p. 312.

II

THE STILLS ON STILL

MY ARKANSAS BOYHOOD

What with all the propaganda being disseminated nowadays, it may be hard for many people to believe that my boyhood was as it was--a typically American one, far removed from the ordinary concept of a little colored boy growing up in the South. I knew neither wealth nor poverty, for I lived in a comfortable middle-class home, with luxuries such as books, musical instruments and phonograph records in quantities found in few other homes of this sort.

All of this was the result of my having had the good fortune to have been born to intelligent, forward-looking parents, as well as to the fact that Little Rock, where I grew up, was considered by many of us to be an enlightened community in the South. This was true to such an extent that in later years, when the city's name was splashed over headlines the length and breadth of the world, those of us who had lived there were amazed and incredulous. We could not believe that of Little Rock, because it was contrary to so much that we had known and experienced!

It is true that there was segregation in Little Rock during my boyhood, but my family lived in a mixed neighborhood and our friends were both white and colored. So were my playmates. In many instances, their friendship lasted over into adulthood. Stanley and Clifford, for example, were two little white boys who played with me. Their father was a friend of my stepfather. Boy-like, we arranged an elaborate series of signals. We would have little flags or semaphores on our houses. These would be up when we were at home and down when were away. This was so that we would not inconvenience our busy selves by calling on the others when the others were absent. When I returned to Little Rock in 1927, after my mother's death, Stanley (who then lived in North Little Rock) came back to see me.

So, while I was aware of the fact that I was a Negro, and once in a while was reminded of it unpleasantly, I was generally conscious of it in a positive way, with a feeling of pride. At the same time, my association with people of both racial groups gave me the ability to conduct myself as a person among people instead of as an inferior among superiors. The fact that this could be done at all in the South represents, to me at least, an open-mindedness on the part of so many of the other residents of Little Rock.

It would be completely unrealistic if I were to suggest that there were no incidents involving racial prejudice in Little Rock, because there *were,* and they did make an impression on me. I even witnessed one such occurrence, which today would be termed "police brutality" on Center Street. It horrified me, but did not change my feeling that the good people in Little Rock overbalanced the bad.

In shaping my attitudes, my mother had a most important role to play. She was constantly "molding my character," trying to keep me from "following the path of least resistance," impressing on me the fact that I *must* amount to something in the world (it never occurred to her or to me that any other course was possible, even though she and I had different ideas as to the means of accomplishing it), correcting my grammar and my accent, and never sparing the rod lest her child be spoiled.

If my father had lived (he died only a few months after I was born in Mississippi) he would have been expected to discipline me. But since he could not, my mother courageously set out to be both mother and father. She gave me chores to do: cutting the kindling and the wood, bringing it and the coal indoors; starting the fires every morning; sweeping the house. When in high school I wanted long trousers like the other boys, I had to go to work to pay for them. My mother could easily have given them to me, but it was part of her discipline to let me earn them.

That work was in an Arkansas heading factory, making barrel heads. It was exhausting, but I stuck to it until I got the trousers. One of my subsequent jobs was in an ice cream factory; another in a soda fountain where I could get lots of fizzy water to drink. Still another was in an electro-therapy office, where I nearly drove the doctors crazy, experimenting with their machinery in moments free from duty.

Although my mother was strict and proud, she had a sense of humor and she loved me dearly. I remember her discipline today with gratitude and affection.

My parents were far removed from the sort of colored people we now term "stereotypes," and their circle of friends matched them in fine upbringing. They both were teachers in secondary schools in the South; both were musical; both were creative in many ways. Charles B. Shepperson, the stepfather who came into my life when I was about eleven, was a postal clerk and a sensitive soul who loved the arts. It was he who bought Victor Red Seal records for our phonograph and took me to see the various stage shows that came to Little Rock. He initiated and fostered in me a love for the stage which has never died.

We had come to Little Rock, my mother and I, after my father's passing. We lived with my Aunt Laura (then Mrs. Oliver) at 912 West 14th Street. Later, my mother bought that house as well as other property in Little Rock.

This was a city comparable to other American cities of that era, with many fine homes, theatres and a thriving business section. Even so, it was not far removed from typical rural life: women in sunbonnets, farms, cane fields. About five miles out of the city was "Sweet Home," where I remember watching horses go 'round and 'round, crushing the cane to make sorghum.

This was around the turn of the century, and yet it was near enough to real frontier days to have sights that today would be unheard-of, such as the two dead bandits who were put on display in Little Rock as a method of deterring would-be criminals. One was a big white bandit who had tried to rob a little white railway clerk of his diamond. In the struggle, the mail clerk's .45 caliber gun went off when it was thrust up against the robber's chest. The big hole it made was left visible by the embalmers, so that we could see it plainly when the body was displayed in the funeral parlor's window. The other was a Negro bandit, whose body was also intended for display. One of my friends and I were enterprising enough to go to the funeral parlor during the embalming process and get a first-hand look. We never forgot it.

During my early years, my maternal grandmother also lived with us, and it was she who sang Spirituals and Christian hymns all day long as she worked. "Little David, Play on Yo' Harp" was her favorite. Outside of that, my early musical experience had to do with songs such as are sung in school, hymns heard in church, and pieces like the "Angels' Serenade"-- later, when I began to study the violin at my mother's insistence. Negro music, as we know it today, was not yet an important part of my life.

As a matter of fact, it was so foreign to what I usually experienced that one summer, when I was still in elementary school, I accompanied my mother when she went to teach in Olmstead, a rural community. These simple people had only a few weeks of school each year, and very few other advantages. Their schoolroom was topped by loose branches instead of a roof, branches which hid scorpions and any other form of insect life which felt that it wanted to take a closer look at learning.

Because she was a visiting teacher, my mother was expected to attend their social functions, one of which was a basket meeting on Sunday, in this case, an affair both religious and social. As a prelude to the variety of food prepared by the housewives, they all gathered in the church, sang Spirituals and shouted. I thought they were very funny and laughed heartily. My mother scolded me and sent me out of the church. The thought that I was "hearing authentic Negro music at its source" never entered my irreverent little mind. All I was interested in was the food. I considered the rest of it a hilarious show put on just for my benefit.

11

Back in Little Rock, my schooling--and that of my friends--was on a more dignified plane. I went first to Capitol Hill School, which wasn't built on a hill at all, but was located in a section named Capitol Hill. It was a school of moderate size, with a main building of red brick, back of which was an old-fashioned frame structure. In the schoolyard were many rocks and trees around which were built rough benches for the children's use during lunch hours. I always ate lunch with my mother, for she taught at Capitol Hill School too, but in the High School Department. In the 8th grade I was sent to Union School for a year, since we lived in that district.

Eventually, Capitol Hill School proved to be too small to be both a high school and a grammar school, so a new high school named after Judge M. W. Gibbs was built. My mother, of course, taught there.

Whenever I was enrolled in one of my mother's classes, such as literature, I suffered through every moment, and won the sympathy of *all* my fellow-students. Mama was determined not to let anyone accuse her of partiality; she was also determined that I *had* to excel. The slightest error found me standing in the corner, being given demerits, or feeling the sting of Mama's ruler as it cracked smartly over my fingers. This happened once when I was reading Chaucer aloud to the class and, coming to the word "dung," I laughed a hearty schoolboy laugh. That ruler was put into action immediately. When I pouted, she said, "Stick that lip in, young man!"

Each time I was involved in a childish prank, I could count on a whipping when I got home, and I was often involved because most of my schoolmates were just as impish as I. Once, but only once, I played hookey to watch the trains pass, and to see the horses being shod in the blacksmith's shop.

Today I can find it in my heart to feel sorry for poor Professor Gillam, whom all the boys loved to torment. We poured water in his chair before he sat down; hit him in the back with little pieces of crayon when he turned around to write on the blackboard. If we had stayed in that school a few years longer we would have regretted our practical jokes, for Professor Gillam eventually became Principal and was in an ideal position to retaliate. He forgave us, though, and became a good friend in later years.

Many times I had to escort my mother to club meetings when Mr. Shepperson wasn't at home, for though the people in our group danced and played cards as people do socially today, they also managed to support events of a cultural nature and to promote Negro artists. Clarence Cameron White, the colored composer, played the violin at one such program; Mme. Azelia Hackley (who helped many Negro artists get scholarships) gave a vocal recital; Richard B. Harrison, later to win fame as The Lord in "The Green Pastures", read a Shakespearean play; others came to lecture.

There were projects in which my mother took the lead, and of course I was always expected to be on hand. At that time, my mother was disturbed over the fact that there was no public library in Little Rock open to colored people, despite the fact that several colored residents had extensive private libraries. So she organized performances of some Shakespearean plays, and with the proceeds bought books which formed the nucleus of the library in Capitol Hill School.

The violin was selected as my first instrument, possibly because I had been inspired to make toy violins when I was little. My first teacher was Mr. Price. Here again, it was my mother who insisted that I practice regularly. However, when I was elected Valedictorian of my class at Graduation time, my mother decreed that my speech should be memorized--which dismayed me to such an extent that she then had to beg me to stop practicing.

High school graduation found quite a few less members in my class than had entered school some years before. Many had left, one at a time, in order to take jobs and help support their families.

For me, college was the next step. And it was after I had enrolled in Wilberforce University that I decided that I *must* become a composer. My mother opposed this because, in her experience, the majority of Negro musicians of that day were disreputable and were not accepted into the best homes. She had wanted me to be a doctor. After many arguments she realized that my mind was made up: nothing but music would do.

After my college years, I was thrown out on my own, a fortunate occurrence as it later turned out, since I entered the field of American commercial music in order to make a living, and there learned many things which my later conservatory training could not and did not give me. It was in Columbus, Ohio that I first worked as a professional musician and it was there, while I was alone one day, that I decided to use whatever talent God had given me in His service. This was a promise which I made in my own way, and which--also in my own way--I have kept.

A few years and many experiences later, in New York, I began to feel that one way to serve God would be to serve my race. Then that in itself began to seem a narrow objective, so I decided that wanted to serve *all* people. All three objectives, I thought, could best be achieved by doing whatever I had been sent on earth to do--in this case, music--to the very best of my ability, so that the accomplishment would in itself count for something.

13

The middle twenties had to arrive before I had committed myself to Negro music, however. This followed periods of conservatory study at Oberlin; learning in the school of experience (i.e., I was self-taught in orchestration); and private study on scholarships, with George W. Chadwick who acquainted me with serious American music, and with Edgar Varèse, who introduced me to the ultramodern idiom. All the while, I had been making it a point to listen to Negro music everywhere I went. On Beale Street in Memphis, where I worked with W. C. Handy, as an onlooker in small Negro churches, and in popular bands.

Although my compositions in Mr. Varese's dissonant idiom brought me to the attention of metropolitan critics, I soon decided that this was not representative of my own musical individuality, and adopted a racial form of expression. Quite a few of my compositions with racial titles were the result of this decision. I made an effort to elevate the folk idiom into symphonic form, though rarely making use of actual folk themes. For the most part, I was developing my own themes in the style of the folk.

Following this period, there came a time when I leaned toward a more universal idiom which, in my opinion, partook of all the others and became an expression of my own individuality as a composer. In other words, instead of limiting myself to one particular style, I wrote as I chose, using whatever idiom seemed appropriate to the subject at hand.

This surely would have won my mother's approval. She lived long enough to know that my initial serious compositions had been successful, and her pride knew no bounds. Although she had opposed my career in music, she finally understood that music meant to me all the things she had been teaching me: a creative, serious accomplishment worthy of study and high devotion as well as sacrifice. She knew at last that the ideals which she had passed on to me during my boyhood in Arkansas had borne worthy fruit.

William Grant Still

WITH HIS ROOTS IN THE SOIL

More than a quarter of a century ago, North Americans were busily engaged in a search for a serious composer whose works would most accurately reflect their country in music. As the search continued, many arguments occurred. What sort of music would be the most representative? Anglo-Saxon music? For everyone knew that all the countries in the Western Hemisphere had been settled by people of many different racial and nationalistic groups.

It seemed to some of the searchers that perhaps a blend of *all* types of music would best represent the melting pot that is the U.S.A. But how and where to find it?

Amid the arguments and the seeking, a composer who combined many of those elements within himself was working quietly, having his compositions played auspiciously at home and abroad, and slowly but surely winning recognition as a genuine American composer. This was William Grant Still, whose mother was of Negro, Spanish, Indian and Irish ancestry, and in whose father's veins flowed Negro, Indian and Scotch bloods. The son of this union naturally came into life with a heritage that was truly American in all its aspects.

More than that: he balanced his academic musical training with a practical experience in the field of American popular music. This happened because he was faced with the problem of making a living for himself and his family, and the commercial field appeared to be the most remunerative. But he also resolved to learn from it and to make use of its valuable assets in his own creative work. Small wonder that, when audiences abroad hear his music for the first time, they are apt to recognize it immediately as being a product of the North American continent. Some European critics have described it as the "most indigenous" music to come out of North America.

In writing about Americans of Negro derivation it has been the custom to mention their lowly beginnings or to dwell upon lurid aspects of their lives. It is not possible to do this in writing of William Grant Still; for his parents both were schoolteachers, both musicians, far removed from the folk. He was born on a plantation near Woodville, Mississippi, on May 11, 1895. When his father died, six months later, his mother took him to live in Little Rock, Arkansas, where she taught school and where he gained his elementary education.

In those years, Little Rock was known as an enlightened community, as compared with other places in the South. The boy thus had an opportunity to grow up among friendly people--people who were interested in cultural matters and who listened to him appreciatively when he began to play the violin.

Later, in Wilberforce University, he found many more appreciative friends when he started to lead the band, to train players for it, and to make musical arrangements for the band to play. It was then that he made his first timid efforts toward musical creation.

At the close of his stay at the college, he and his mother had a disagreement, as a result of which he left home and began to earn his own living in a strange city. Upsetting as this was, it undoubtedly had a profound effect on the music he was to compose later. Had he stayed at home, accepting his mother's bounty, he might have gone to a Conservatory of Music and there might have learned no more than the academic way of composing music. As it was, he chose to work among professional musicians, thus automatically absorbing a different approach to music than a Conservatory might offer.

Meanwhile, he realized that he must not neglect academic knowledge. So he went to the Oberlin Conservatory of Music, at times working to get enough money to pay for his tuition and at other times being the recipient of scholarships.

Later, he was given scholarships with two men of widely divergent musical tastes: George W. Chadwick of the New England Conservatory, a pioneer North American composer, and Edgar Varèse, French ultramodernist. From each of them, he acquired valuable knowledge. Mr. Chadwick sharpened his own self-critical faculties, while Mr. Varèse led him into new and untried paths of musical expression.

Meanwhile, the commercial work he engaged in (playing in orchestras, orchestrating for Broadway shows, conducting radio orchestras, and so on) supplied an education of an entirely different sort. Because of it, he was entirely self-taught in the field of orchestration. His desire to experiment and to create new orchestral tone colors quickly marked him as an innovator and a pioneer. Many of the instrumental effects used today by other orchestrators actually stem from his early efforts.

He has considered it a blessing that he never learned to play the piano. Had he done so, he might have written first for piano and then orchestrated the piano scores. As it is, he now writes directly for orchestra, and his playing knowledge of orchestral instruments--the oboe, violin, and cello--has helped him to write playable and enjoyable parts for each instrument.

Before his study with Mr. Varèse was over, Mr. Still had tried--and found wanting--many of those unusual ultra-modern experiments in sound that are still incorrectly labeled "music." He had become more dissonant than some of the acknowledged disciples of dissonance, to such an extent that those disciples hailed his early efforts joyfully. After a few of those compositions had been played in New York, however, the young composer began to have grave doubts about the value of the idiom, and particularly about its suitability for him.

Second Period

He then discarded dissonance for the sake of dissonance in favor of a Negroid musical idiom. This seemed to him to be more in keeping with his own individuality at the time. Some of the works he wrote after making that decision are still played and have become, in fact, among the best known of all his compositions. They are the *Afro-American Symphony, Africa, From the Black Belt* and the ballet *Sahdji.*

It was not long before he began to feel about the racial idiom exactly as he had felt before about the discordant idiom: that it was too confined, and that it should not be an end in itself. So, in the early thirties, he embarked upon a creative period which has not yet ended, and during which he has utilized any or all idioms which have seemed to suit the purpose of the particular composition he was writing at the moment--but always with a singleness of purpose and with good taste, never in haphazard fashion.

He still feels that this method is the answer to many of the problems arising among contemporary composers. If followed, it would bring variety to the concert hall and rekindle the waning flames of audience interest in new music.

For audiences happen to be one of the major interests of this composer. Not in the sense that he believes in "writing down" to people, nor in writing what is generally termed "popular" music. Rather, with the knowledge that an audience is, after all, the ultimate consumer of a composer's product, and that it must find in that product something that it needs and wants, or else it simply turns away.

Mr. Still believes that it is possible to compose serious music that is truly serious and yet will still fill an audience's needs. He deplores the ego which causes some composers to expect people to hear and applaud their works, whether worthy or not, as much as he deplores the insistence of some schools of musical thought that their way is the *only* way.

Another type of composer with whom Mr. Still is in disagreement is the one who listens too carefully and too often to other composers' works, with the idea of finding out what is being done currently, in order to follow the general trend. Mr. Still, on the contrary, tries not to listen to the works of others beyond getting acquainted with them, for fear of being influenced, consciously or unconsciously. It is not a disinterest on his part. Rather, it is a reluctance to assimilate what does not belong to him.

Similarly, he finds it hard to accept arguments over atonalism vs. nationalism in music. To him, there is something useful in both idioms. He finds dissonance effective when dissonance is needed (but he does *not* agree that dissonance is the sole end of all music) and he also finds a great deal of beauty in various schools of nationalistic thought. Each nation, in his opinion, has something distinctive and valuable to contribute to the world's cultural aspects; each nation's composers, artists and writers should consider it a duty and a privilege to preserve their national heritage for posterity.

In the early thirties and afterward, when Mr. Still lived on the West Coast of the United States, away from New York and away from the compulsion to do as others in his field were doing, he wrote many compositions which demonstrated versatility in the variety and type of music composed. At the same time, he also succeeded in developing a decidedly personal idiom, one that is clearly recognizable as his in all his works. This is something that few composers in all history have achieved.

Closest to his heart are his operatic works, some of them as yet unproduced. Altogether, seven operas and four ballets have come from his pen, each one different from that which preceded it. Among the choral and orchestral works are many which express his own sharpened social consciousness, and his selection of subjects which speak of the brotherhood of man. Some of these are his *And They Lynched Him on a Tree* (for double mixed chorus, narrator, contralto soloist and orchestra); *In Memoriam: The Colored Soldiers Who Died for Democracy* (for orchestra); *Rhapsody* (for soprano and orchestra); *The Little Song That Wanted to be a Symphony* (for narrator and orchestra, a work for children) and so on.

Such compositions as *Poem for Orchestra* and *A Psalm for the Living* are the outgrowth of one of his earliest ambitions: to be able to serve God with his creative ability and to try in every way to make his music point to the Supreme Creator. It is for this reason that every one of his scores, from the smallest to the five symphonies, bears the inscription, "with humble thanks to God, the Source of inspiration."

His works for piano, such as the *Three Visions* and *Seven Traceries* are reminders of his early interest in the modern idiom, yet are distinctly personal in their harmonic treatment. For this composer is one who does not believe that harmonic resources have now been exhausted. With a little searching, a true creator can open up vastly new horizons without going to extremes in the matter of discords.

Another fertile field for investigation has been the folk music area. Not only has Mr. Still interested himself in setting North American Negro Spirituals but also in arranging some of the ingratiating melodies coming from other countries in the Western Hemisphere, such as his string quartet, "Danzas de Panama," his "Miniatures," "Vignettes" and "Folk Suites" nos. 1, 2, and 3, for various small chamber ensembles.

During his lifetime, this composer has received many honors: honorary degrees from nine universities in the United States, commissions from the League of Composers, Paul Whiteman, the Cleveland Orchestra and the Columbia Broadcasting System. In 1939 he was selected to write the Theme Music for the New York World's Fair; in 1944 he won the Cincinnati Symphony's prize for the best overture to celebrate its Jubilee season; and in 1961 he won the prize offered by the National Federation of Music Clubs and the Aeolian Music Foundation for a composition dedicated to the United Nations. This was *The Peaceful Land*, introduced by Fabien Sevitsky and the University of Miami Symphony Orchestra. On May 13, 1963, his new one-act opera, "Highway No. 1, U.S.A., " was given its premiere at the close of the University of Miami's fourth annual Festival of American Music. Mr. Still is today a respected member of ASCAP, and a life member of Local 47, A.F. of M.

The Simple Life

He prefers to live and work simply and quietly at his home in Southern California, where he fills each day with a varied assortment of chores. In the morning, music. In the afternoon, constructing useful objects for the home, tending the plants. His interest in young people has been stimulated by his own children, so that of recent years he has composed several works especially for youngsters. Occasionally, he leaves home to conduct his own works, or to speak. That he has a genuine message for listeners is apparent not only in his music, but in his clear-thinking approach to matters of musical moment.

Contemporary audiences have so often been told that they *must* accept what is known as "ultra-modern" music and art, that they breathe a sigh of relief when an authoritative voice tells them they do not indeed have to accept what they do not like. Nor do they have to force themselves to listen to people or music whose sole virtue is that of having been publicized out of all proportion to its true worth. Merit should be the only basis for advancement, and the day will come, Mr. Still firmly believes, when it will be.

His is a warm, sincere and friendly personality, even as is his music. So it is fitting that he has dedicated himself and his work to the task of bringing men together in brotherhood. Successful thus far, he hopes only that his work will have made a resounding contribution to that goal when the last note has been played and the last song sung.

Verna Arvey

MEMO FOR MUSICOLOGISTS

It was with considerable surprise that I read in a recent book (*Music in the 20th Century*, by William W. Austin, published by W. W. Norton and Company, 1966) by a Cornell University professor, the statement that "Gershwin's *Rhapsody* helped inspire William Grant Still to make use of Jazz and Negro folksong in his symphonies and operas." Surprise, because it seemed so unrealistic to assume that a Negro composer could have been motivated by a White composer who had made no secret of his own devotion to Negro musicians and their music.

For Gershwin's indebtedness has been well documented over the years, and it does no disservice to his memory to acknowledge it, since he himself did just that during his lifetime. One of these acknowledgments came when, on August 30, 1926, he autographed a copy of his *Rhapsody in Blue* to W. C. Handy. "For Mr. Handy," he wrote respectfully (for at that time the beloved Father of the Blues was almost twice his age) "whose early 'blue' songs are the forefathers of this work. With admiration and best wishes."

Those people who lived--as did Gershwin--through the exciting Twenties in New York can attest to the presence of both Gershwins (George *and* Ira) at nearly every place where Negroes were performing, or even enjoying themselves at parties. As the veteran songwriter Jack Yellen put it in an article in the Autumn 1966 issue of the *ASCAP News*: "Among the young White composers who frequented the hot spots of Harlem were the already-famous George Gershwin and a novice named Harold Arlen, and their visits undoubtedly influenced their subsequent compositions. It was soon thereafter that Gershwin wrote his classic *Rhapsody in Blue*."

Kay Swift (herself the composer of the New York musical hit, *Fine and Dandy*, and often a sort of musical secretary to Gershwin) in an interview given for the April 1948 issue of the West Coast magazine, *Opera and Concert*, told of going with George Gershwin at 3, 4, and 5 a.m., after their respective shows were over, to little places in Harlem where there were recordings by Negro artists that couldn't be gotten downtown. There Gershwin would listen intently, making mental notes and absorbing the style. She also told of the Macedonia Church in Charleston, where Gershwin used to go to hear the Gullah Negroes who formed the congregation sing (or shout) and to join in the singing and shouting. This is a fact also documented by Dubose Heyward in the chapter he contributed to Merle Armitage's book on Gershwin.

Also clarified by Miss Swift was the relationship between Gershwin and

Will Vodery, the colored orchestrator who was so well established in New York when Gershwin was just starting. Their relationship initiated the rumor that Gershwin had a colored ghost writer--which was not true. What *was* true was that Vodery befriended Gershwin in the early days and--recognizing talent--got him a job with a big publishing house. Gershwin never forgot the kindness and later asked Vodery to orchestrate for him.

In addition to haunting spots where Negroes of the primitive type could be heard, Gershwin also made it a point to be present at any concert or show in which a Negro was doing something new in music. If getting there was difficult, according to Miss Swift, he would make the effort somehow and arrive in time to hear it. Thus it was inevitable that Gershwin should attend some of the early concerts in New York in which William Grant Still's music was featured. One such was at Aeolian hall on January 24, 1926, given by the international Composers' Guild with the unforgettable Florence Mills as soloist and Eugene Goossens conducting.

This was an early effort to place the American Negro folk idiom in the context of concert music, the result of a dream of Still's dating back to 1916 when he, as a young man, went to Memphis to work with W. C. Handy. Before that, he had led a sheltered life with a family composed of teachers, civil service workers, and so on. Now the full impact of Negro folk music came to him as a welcome addition to his own formal musical training. On Gayoso Street, in Memphis, he heard for the first time unadorned Blues singing. However, he heard the Blues, not as something immoral and sexy, but as the yearnings of a lowly people, seeking a better life. Then and there he resolved that someday he would elevate the Blues so they could hold a dignified position in symphonic literature, and from then on he was making countless musical experiments toward that end--sometimes in the commercial arrangements he made for other people, sometimes in original compositions which he would write, revise and then discard as being not yet good enough. Most of these early efforts were lost before they were performed publicly, and more than a dozen years were to pass--years occupied with study, first-hand experience with orchestras, more observation of the Negro folk idiom, etc., before his dream finally crystallized in the *Afro-American Symphony*.

One Negro musical show which took New York by storm in the early Twenties was *Shuffle Along*. George and Ira Gershwin and most of the other Broadway celebrities attended it, some more than once. The Eubie Blake and Sissle orchestra was the one used in *Shuffle Along*; and, in it, William Grant Still played oboe. As the show went on and on, the players in the orchestra began to get tired of playing the same thing over and over again, so very often they would improvise. Most of them had a special little figure that they added, as they felt so inclined. Still's figure was melodic. Later, when he was composing the *Afro-American Symphony*, he used the small little figure, wedded to a distinctive rhythm which he had originated in the orchestration for a soft-shoe dance in the show, *Rain or Shine*. It became a brief accompanying figure in the Scherzo movement of the *Afro-American Symphony*, not at all related to the original theme in the Blues idiom on which Still had constructed the entire symphony.

Apparently, at the same time Still was composing the *Afro-American Symphony*, Gershwin was writing *Girl Crazy*, in which *I Got Rhythm* appeared, for that show and the *Afro-American Symphony* were brought to public attention about the same time (1930). Naturally, the people who had heard more about Gershwin than about Still assumed that the latter had copied the former in that tiny phrase.

Gershwin felt that he was not "borrowing" any musical material exactly. He was listening and absorbing, then transferring the Negro idiom to his own musical speech. Yet we might assume that sometimes there actually was unconscious borrowing, not only in the *I Got Rhythm* episode, but in others. How else can the similarity of the opening notes of his *Summertime* (in *Porgy and Bess*) to the opening notes of the *St. Louis Blues* be explained?

As composers, the difference between Gershwin and Still is obvious. Gershwin approached Negro music as an outsider, and his own concepts helped to make it a Gershwin-Negro fusion, lusty and stereotyped racially, more popular in flavor. Still's approach to Negro music was from within, refining and developing it with the craftsmanship and inspiration of a trained composer.

Gershwin and Stephen Foster and certain American songwriters were not alone among White musicians in their appreciation of the possibilities of Negro music. Years before, Antonin Dvorak had come to America and had written chamber works and the *Symphony No. 9* ("From the New World") which were so infused with the feeling of Negro music that ever since some people have been trying desperately to prove it was not so, while others have been trying just as hard to find precise Negro melodies which could have been the basis of his work. In the main, the latter has been an unsuccessful quest, for Dvorak (like Gershwin) discounted any conscious "borrowing." "All I tried to do," he claimed later, "was to write music in the spirit of national American melodies."

However, the presence and influence of Harry T. Burleigh, the colored composer, in Dvorak's life *cannot* be discounted. Mr. Burleigh for four years was a student at the National Conservatory in New York during Dvorák's tenure as its director. He repeatedly visited Dvorák at his home on East 17th Street in order to sing Plantation songs and Hoe-downs to him. There was no question in Burleigh's mind, the mind of Walter Damrosch and that of Camille W. Zeckwer of Philadelphia (another student in the Conservatory) as to what Dvořák had in mind. He repeatedly announced his intention to use Negro melodies in the "New World" symphony to all his students. He also, according to Mr. Burleigh, saturated himself with the spirit of the old tunes and then invented his own themes. Sometimes, when Burleigh was singing the Spirituals, Dvořák would stop him and ask if that was really the way the slaves sang.

One actual Spiritual, *Swing Low, Sweet Chariot,* did find its abbreviated way into the symphony in the second theme of the first movement, a sprightly theme in G Major, first given out by the flute. Mr. Burleigh remarked later that Dr. Dvořák had been especially fond of hearing him sing that Spiritual.

Wrote Dr. Dvořák himself in an article for *Harper's New Monthly* for February 1895: "A while ago I suggested that inspiration for truly national music might be derived from the Negro melodies or Indian chants. I was led to take this view partly by the fact that the so-called plantation songs are indeed the most striking and appealing melodies that have yet been found on this side of the water, but largely by the observation that this seems to be recognized, though often unconsciously, by most Americans."

Nor was the inclination toward Negro music confined to this famous example of the Czech composer and his Symphony. William Grant Still himself was startled when one of his later symphonies received its first performance on the East Coast, to read that it reminded one critic of Delius. At the time, Still was completely unfamiliar with Delius' music. But much later, in the book, *Delius as I Knew Him,* by Eric Fenby, published in London in 1937 by G. Ball and Sons, Ltd., he found this paragraph: "*Ol' Man River* and other such records gave him great pleasure, for the singing was reminiscent of the way his Negroes used to sing out in Florida, when as a young orange planter he had often sat up far into the night, smoking cigar after cigar, and listening to their subtle improvisations in harmony. 'They showed a truly wonderful sense of musicianship and harmonic resource in the imaginative way in which they treated a melody,' he added. 'And, hearing their singing in such romantic surroundings, it was then and there that I felt the urge to express myself in music.'"

Add to this the names of composers like Debussy, Ravel, Tansman, Milhaud, and even Brahms. The book, *The Unknown Brahms,* by Robert Haven Schauffler, published by Crown Publishers in New York in 1940, carries a statement by Arthur Abell, an American violinist who was one of

24

the few who could inspire the master to talk intimately of his own work. "A year before Brahms died," said Mr. Abell, "he asked me whether I played the banjo. 'No,' I replied. 'Why?' 'Because at Klengel's I met an American girl who played for me, on that curious instrument, a sort of music which she called Ragtime. Do you know this?'--and he hummed the well-known tune which goes to the words:

"If you refuse me,
  Honey, you lose me."

'Well,' the master continued with a faraway look in his eyes, 'I thought I would use, not the stupid tune, but the interesting rhythms of this Ragtime. But I do not know whether I shall ever get around to it. My ideas no longer flow as easily as they used to!'"

Brahms' inclination toward Negro music was no more than that--just an inclination which never found fulfillment. But the experiences of other White composers in the Negro idiom would lead one to accept the statement made by Carl Van Vechten in *Parties*: "Both critics and public are so unaware of the Negro origin of much American dancing that they continue to revive the hoary old lament that the Negro cannot create anything for himself, but must continue to imitate the White man's creations. A scrutiny of the facts must bring us to the inevitable conclusion that neither in music nor in dance is the Negro the imitator."

Verna Arvey

25

STILL OPERA POINTS THE WAY

Menotti's operas had followed a successful City Opera Company seven week Fall season, which came close to breaking even. Indeed, its Spring season, too, lost less money than expected because of the success of several new productions, one of them a landmark. Remember this was 1949, and the new work, *Troubled Island*, based on the historic uprising of slaves in Haiti, was the first production of any opera company of an opera by gifted Black men--Langston Hughes, the librettist and William Grant Still, the composer. It was splendidly produced and extraordinarily well-cast, taking into consideration that White singers were playing Black parts, which would probably be unheard of in the New York City opera today. Robert Weede was Dessalines, the leader of the revolt, and Marie Powers was Azelia, his wife. They were unforgettable. Azelia's lament when Dessalines was slain still haunts me. The critics were a bit pro and con in their opinion, but our audiences loved it all, including the "authentic voodoo dances" by Jean Leon Destine and his group and the ominous thudding of the distant drums.[1]

A new feather adorns the cap of the New York City Center Opera Company as a result of last season's successful presentation of William Grant Still's opera *Troubled Island*, based on a libretto by Langston Hughes. Warren Storey Smith, distinguished New England music critic, wrote in the Boston *Post* for April 17, 1949, that this opera is not only "better than the general run of American operas," but also "a better show than that current sensation of the Lyric Theater, Benjamin Britten's 'Peter Grimes.'"

Certainly *Troubled Island's* success with its audiences and the ovations it received at its two initial performances have made Laszlo Halasz and other City Center officials decide on a policy of furthering the cause of native American opera in forthcoming seasons. It is not the first time that a stage work by William Grant Still has paved the way for other American music. For instance, when the American Music Festivals were started in Rochester, they consisted solely of music. Then, in 1931, Dr. Hanson decided to test audience reaction to a new venture and, together with choreographer Thelma Biracree, he presented Mr. Still's impressive African choral ballet, *Sahdji*. So successful was it that, ever since, one entire Festival night in Rochester has been devoted to American ballets--

---

[1] Dalrymple, Jean. *From The Last Row*. New Jersey: James T. White & Co., 1975, p. 101.

others by Mr. Still (*La Guiablesse* and *Miss Sally's Party*) being presented incidentally.

The story of the opera *Troubled Island* begins back in its composer's boyhood. Early in his life, William Grant Still, fascinated by the music on the Red Seal records owned by his family, decided to write operas. He grew to love the theater so much that he used to sneak backstage in the theater in Little Rock, Arkansas, where he then lived. He even loved the smell of a theater: musty, old and, to him, tremendously appealing! When he was in college, he made trips to Dayton, Ohio, to hear operas performed, and one of his greatest thrills came when he heard "I Pagliacci" done in Cincinnati. All of these things were directed toward gaining knowledge that would help him later in composing operas, as were his readings of plays and study of dramatic technique, in addition to his actual contacts with the theater as a member of pit orchestras and as arranger for Broadway shows in his early professional years. Then, in the belief that in order to learn to walk one must first attempt walking, he began to write operas and, one by one, to tear them up. *Troubled Island* was the second opera he considered good enough to keep, and to try to get produced.

When both he and Langston Hughes were living in New York, Mr. Still asked the poet to supply him with a libretto for an opera. This did not come at once, but several years later, when the composer had moved to California, Mr. Hughes came to him and outlined the plot of an opera to be based on the life of Jean Jacques Dessalines, the Haitian liberator. (He had previously written a play called "Drums of Haiti" on this subject, and now proposed to convert it into an opera libretto.) Mr. Still was strongly gripped by the bare recital, and agreed to write the music.

In the company of friends, the two artists went to a cabin in the California hills, and there the composer indicated the position of arias, choruses and so on. Mr. Hughes then returned to New York. After some months had passed (during which Mr. Still was eager to get to the composition of the music, but had no libretto to work from) he again came to California, settled down in a hotel room, left orders that he was not to be disturbed until 11 a.m. every morning and there, in a prosaic setting quite different from the pastoral countryside in which the libretto had been first outlined, turned out his libretto quickly. After that he left California to go to Madrid, which was then in the throes of war.

From that point on, work on the opera belonged entirely to Mr. Still. The music was begun in 1937, when a portion of Act I was completed. An extension of an earlier Guggenheim Fellowship made it possible for the composer to resume work in 1938, during which year the actual creation of the music was completed. A portion of 1939 was devoted to completing the orchestration. The work was interrupted only by a commission to write the theme music for the Perisphere in the New York World's Fair, and it was on one of the composer's visits to New York for the purpose of finishing the Theme Music that Robert Weede first saw, and sang at sight, excerpts from the principal baritone arias in *Troubled Island.* Kay Swift, of the New York's World's Fair staff, had introduced the two men. The composer was thrilled by Mr. Weede's voice and decided then that he would like to have him create the leading role in the first performance of the opera. This he actually did, eleven years later, giving a powerful performance, and adding to his already-great stature as an artist.

During the creation of the music, Mr. Still spent many hours in research, only to discover that at that time there was almost no authentic Haitian musical material to be found in the United States. Accordingly, with the exception of two native themes (a Meringue, used in the last act; and a Voodoo theme, greatly altered, in Act I) which were supplied by John Houston Craige, author and former U. S. Marine officer stationed in Haiti during the occupation, all the themes and their various treatments were original with Mr. Still. He devised his own musical idiom to fit the subject and the locale.

Creatively, there were many things to be borne in mind while the music was coming into being. Some of them will bear noting here. Believing that opera is primarily entertainment, Mr. Still tried to write music that would arouse an emotional rather than a cerebral response in his hearers. He thought always of those who would listen to the finished product. "The latter statement," he once declared humorously, "does not include other composers!"

Harmonically, Mr. Still employed both consonance and poly-tonality with a view to maintaining interest and to achieve a sort of unity through the use of diversified styles. To each act, moreover, he gave a distinct musical flavor--but managed to retain an overall effect of one-ness.

Especially did he try to make the recitatives more interesting by constructing the vocal lines on the motives having a direct bearing on the action of the moment or upon the thoughts underlying the words. He tried to let the text be clearly understood by approximating musically the speed and rhythm of the natural speaking voice and to have the music conform to the inflection of each word as it would be spoken. He also departed from tradition by restricting the recitative--that is, limiting its freedom by making it more metrical.

He chose his themes thoughtfully. For example, there is a reiteration of notes in both the Azelia and intrigue themes, but they are quite different. One (Azelia) is working for Dessalines and the other (intrigue) works

28

against him. Today, a reference to the composer's original notes shows that all his themes underwent extensive alterations before emerging in their final forms.

Mr. Still divided his working hours into creative effort (sometimes he wrote only 1 1/2 measures a day, sometimes as many as 25 measures, and generally around 12) and into mechanical work--the latter consisting of making the final piano-vocal score on the music typewriter, and on master sheets so that it could be reproduced by a black and white blueprint method, and also of orchestrating, extracting chorus and orchestra parts, and so on. The opera was scored first by its composer for very large orchestra, later rescored for a smaller group. In all this, Mr. Still was a lone wolf--not even calling in an outside copyist. He also made his own miniature sets for each act, to gauge the action. These have since been destroyed.

The opera is set in the year 1791. The Haitian slaves led by Jean Jacques Dessalines, revolt against their masters. Azelia, Dessalines' slave wife, stands by his side in all his dangerous enterprises, but as soon as he becomes Emperor, he casts her off and lives in splendor with his lovely mulatto Empress, Claire. His downfall begins when he, through ignorance and shortsightedness (he wants freedom for the blacks only, while his aged African counsellor, Martel, dreams of a world where *all* men will be free) he is unable to prevent the secret plot against him by his Empress, and those members of his court who wish to supplant him. The sumptuous banquet of state, at which the slightly sardonic Minuet is danced by mulatto girls trained in Paris, is interrupted by a voodoo dance and voodoo drums from outside: an insistent throbbing that bodes ill for Dessalines. Dessalines rides to quell the uprising against him. In a distant marketplace by the sea he meets his traitorous generals and is on the point of winning a duel with one of them when another shoots him in the back. His body is left in the square to be robbed by ragamuffins and to be wept over by Azelia who, now crazed by her harrowing experiences, alone remains faithful to her husband, that broken Dessalines who once had all Haiti at his feet.

Because his librettist remained in Madrid, Mr. Still called upon his wife, a journalist, to supply alterations and additions to the libretto when they were needed. To her also fell the job of playing over for him, on the piano, the music that had been written every day, so that he could hear it objectively and study it with a view to improvements.

Once written, the question of a production came up, and for many years thereafter, it remained an unsolved question. It was twice submitted to the Metropolitan, whose rejection was "In advising you that, to our regret, we do not see our way clear to accept this work, we should like to point out that this conclusion should in no way be taken as implying any criticism as to the artistic merit of the work." After other rejections, Leopold Stokowski became interested in the work and wished to produce it. At City Center he joined with Mayor La Guardia, Newbold Morris, Mrs. Franklin D. Roosevelt and others to establish a fund for its production. Eventually the fund was discontinued, the money returned to donors all over the country. But Mr. Stokowski's enthusiasm had communicated itself to Laszlo Halasz, who finally decided to produce it and who, with Eugene Bryden to stage the work and with a large and cooperative staff, at last brought it to the public.

It must be added that some of the metropolitan critics hedged as to the opera's real worth, despite the ovation it received from the audience. Years before, Puccini had had the same experience with many of his operas, notably "La Bohème," of which critic Carlo Bersezio, writing in the *Stampa*, said "even as it leaves little impression on the minds of our audience, it will leave no great trace on the history of our lyric theatre." The New York critics did, however, term *Troubled Island* interesting, imaginative, atmospheric, and colorful. They also spoke of its "music of sensuous richness" and its "structure of considerable breadth" and "melodic curve" which commended it to the audience. Carl Van Vechten wrote to the composer afterward that "It is never a bore. Of how many other operas can this be said?"

Our State Department recorded *Troubled Island* for distribution abroad and presented recordings of its dress rehearsal on a Voice of America broadcast.

All in all, an important step forward for William Grant Still, and for Laszlo Halasz and the New York City Center!

Verna Arvey

MODERN COMPOSERS HAVE
LOST THEIR AUDIENCE: WHY?

Early in 1956, a visiting European composer declared in a Los Angeles interview that "The composer today is in a situation that has never before occurred in musical history. We have completely lost our audience."

Soon after that, the music critic on another Los Angeles paper wrote that "Today's American composers, at best, encounter patronage rather than championship. And their greatest enemy is blank indifference."

Surprising? Not to those of us who had long noted the trend and had been sounding warnings--warnings that had all too often gone unheeded. Year after year, we spoke of the fact that the public was making known its likes and dislikes by the simple expedient of attending, or not attending, concerts.

Laymen were expressing their disapproval by writing letters to editors; artists such as Geraldine Farrar were saying that they did not care for "that sort of calculated noise;" even music teachers (who had tried hard to understand and appreciate the so-called "new" trend) were frequently having to admit that they had failed to grasp it, or to make their pupils accept it.

One of them confessed, in print, that she much preferred jazz!

And yet, year after year, the propagandists of meaningless music continued to insist that their products--and only their products--HAD to be accepted whether anyone cared for them or not!

It is just such a ruthless spirit that must animate dictators, and it may be that same spirit that antagonizes audiences, when they are asked to listen to music that they have rejected time and time again.

It does no good to present this music as the "new" music, the "music of the future." It has been so labelled for more than forty years, and is less successful now than it was at its outset.

When it first came to public notice, this type of music was electrifying. What not everyone realised after that was that it succeeded because its dissonance had a reason for existing. For dissonance does have a value, and can be used with pleasing effects. Later, when some composers began to write dissonance just for the sake of dissonance, there arose a sameness in the greater part of the music that was composed. Rare was the composer who succeeded in developing an idiom recognizable as his own; most of the contemporary music fell into a seldom-varied pattern.

It became the fashion to write thus and so, and those who did not follow the fashion slavishly were disparaged. Their music was sneeringly termed "popular" and "reactionary." Many people claimed to be seeking a musical Messiah, who would shed light on the contemporary musical situation, but whenever anyone dared to speak out, he was met head-on by the pronouncements of the dominant group.

Mathematical formulae were often used by certain of the leading contemporary composers as a basis for musical creation. (How the inspired composers of the past would have scorned such mechanical devices!) The intellect usually took precedence over the emotions, and while intellect is necessary to musical creation, it should be no more than subordinate to inspiration. Even when some of the composers spoke or wrote of the importance of inspiration, it was not always apparent in their works.

The demand for inspired music has had its effect, however. Some composers, long steeped in the intellectual tradition, have felt the need to respond in some measure and have devised long statements to describe and justify their methods. Nonetheless, words can not disguise the basic qualities of music. Simply saying something is devout and spiritual does not make it so. Simply declaring that a succession of notes is a melody does not make it a melody, nor a few odd beats a recognizable rhythm.

These things the public senses intuitively because the public is, after all, the final judge of what will live and what will not live. It resents being forced, it refuses to be intimidated. Just as the spark of freedom burns in the hearts of people all over the world, whether they be free men or oppressed, so does the inner love of beauty, and so does the public appreciation of all that is worthy in the arts.

Because the public *is* beginning to express its wishes now, it will soon be able to hear contemporary music that it can and will enjoy, music that is contemporary because it is composed *now* and because it is the expression of a modern world that isn't necessarily ugly.

Such music is being written by composers who are waiting for a chance to make their products known to the world, free of sneers and false propaganda.

We venture to predict that among them there is indeed a composer whom God (not man) has appointed, probably unpatronised and unpublished by commercial interests.

As our musical horizons broaden, we may find this composer. But the horizons *must* broaden. We can not limit ourselves to what a small group insists has to be our "new" music and expect a miracle to come from it. It hasn't happened yet, and the chances are it never will!

As Ivor Brown wrote from London (in an article titled "And Why Not Write Of Daffodils?" in the *New York Times* Book Review for February 18, 1951):

The skies are still blue and the grass is still green where war does not befoul them, and there are vast tracts of decency and compassion in the great continent of human nature. Let the writer continue to say so, unfevered and unabashed . . . And we should not have to find our relief in the serenity and sagacity of the classics alone. The contemporary writer can offer confirmation of our values of truth, beauty and wit by being true to his own way of narrative, play-writing, reflection, or poetry. He will do so far more effectively by believing so than by tearing up his technique, by making anarchy in art his reaction to anarchy in world affairs, and by meeting chaotic facts with chaotic composition.

If we substitute the words "contemporary artist" or "contemporary composer" for Mr. Brown's "contemporary writer" we will have just as true a statement. And if we accept his suggestion, we will soon find that modern music will have regained its audience. But it undoubtedly won't be the same music we have been taught to call "modern" for, lo! these many years.

Verna Arvey and William Grant Still

NOTE:
"One other who must be mentioned in speaking of the development of arranging for radio is Willard Robison, who conducted a show called *Willard Robison and His Deep River Orchestra* on most of the networks some years ago. Mr. Robison's orchestra was a small one, but the effects he attained with it were so unusual and distinctive as to gather great attention not only from the public, but from other radio conductors and arrangers. I am told that the distinctive quality of his orchestra was first set by a then unknown symphonic composer, who is currently engaged in scoring films on the West Coast."
  -- From the chapter on "Arranging Music For Radio" by Tom Bennett in *Music In Radio Broadcasting*, edited by Gilbert Chase, McGraw-Hill Book Company, Inc., 1946, page 78.

As most people in New York knew, it was William Grant Still who was both arranger and conductor of the Deep River Hour.

The speech which follows is an early one William Grant Still delivered at the Eastman School during the time of his orchestral innovations for the Deep River Hour--which, by the way, have been widely imitated through the years, so that today they no longer sound unique.

Robert Bartlett Haas

ON ORCHESTRATION

Dr. Hanson's invitation to tell you of my theories of orchestral scoring led me to discover that I had given but little, if any, thought to formulating such theories. Of course, they existed. But I had been so busy trying to learn more of the art of orchestration that I was not conscious of them. Although what I am about to say may seem paradoxical, it is nevertheless true. The more I learn of orchestration, the more I know how *little* I know of it. Thus you may understand why the theories were so long neglected. Even now, after having given some thought to the matter, I hesitate to term the thoughts I'm about to express "theories." I'd rather call them experiences and resultant conclusions.

The major problem confronting one who sets out to score for an orchestra is that of presenting the music most effectively. For the solution of this problem, three factors are absolutely essential: clarity, balance, and a tasteful variety of tone color.

Clarity is the quality that tends to make every effect clear and each voice proportionately distinct. In order to acquire this quality it is necessary to refrain from over-orchestrating. I use the term "over-orchestrating" to define the excessive use of embellishments, ornate accompaniments, and masses of sound. Very often, one who scores is tempted to indulge in such excesses, perhaps due to his desire to avoid thinness. Thinness should indeed be avoided, but not by going to a worse extreme. Such excesses may also be due to the pleasing effect an elaborate, over-orchestrated score has on the eye. It is true that a score of this sort displays visual evidence of skill. But one must not for a moment lose sight of the fact that the message of music can be comprehended only by man's aural sense. A florid orchestration is generally thick and indefinite; masses of sound always confuse the ear.

If one employs a contrapuntal style it is best for the sake of clarity that he limit the number of counterpoints. The rather simple combination of a melody with one striking counter-theme against an appropriate background will often be more pleasing than the more complicated contrapuntal treatments. I don't mean to give the impression that I believe such a limitation as that just cited should be strictly observed. Use as many counter-themes as may be effectively employed, but dovetail them in such a manner that each will stand out distinctly. Remember always the limitations of the ear!

Another thought of great importance in orchestrating is that the melody should always stand out prominently. All else that accompanies it should be subordinated to it, and constant caution must be exercised lest the melody be obscured by having too much going against it.

I've mentioned balance separately despite the fact that balance and clarity are related. Clarity depends to a large extent on balance, for a poorly balanced orchestration can never be clear. My reason for considering balance separately is that it lies principally in the sphere of physics, being gained by cold calculation more than through the artistic sensibilities. Undoubtedly, this is the reason it is so difficult to attain! Such a conclusion appears logical when we remember that the artistic mind is prone to shun cold reasoning. Balance can be a great problem to the beginner, but as experience broadens the difficulty lessens. In other words, proficiency in balancing instruments can be acquired only through experience. The first step toward the necessary experience should be to become intimately acquainted with each instrument: its dynamic possibilities as well as its tone quality in each register. With this knowledge, it is easier to reckon the effect of any combination of instruments and to distribute the voices so as to avoid having any stand out with undue prominence.

The third factor, a tasteful variety of tone color, is purely artistic in nature, and the extent to which it may be attained depends solely upon the degree of taste possessed by the arranger. Pleasing contrasts that bear some relation, one to the other, define "tasteful variety." Probably the first question that arises when one prepares to score is, "What color is best at this or that point?" This question shouldn't be settled at random. Neither should a passage be assigned to some instrument merely because it can be played easily upon that instrument. The desired mood should be considered first, and that mood should govern not only the choice of instruments for that passage but also the choice of color for the passage that follows. You will remember that my definition of "tasteful variety" is "pleasing contrasts that are related." This relationship, then, should be one of mood.

At this point, I must stress the importance of choosing the instrument that will portray exactly the mood desired. I will also illustrate a variety of moods that may be obtained through assigning one passage, with unaltered accompaniment, to different instruments. Suppose we had a melody in the minor mode lying above a throbbing string accompaniment. Let us also suppose that the compass of this melody makes possible its performance upon flute, English horn, horn, or 'celli. (Remember that the string accompaniment remains unaltered.) If we assign this melody to the flute we gain the passive mood of tender longing. If we give it to the English horn the resultant mood is one of melancholy. If we give it to the horn it assumes an ominous aspect, especially if the horn be closed. If we have the 'celli sing it the effect is one of deep-seated grief that knows no repression. This illustration should serve to show the care that must be given to the choice of instruments.

I scarcely need to emphasize the necessity for contrasts, because we all know that man's craving for variety is inherent in his nature. Tone color *must* change, and it is important that the changes occur at the proper place. It is, of course, impossible to make any definite statement concerning the proper places for such changes as this depends upon the style of the music. There are times when it is advisable to give an entire passage to one instrument or choir. At other times it may be advisable to assign the first part of a passage to one instrument or group of instruments and the latter part to another instrument or group of instruments in a sort of antiphonal manner. And then the style of the music may call for more or less frequent changes. But no color should at any time be retained too long, for the most beautiful effect will become monotonous if it lasts overlong. It should be continued only long enough for the hearer to grasp its beauty. Then a new color should be introduced.

A nude style of orchestrating (i.e., one that leans not so far toward reinforcing) is best suited for attaining variety of color. I don't mean to imply that reinforcing should be avoided, for it has its uses and is particularly valuable when intensity is desired. But *restraint* in the practice of reinforcing will tend to heighten the brilliance of an orchestration, and to produce contrasts that are more striking.

Now, for some of the experiences and practices that have proved helpful to me personally. At the beginning it was, as may be expected, necessary for me to imitate. During my period of imitation, I learned two valuable lessons. The first: it's best for a beginner to choose as examples only the works of the best orchestrators. The second: one shouldn't confine his imitation to the works of a single composer or orchestrator for, in so doing, he is likely to fall under an influence which will be hard to cast off later.

During my period of imitation, which was rather long-lasting, I grasped every opportunity to become familiar with the various instruments, learned to play some of them, and jotted down in notebooks combinations of instruments which I thought might portray moods of all sorts. You would certainly be amused if you could see some of the impossible and far-fetched ideas my notebooks contained!

All the while I was drawing nearer the starting point--the period when one has gained enough experience for his own individuality to begin its development. That period finally came for me, heralded by an ungovernable impulse to combine instruments in many new ways. And then another lesson was learned: that some of the most striking effects are comparatively simple. Since then, I have learned many more lessons and have made many errors, but the more I progress the more convinced I am that a simple style of scoring achieves best results. In fact, the clearly defined effects which should be the aim of everyone who scores for orchestra can be obtained *only* through simplicity.

This has been particularly impressed upon me during the past year because of having been forced to adopt an altogether different style of orchestrating in order to get certain results with a limited group of players. This experience taught me how to employ individual instruments in a simple but effective manner, and caused me to believe that beauty can be expressed only in terms of simplicity.

Another valuable lesson I've learned is that one should never fail to give the members of the orchestra consideration. Indifferent playing will spoil the most beautiful passage, and unless the interest of the players is gained, their execution is apt to be more or less indifferent. Their interest can only be gained by giving them, whenever possible, something to play that they will enjoy playing.

Experience has also taught me that it doesn't always pay to accept statements regarding impossible orchestral combinations without first testing them and proving their value. Once I was told that a bass clarinet should never be combined with brass instruments. Later I discovered that there are ways in which they may be combined, and I was fortunate enough to gain a very pleasing effect by combining three muted trumpets, solo 'cello and bass clarinet.

On another occasion, it was said that celesta and chimes should never be combined. Yet a satisfactory pianissimo effect results from the combination of three clarinets playing sustained chords in the low register, chime struck lightly near where it is suspended with triangle beater, and celesta. A short interval between the chime struck and the entry of the celesta is necessary.

There is one overall truth that I've learned. Probably it's best that I approach it by way of another truth. Although material means must be employed in the production of music, music is actually spiritual in nature, and its message is addressed to the soul. I became aware of this truth long ago, together with the other truth that goes hand in hand with it. That is that the voice of inspiration is the voice of God, and the soul of man must first hear it before its message may be transferred to the intellect. Anyone who wishes to hear the voice of inspiration clearly must be in accord with its possessor, and he may attain this accord through prayer.

Before beginning to work on any musical problem, I pray. And my prayers are always answered.

William Grant Still

REVIEWING THE VOCAL WORKS WHICH PARALLELED
THE CREATION OF WILLIAM GRANT STILL'S SYMPHONIES

Of his two loves--opera and symphony--William Grant Still found opera the more compelling. Just as when he was a youngster studying the violin, he no sooner learned to read notes than he wanted to write them, so on hearing his very first operatic recordings in his early teens, he resolved that this was the sort of music he wanted to compose. Boylike, he went ahead and tried, even though at that time he had had so little preliminary training.

He entered contests for composers, carefully making his own manuscript paper when there was no printed paper available to him. Some of the contests were for original operas. When his entry for one of these was returned, the judges sent a note saying his work had merit, though they couldn't completely understand it. On another occasion, the judges returned his "opera", asking what on earth he had sent them! No wonder, for this ambitious effort was a scant twenty pages long.

The rejections did not dampen his enthusiasm, however. As the years went on and his formal training progressed, he wrote more and more operas and then discarded them when he decided they were not good enough. In perspective, he was able to act as his own judge and jury. Today he has even forgotten the names of many of those works. To him, they exist simply as exercises in composition which paved the way for works he *did* consider good enough.

Meanwhile, as he worked on opera after opera, he was also trying to make the connections which would make it possible for him to get public hearings in this medium, but he was constantly frustrated. Operahouses were few and were largely devoted to repeating those European operas which had won favor in the past. Many leading American composers found it impossible to break this barrier, and in Still's case there was the added difficulty of color.

At long last, he was forced to accept the fact that he could not break into the musical world that way, so he turned to writing symphonic music, and in this field he *was* successful. Nonetheless, his early desire persisted. He still wrote for voices (even including vocal sections in three of his four ballets) and he still wrote opera and more opera, until he finally was able to get some of it to public attention.

Notably, in the Twenties, his vocal works were *Levee Land*, which won great acclaim in 1926 when sung in concert at Aeolian Hall by the incomparable Florence Mills, with Eugene Goossens conducting the orchestra, a concert attended by such luminaries as Arturo Toscanini, George Gershwin, Carl Van Vechten and many others--also the large-scale African choral ballet *Sahdji*, dedicated to and first performed by Dr. Howard Hanson in Rochester. This, too, was received with enthusiasm by public and press.

The successes of these works helped to bolster his basic passion for the writing of operas, but here, he soon found that another of his problems was the same as that of many other contemporary composers: getting a suitable libretto. He did not want to adapt plays that had been successful as plays, as some other composers did in later years, and he did insist that whatever he attempted had to be good theatre. Accordingly, he approached several Negro poets, asking for libretti but, for one reason or another, they promised but did not deliver. Then he tried writing a libretto of his own, called *Chloe*, set in Mississippi in modern times. Its plot dealt only with the conflict in the lives of several individuals and had no sociological connotations whatever. However, this too, he discarded.

Finally, he was awarded a fellowship specifically to compose an opera. He came from New York to the West Coast to work with librettist Bruce Forsythe on a scenario supplied by Carlton Moss. From this effort emerged *Blue Steel*, in three acts, a story of a mysterious voodoo cult in an inaccessible swamp, at odds with a strong-minded, arrogant man from the outer world. Granted, the plot smacked of the particular sort of sensational elements that were joyfully accepted on the stage of the Twenties and Thirties--but it also contained popular elements that later led the composer to feel that the story itself would not make a lasting contribution. For that reason, he discarded the opera once it was completed, and later made use of sections of its music in other works.

This was a wise decision, for the music itself was unique: lush, exotic and appealing in melodies, harmonies and rhythms. It was composed at a time when its creator was fresh from the confines of commercial work, with many plans made and many preliminary sketches in his notebook. He was, in short, bursting with ideas and eager to get them down on paper. Inspiration flowed, morning, noon and night, and for as long as the work continued, *Blue Steel* was a pet project. In fact, one night immediately after it was completed, several singers (friends) came to his home to sight-read the score. As their voices rose and fell in the to-them unfamiliar music, its inspired quality became evident to all, even the neighbors who sat on their front porches to listen and applaud. The composer knew at that moment that he had not been wrong all along. This, indeed, was his field, and in this field he meant to persist, despite opposition.

Other compositions, mostly instrumental, occupied Dr. Still in the mid-Thirties, at the same time that there came a new operatic ray of hope. Langston Hughes, who had been asked for a libretto long before, suddenly found he had an unused libretto on his hands, after all. He had written the text of *Troubled Island* for the composer Clarence Cameron White, who had then rejected it. At that point, Mr. Hughes' economical soul recalled the earlier William Grant Still request, so he brought his Haitian libretto to the West Coast. Still was only too happy to have a text based on the dramatic story of Emperor Jean Jacques Dessalines of Haiti. He and the poet immediately set to work to make it conform to Still's concept of the needs of the music: the proper places for arias, for the ballet, and so on. It developed into an opera of three acts, four scenes.

While Mr. Hughes was adapting his libretto to the new requirements, Dr. Still was creating his leit-motifs which would, of course, re-appear in various guises throughout the opera to clarify and emphasize the action. There was a harsh motif designating the ugly scars left on Dessalines' back by the whips of slave-drivers; a warm theme to express the slave-wife Azelia's love for Dessalines; glittering sensuous music to depict the illicit affair of Empress Claire with the Emperor's secretary; a motif for intrigue, another for the Voodoo rites, and still another for Martel, who was described as being a symbol of world peace.

Since *Troubled Island* is on a Haitian subject, one might conclude that the music would contain authentic Haitian material--and indeed, there really is a snatch of one authentic folk tune in the final act. But, generally speaking, such an obvious device failed to capture Still's fancy, and in this opera, as in his earlier African ballet *Sahdji* and his Martinique ballet *La Guiablesse*, he tried to steep himself in the subject and then create his own musical material in that style and mood. As it turned out, it was a sound decision in more ways than one, because at that time, very little authentic African, Haitian or other West Indian material was available for study in this country. The field was then new and largely unexplored by North Americans.

Once completed, *Troubled Island* became, as the previous operas had become, a source of anxiety because again, despite the composer's undeniable symphonic successes, a performance seemed out of the question. Apparently, there were some who felt that this was an exalted field that should not be opened to him. But, while making efforts toward a production, Dr. Still was not content to be idle, and one important factor emerged from the creation of *Troubled Island* that was to have a significant effect on many of his future vocal works.

This happened when the librettist, having finished his libretto, went off to Spain. He was, for that reason, not available when the composer needed to make changes in the text--even, in one important instance, in the drama itself. Somehow, Dr. Still had to improvise. He wrote the necessary music and then asked me to set words to it. Neither one of us was sure that I could do it, for I considered myself then, as now, a journalist rather than a poet. However, I tried to fill the need, and the result made Act II Scene I one of the highlights of the opera. After that, we decided that I could be the librettist for succeeding operas since I had one attribute that many poets lack: a knowledge of music.

So, while awaiting a production of *Troubled Island*, William Grant Still wrote two operas, both on my libretti. One, *A Southern Interlude*, was short and set in our contemporary South. It, too, was later discarded and many of its elements were incorporated into another work. The other, *A Bayou Legend*, in three acts, has not been discarded. Instead, it was once revised and now also awaits production. Its plot was developed from an authentic legend of the Biloxi region, concerning a man who fell in love with a spirit. Although the characters in the opera are of French descent, the musical allusion to this is of a subtle, rather than a direct, nature. Nor is the music concerned with characteristics peculiar to the geographical area. Instead, its purpose is to describe and color the story. The plot has to do with simple people, caught up in a drama that ends tragically.

During the waiting years, Dr. Still also composed *And They Lunched Him On A Tree* for white chorus, Negro chorus, contralto soloist, narrator and orchestra, on a text by Katherine Garrison Chapin, a stirring work which pointed to ultimate brotherhood in America. A year later, also on a text by Katherine Garrison Chapin, he wrote *Plain-Chant For America* for baritone soloist and orchestra for the Centennial celebration of the New York Philharmonic Orchestra. This was a patriotic composition which, when converted into a choral work almost thirty years later, proved to be just as timely and moving as when it was first performed.

The mid-Forties were a time of many new works, many auspicious performances and one prize of national import (that given by the

Cincinnati Symphony Orchestra for the best Overture to celebrate its Jubilee season). Yet there was also time for more vocal works. One of these was the choral composition *Those Who Wait*, a dialogue between soloists and chorus clarifying the racial problems of the day. Another, *Wailing Woman*, for orchestra, soprano and chorus, had a definite Semitic quality and emphasized a bond between members of different minority groups. These two were based on my texts. Still another, also Semitic in flavor, was *The Voice Of The Lord*, or *Mizmor Ledovid*, for tenor, chorus and organ. This was a setting of the 29th Psalm, requested and performed by the Park Avenue Synagogue in New York City. Then there was *From A Lost Continent*, a unique suite for chorus in four sections, using syllables instead of words to impart an archaic flavor. It was inspired by accounts of Mu, the continent that once existed in the Pacific area. And, of course, there were the charming *Songs Of Separation*, a cycle of art songs for solo voice and piano, set to poems by five Negro poets: Arna Bontemps, Philippe-Thoby Marcelin of Haiti, Paul Laurence Dunbar, Countee Cullen and Langston Hughes--each one having to do with lovers who have separated. From the tropical languor of the Marcelin *Poéme*, set in its original French, to the pert sarcasm of Dunbar's *Parted* and the tenderness of Cullen's *If You Should Go*, this group of songs is unusual in that the composer carefully selected the poems from collections by the five poets and then placed them in sequence so that together they formed an effective unit.

This creative activity accompanied, but did not supplant, constant efforts to get a production of *Troubled Island*. Finally, Leopold Stokowski became interested in it and offered to present it at the New York City Center of Music and Drama with which he had just become affiliated. He was as good as his word, and quickly started a campaign to arouse public interest and to give it the sort of presentation he felt it should have. Years were to pass, and Mr. Stokowski eventually resigned from the City Center. But the production itself, after many maneuvers and counter-maneuvers, did finally get underway. To its opening came a blue-ribbon audience, which at first sat quietly, waiting to be convinced--and then applauded warmly and continuously as the opera progressed. The composer was supremely happy; the stage director (Eugene Bryden) left New York for his home in California feeling that he had a hit on his hands, and the director (Laszlo Halasz) lost no time in asking for another opera.

The next morning the reviews appeared. It was obvious that the critics had banded together to overrule the audience's verdict. While they were in no sense unfavorable, they still (as Carl Van Vechten later wrote)* sat on the fence so that they could jump either way when they saw how things were going later. So *Troubled Island* despite its enthusiastic acceptance, was *not* permitted to open the door for more operatic performances.

Nonetheless, William Grant Still went home to write not one, but two, new operas. These were *Costaso* (in three acts, four scenes) and *Mota* (also in three acts, four scenes) both based on my libretti. Since Mr. Halasz also did not stay at the New York City Center, these two were unperformed.

In these new operas, the composer discovered, as he had discovered in working on *A Bayou Legend* and *A Southern Interlude*, that he worked better when he could have a firm hand in the pre-compositional stages of the work. For instance, once the locale of the opera and the germ of a plot is established, it is he who does all the research, both musical and otherwise, and this is his exclusively, in every sense. As he gathers his notes, the complexities of the plot begin to unfold, much of it determined by what the characters themselves would do under the same circumstances in life. Then he decides where the arias will come, and then I step in to write the dialogue and to indicate the opening line of each aria. After that, he writes the music and my words are set to it, thus giving him freedom to write as he wishes, and not limiting his musical expression to a rigid series of lines.

Costaso's setting was one we both loved: Spanish-Colonial America, with its romance, its colorful costumes and its all-pervading religious aura. The *Ave Maria* at the end of the second act, is in my opinion, one of the most devout and uplifting pieces of music ever written. The plot of *Costaso* was evolved by us from a germ of an idea in a legend of Colonial New Mexico, and as the characters developed, they told their own story. The Spanish atmosphere throughout is so authentic that the music often gives the feeling of the folk, though there is no actual folk material employed.

Quite different was *Mota*, the succeeding opera. This too was an original story, set in ancestral Africa, with the conflict coming between individuals who represented stubborn tradition on the one hand, and

---

* "The critics hedge a little at first, rather than have to eat crow later. The principal thing to notice is the way the audience ate it up. It is never a bore. Of how many other operas can this be said?"

45

progress on the other. In the end, the cunning exponents of tradition, led by the witch doctor, eliminate Mota, symbol of a better life, by means of what today would be termed a "rigged" trial. He is branded a young upstart and is asked, "If the world is left to such as you, what will happen to the rest of us?" In the end, the traditionalists lose too, for the sword of their vengeance cuts down more than the crusader. It also takes the life of the witch doctor's beloved daughter and, too late, he realizes that his own lust for power has turned back on him.

As for all of his operas, Dr. Still constructed miniature sets for *Mota*, so that he could best visualize the action while composing.

A three-act opera called *The Pillar*, on an American Indian theme, and several art songs (notably *Song For The Valiant*, *Song For The Lonely*, *Grief* on a poem by LeRoy V. Brant, and *Citadel* on a poem by Virginia Brasier) followed *Mota* and *Costaso*, in addition to *A Psalm For The Living*, for chorus. The latter was, again, a setting of my text (this one pre-written), having to do with the premise that our Father is not only in Heaven, but is living among us, guiding our footsteps and inspiring our earthly achievements. This reverent work has been performed repeatedly with great success. Its lovely opening cadence gives a hint of the melodic line to come. The *Rhapsody*, a suite in four movements for soprano and orchestra, followed closely. It details the growth of awareness in a girl who grows from carefree childhood into maturity and into a realization of her function, as a mother, in the world of brotherhood to come. It was a commissioned work. Somewhat different in concept was the succeeding four-part song cycle titled *From The Hearts Of Women*. In this, a child sang to her doll; a woman reached middle age; a girl gloried in being a coquette; and a woman lamented the death of her son. Both of these suites were set to my texts--or, to be completely accurate, my words were set to his music.

Then, in 1958, we completed another opera set in a locale which fascinated us: New Orleans. The principal character, Minette Fontaine, was a prima donna in the old New Orleans Opera Company, around mid-Nineteenth century. Her name became the name of our opera, though of course, we *created* Minette Fontaine. As far as we know, there was no actual singer of that name in the New Orleans of that period. We also invented the plot of the opera. Naturally, a colorful spot like New Orleans gave plenty of opportunity for interesting action and interesting settings: The French Market, the home of a social leader, a plantation near the city, and even a séance room in the home of a Voodoo priestess. Though there

46

is a slave chorus, the drama itself is played out between the other characters, Minette (strong-willed and selfish) gaining what she wants, but in effect, losing in the end, in a poignant and bitter finale.

It was Dr. Fabien Sevitzky, then of the University of Miami, who (after he had given a first performance to Dr. Still's prize-winning composition *The Peaceful Land*) asked for a new short opera which he could introduce at his Fourth Annual Festival of American Music in Miami. It was a new experience for us: to have an opera requested and a performance secure before the work actually began! So we set to work and very soon *Highway I, U.S.A.*, in two acts, was completed. It was set in contemporary America, in the living quarters adjoining a filling station near the busy highway, and the theme was one of our favorites: a man and his wife who love each other, despite the interlopers who try to come between them. This, too, turned out to be a simple story about simple people, avoiding the Freudian pitfalls that beset so many of our modern dramas. The music is thoroughly American in flavor, direct and to the point. It was received with warm enthusiasm at the Miami premiere, and at subsequent performances in other parts of the country.

The variety of locales for the Still operas (the Bayou country, Haiti, Africa, Spanish Colonial America, New Orleans and American Indian land) automatically gave each one an individual musical flavor and style, though over all, the composer's own distinctive personal idiom prevailed. As the late Wladimir Bakaleinikoff once remarked, after hearing several Still compositions of different types, "Already I begin to hear him!" indicating that the composer had succeeded, as few other contemporaries had, in making his own individuality apparent in his music.

Only one major vocal work followed *Highway I, U.S.A.* This was the suite for bass-baritone soloist and orchestra called *Path Of Glory*, set to my text concerning the fall of the Aztec Empire after its leaders had turned away from God.

And what of the future? There is yet another opera in the process of conception. Dr. Still wants it to be a large, climactic work. What ultimate form it will take, and what its theme will be, even he is not now sure. But it *is* taking shape.

Verna Arvey

47

WHAT A COMPOSER IS

Today, there seem to be varying ideas as to just what a composer is. Some people think that anyone who writes a song is a composer; others think that anyone who arranges a Spiritual is a composer. My own view is that a real composer should be one whose studies in many fields, added to his natural talent, enable him to try, at last, to walk in the paths of those master musicians who wrote in larger forms: symphonies, operas, chamber music, and so on. Of course, writing songs and arranging Spirituals do call for many of the abilities of a real composer, and many composers do make excursions into those realms, with great success. In other words, a composer can write songs or make arrangements, but not every arranger or songwriter can be a composer.

It is for this reason that I would like to consider first the qualities a composer must have, then to tell you of my own approach to a new composition and of the steps taken in building the composition from its inception, illustrating this with excerpts from my *Afro-American Symphony*.

What are the qualities which must be inherent in the person who aspires to write music? First, and most important, is the ability to induce the flow of inspiration, that indefinable element which transforms lifeless intervals into throbbing, vital and heartwarming music. Brahms looked on it as a spiritual communion. Wagner also realized its importance. Experience has taught me that the ability to induce the flow of inspiration is of the greatest importance, for without it one's efforts often have little value. There is a spontaneous kind of inspiration that comes of its own accord and, more often, an effort must be made to contact it and that can be very painful. Many composers keep notebooks of themes that have come to them spontaneously and refer to them when they need thematic material for a new work. This is a helpful practice.

Very often I have had the experience (as I understand many writers and other composers have had) of getting a theme after I've gone to bed at night. At such times it is always difficult to retain it long enough to put it on paper, so I developed the habit of visualizing it and thus helping to keep it in my memory until I could get to my notebook, usually in the following morning, and recording it for future use. It has sometimes been my feeling that I have heard such themes with the inner ear, a sort of psychic process.

48

One of the results of being able to tap the fount of inspiration is a melodic gift, and I can not emphasize too much the importance of this gift, which seems to be so woefully lacking in so many contemporary composers. The so-called "creators" who lack the gift of melody always direct their messages to the intellect rather than to the heart, or soul--and this explains the dry, boring music they turn out.

Probably next in importance is a well-developed sense of proportion. Whether the listener is aware of it or not, the form (or architecture) of a composition can do a great deal to help or hinder his enjoyment. Poor form may produce a fragmentary, lopsided or insufficiently balanced piece of music, whereas hearing a well-formed musical work gives as much satisfaction as that derived from seeing an artistically designed building. In fact, in one way or another, form plays an outstanding role in all of the arts. Most people, even when they do not think of it in technical terms, are intuitively aware of it, or of its lack, when hearing music, or viewing works of art.

All of us have heard music which seems to be so lacking in contrast that it becomes boring. The only way this can be avoided is for a composer to be gifted with inventive ability. In order to sustain the listener's interest, the themes of a piece of music must undergo changes in rhythm, harmony, melody, and so forth--all of these changes being dominated by the musical intellect so that there is an effect of unity without undue repetition.

Now let's explore the approach to the creation of a new piece of music. The first step is to obtain thematic material and, if the composer has followed the practice of keeping a notebook such as I mentioned earlier, he may find satisfactory themes in this. If he doesn't, he must rely on the inspiration of the moment to produce what he needs. I prefer to do this after retiring at night and just before falling off to sleep. The following day, I decide on the way in which the thematic material will be presented.

Once having decided on which themes to use, I then go to planning the form of the new composition. My usual practice is to map out a plan which conforms loosely to the established rules of musical form, and then deviate from it as I see fit. This method serves as a stimulant to invention and inspiration.

It goes without saying that the harmonic pattern of the Principal Theme will influence the overall harmonic treatment of a movement, yet the composer doesn't have to limit himself to that particular harmonic idiom. As his work progresses, new ideas will develop that will fit harmoniously into the general pattern. If one works at a rate of speed which allows him to understand his own material better, it will unfold itself in such a way as to seem to dictate its own treatment. This conforms to what some playwrights have said of their work: that, as their characters grow within the framework of the drama, they often seem to dictate their own speech, actions, and even the direction of the plot.

After the preliminary period of planning and the initial creative steps have been taken, the composer may begin the sketch of his composition. This rough draft always undergoes numerous changes as it grows. Some composers wait until they are satisfied with the sketch before planning the orchestration. I don't, because I generally compose directly for orchestra. In other words, as each idea comes, I hear it orchestrally, and my notations for the orchestra score are written into my sketches. But before turning to the actual writing of the orchestration there is the additional task of testing and polishing what has been written. This includes a thorough examination of the music in order to determine nuances, tempi, phrasing, and so on.

Next comes the writing of the orchestra score, which is followed by the extracting of the parts. Many composers consider this a chore and try in every possible way to get out of it--some assigning it to their pupils and some asking for funds to employ professional copyists. I, however, gladly do my own copying since it gives me a pleasant way to read proof on the orchestra score. This is the final step, provided that the music proves to be satisfactory when it is performed. If it is not, then revisions are necessary.

Incidentally, all of the music following the sketch is written on onion skin, or transparent reproducing paper from which any number of copies can be made, thus reducing the cost of providing all the copies needed for an orchestra performance. Before leaving this aspect of the composing process, I would like to stress the necessity for legibility. The initial sketch may be as haphazard as the composer wishes as long as he can read it--because he is the only person who has to deal with it. But everything that follows must be done with the greatest of care, for if the musicians cannot read the music well, they will inevitably make mistakes and this leads to a useless waste of rehearsal time, and could also result in a bad performance.

Now, to demonstrate the progress of a composition after the first steps of planning, I will use brief extracts from the *Afro-American Symphony.* Long before writing this Symphony I had recognized the musical value of the Blues and had decided to use a theme in the Blues idiom as the basis for a major symphonic composition. When I was ready to launch this project I did not want to use a theme some folk singer had already created, but decided to create my own theme in the Blues idiom.

William Grant Still

AN AFRO-AMERICAN COMPOSER'S VIEWPOINT

Melody, in my opinion, is the most important musical element. After melody comes harmony; then form, rhythm, and dynamics. I prefer music that suggests a program, to either pure or program music in the strict sense. I find mechanically produced music valuable as a means of study; but even at its best it fails to satisfy me completely. My greatest enjoyment in a musical performance comes through seeing as well as hearing the artist.

The exotic in music is certainly desirable, but if one loses sight of the conventional in seeking for strange effects, the results are almost certain to be so extreme as to confound the faculties of the listeners. Still, composers should never confine themselves to materials already invented, and I do not believe that any one tonality is of itself more significant than another. I am unable to understand how one can rely solely on feeling when composing. The tongue can utter the letters of the alphabet, but it is the intellect alone that makes it possible to combine them so as to form words. Likewise a fragment of a musical composition may be conceived through inspiration or feeling, but its development lies altogether within the realm of intellect.

Colored people in America have a natural and deep-rooted feeling for music, for melody, harmony, and rhythm. Our music possesses exoticism without straining for strangeness. The natural practices in this music open up a new field which can be of value in larger musical works when constructed into organized form by a composer who, having the underlying feeling, develops it through his intellect.

William Grant Still

HORIZONS UNLIMITED

We live in a country where men are free to express themselves as they wish in every field of endeavor, particularly in the arts. And yet, despite this freedom, some of us in the creative field of music find ourselves apparently with our horizons limited. This can not be a limitation placed on us by outsiders--though their opinions may certainly have something to do with influencing us. Instead, it is a limitation that some of us have placed on ourselves, thinking perhaps that it will please outsiders.

In hearing the work of many young composers lately, I've been astonished to see how much of it follows a pattern. Now, I don't disagree totally with that pattern. I simply don't see how it's possible for so many to fall into it and still retain their identities as individuals.

There are people who seem to have decided that a certain type of music is the only acceptable music for our modern times. There are musicians who seem to feel it necessary for *all* to compose that type of music, just as so many novelists feel it necessary to write brutally realistic books in order to succeed. There is a tendency in all the arts toward the new, the sensational, the cerebral, rather than the beautiful and the worthwhile. It's important to have the new, sensational products, but it's important to have beauty too. How can we afford to emphasize one more than the other?

First of all, I don't think that it is good for the world of music to have everything come out of the same mold. God didn't place only roses on earth, or only lilies or only violets. He put flowers of many sorts and many colors here, the beauty of each enhancing that of the others. Anyone who underestimates the great value of differences would do well to remember that life would indeed be dull without variety. Progress would be impossible if all thought alike. It follows, then, that everyone should work toward variety, each individual expressing himself, particularly if he has decided to enter the creative field. He should begin by analyzing himself and his capabilities, in order to learn whether he is really doing--or will be doing--what he *really* wants to do.

Supposing someone has an inclination to write in the traditional style. Should he let someone else talk him out of it? By all means, no. Nor should he allow himself to be persuaded to drop the so-called "ultra-modern" style, if he honestly feels inclined toward that. I stress the word "honestly" here, because (as I said before) I sometimes wonder how many of the people who write in that style do so out of a sense of deep conviction, and how many of them are simply agreeing with the fad of the moment. At any rate, a composer should follow his own leanings. If all composers would do that, and would develop their own capabilities to the best of their abilities, we would soon have an infinite variety and a host of new colors in the music now being composed.

I speak as a composer who has, in a very real sense, been through the mill. In my early years, I studied at Conservatories with Conservatory-trained teachers. There I learned the traditions of music and acquired the basic tools of the trade. If I had stopped there, the sort of music I later composed might have been quite different. But necessity forced me to earn a living, so I turned to the field of commercial music.

Back in the days when America became aware of the "Blues," I worked with W.C. Handy in his office on Beale Street in Memphis. This certainly would not seem to be an occupation nor a place where anything of real musical value could be gained. Nor would nearby Gayoso Street, which was then a somewhat disreputable section. But, in searching for musical experiences that might later help me, I found there an undeniable color and a musical atmosphere that stemmed directly from the folk.

Any alert musician could learn something, even in that sordid atmosphere. W. C. Handy listened and learned--and what he learned profited him financially and in other ways in the succeeding years. He, of course, belongs in the popular field of music. But if a popular composer could profit by such contacts with folk music, why couldn't a serious composer? Instead of having a feeling of condescension, I tried to keep my ears open so that I could absorb and make mental notes of things that might be valuable later.

As the years went on, and I went from one commercial job to another, there were always people who tried to make me believe that the commercial field was an end in itself, and who argued that I should not waste my time on what is now often called "long hair" music. In this, I disagreed. I felt that I was learning something valuable, but only insofar as I could use it to serve a larger purpose.

The next important step was my study with Edgar Varèse. He might be classed as one of the most extreme of the ultramodernists. He took for himself, and encouraged in others, absolute freedom in composing. Inevitably, while I was studying with him, I began to think as he did and to compose music which was performed; music which was applauded by the avant-garde, such as were found in the International Composers'

Guild. As a matter of fact, I was so intrigued by what I learned from Mr. Varèse that I let it get the better of me. I became its servant, not its master. It followed as a matter of course that, after freeing me from the limitation of tradition, it too began to limit me.

It took me a little while to realize that it *was* limiting me, and that the ultra-modern style alone (that is to say, in its unmodified form) did not allow me to express myself as I wished. I sought then to develop a style that debarred neither the ultra-modern nor the conventional.

Certain people thought this decision was unwise, and tried to persuade me to stay strictly in the ultra-modern fold. I didn't do it, but at the same time, the things I learned from Mr. Varèse--let us call them the horizons he opened up to me--have had a profound effect on the music I have written since then. The experience I gained was thus most valuable even though it did not have the result that might have been expected.

After this period, I felt that I wanted for a while to devote myself to writing racial music. And here, because of my own racial background, a great many people decided that I ought to confine myself to that sort of music. In that too, I disagreed. I was glad to write Negro music then, and I still do it when I feel so inclined, for I have a great love and respect for the idiom. But it has certainly not been the *only* musical idiom to attract me.

Fortunately for me, nobody tried to talk me out of the two things that strikingly influenced my musical leanings, possibly because those influences were not the sort which make themselves known to outsiders as readily as others. The first was my love for grand opera, born around 1911 when my stepfather bought many of the early Red Seal recordings for our home record library. I knew then that I would be happy only if someday I could compose operatic music, and I have definitely leaned toward a lyric style for that reason.

The second influence had to do with writing for the symphony orchestra, something which has deeply interested me from the very start of my musical life. Many years ago, I began to evolve theories pertaining to orchestration, and to experiment with them from time to time. Applying those theories has tended to modify, perhaps even to curtail, the development of a contrapuntal style as it is known today. However, their use has enabled me to better achieve the result I sought.

Today the music I write stems in some degree from all of my experiences, but it is what *I* would like to write, not what others have insisted that I write. Some people have been kind enough to say that I have developed a distinctly personal style of musical expression. I hope they are right, and if they are, I'm sure it has come from keeping an open mind, meanwhile making an effort to select what is valuable and to reject what is unimportant, in my estimation.

Ask yourselves, for instance: What would Wagner have become if he had been willing to mold himself to suit the whims and tastes of the critic Hanslick? What would have happened to Puccini had he allowed himself to follow the dictates of the critics who wrote so unkindly of his work?

In this respect, may I say that no one on earth, be he musician or critic, has the right to decide arbitrarily what form music shall take and to renounce what doesn't conform to his dictum. I recall a music-lover who heard a new work by Stravinsky and did not like it. In commenting on it he said, "If this is the direction *music* is going to take, I do not approve." I believe that Stravinsky himself would be the last person to feel that*music* had to take a certain direction just because he composed in a particular way. He, as a creator, has always composed according to his own artistic conscience. If the general trend of music follows him, it is not--to the best of my belief--because he has consciously tried to force it.

It was, I believe, the critic Olin Downes who long ago made up his mind that the great American opera would have to come from a composer belonging to the field of American light opera, or the field of musical comedy. His reasons for thinking so may have been very good indeed, but how could he, or anyone else, possibly anticipate what might come from a creative mind in the future? If he had been living in Bach's time, could he have anticipated Beethoven? Or, in the time of Pergolesi, would anyone have anticipated Verdi? That being the case, Mr. Downes shouldn't have presumed to limit in advance the direction American opera should or would take.

People who assert that *their* way is the *only* way retard progress. They aren't wise enough, or just enough, to realize that even though they may be at variance with a school of thought, that school of thought must not be denied the right to express, for it too must contain elements of truth, just as everything contains elements of truth. Probably the acid test of a composer's right to wear the mantle of freedom is his willingness to accord others the same rights that he enjoys.

There is someone else who has the right to freedom where music is concerned. That someone is usually the last to be considered, but the most important of all, namely: the audience. Remember, just because you write something and you hope the audience will like it, the audience doesn't have to do so, and if it doesn't, that is the privilege of each individual listener. A composer's failure to consider the audience is an abuse of his own freedom.

One very well-known contemporary composer has been threatening lately that music will come to a dead end if audiences and performers refuse to give consideration to the type of music he and others like him are turning out. I don't think that will be true at all. In my opinion, and in the opinion of composer George Frederick McKay, audiences are more astute in the aggregate than most people imagine. And it is my feeling that their *spontaneous* response should be the strongest influence on a composer.

Now, this should not be a limitation for the composer; it should be a challenge. To be able to reach an audience without "writing down" and without becoming cheap should be the goal of everyone in the creative field, for a composer fails to do his duty to the development of music when he writes down to his hearers, nor does he edify, uplift, please or compliment those hearers when he does so. Just as every new doctor takes the Hippocratic oath, so should everyone who undertakes the job of composing music realize that it means a life of service.

American industry should have proven to all of us that *everything* is, or should be, created to fill a human need. Music is no exception to this rule. If the composer expects to have his music performed for people, he must give those people something they want and need. If he does not, then he had better not have his music played in public at all. He might just as well isolate himself in an ivory tower where he can compose for himself alone. When an industrial plant finds that one of its products has not succeeded in serving the public, it discontinues that product, even though its manufacturers may reserve the right to disagree with the public's verdict.

In other words, music shouldn't only appeal to the vanity of the person who writes it. It should serve others just as religion serves mankind, by helping people to live better lives and by giving them--even if only for an instant--a glimpse of real inspiration. And, if we want music to appeal to more people, we must address our message to the heart as well as to the intellect. In trying to understand the needs of others a whole new world will open to us.

There are always scoffers who will insist that a composer who writes within his audience's reach is "popular." Well, Christ spoke in simple, easily-understood terms that everyone could understand. His message has proved to be popular throughout the ages--but not the sort of "popularity" implied by people who scorn the easily-understood composer. To be understood as Christ is understood, one's message must be clear, satisfying and important.

A further sidelight on those scoffers who lightly use the word "popular:" they are, I think, the first to be delighted when audiences approve of their work, and the first to have their feelings hurt when audiences don't understand them. I recall only too well some composers in particular, many years ago, who smugly turned up their noses at Puccini. In all the intervening years, they haven't turned out a single work that could approach Puccini's in inspiration, even though they have tried. I wonder if they, in secret, do not envy the qualities they profess to scorn.

Let's return momentarily to listeners. One thing I will say about the American audience: in the past it has been willing to listen to something new. The audiences for Dr. Hanson's American Composers' Concerts in Rochester performed a great service for native composers by that willingness; the same may be said of the audiences who came to concerts of the International Composers' Guild in New York's old Aeolian Hall. They provided sharp and immediate reactions: sometimes approval, sometimes disapproval. As the years went on and the music that was offered continued to be, in a large degree, the same sort of music which had been disapproved, the audiences lost much of their early interest, and even lost the energy to hiss and protest. They simply turned the dials when it was broadcast, or just didn't pay admission to attend the concerts at which it was performed.

In accepting the verdict of the public, however, the composer ought always to be analytical. He should be sure that it *is* public opinion that speaks, rather than the opinion of a few people who hope to trick the masses into accepting *their* beliefs. In my case, the people who sought to exert influence belonged to small groups; the general public's verdict was often quite different from theirs. When such individuals or small groups start to try to persuade creators to come around to their viewpoints, they invariably try to induce a fear of being called "unsophisticated," "old-fashioned," or "ignorant." It's sometimes very difficult to be immune to such pressure, because no one likes to feel that he is ignorant, old-fashioned or unsophisticated. But it's always possible to recognize these things for what they really are: just taunts, and so to resist them.

Only the intellectual coward fails to analyze such terms and to accept them at their face value, which is the simple need for some individuals (usually those who are not capable of creating on their own) to feel that they have gained power or influence over some other individual.

With that in mind, I think it would be interesting now to consider some of the musical terms that are used while people are trying to persuade other people to one view or the other. The first one might be the word, "contemporary." This has often been mis-used as far as music is concerned. For example, some years ago, a New York composer made a trip to Southern California and, while here, heard some of a West Coast ultra-modernist's new compositions. He said, according to report, that he was astonished that the Westerner could live 'way out here in California and yet write music that is just as "contemporary" as the music being composed in the East.

Now, quite aside from the wisdom of believing that a composer has to live in a particular place to be able to write a particular sort of music, I would also question the Easterner's use of the word "contemporary" in this respect. As a matter of plain fact, the music I write, the music you write, or that written by any other living composer is "contemporary" music, no matter what the style of its composition, because we are living at the present time which, according to my dictionary, means a contemporary time. So, if the Eastern composer was implying that only one type of composing can be considered contemporary, I think he was limiting his own thinking.

Next, the terms "idiom" and "style." These are often heard nowadays, and are sometimes used interchangeably. I myself have been guilty of using them interchangeably, when my speech runs too quickly ahead of my thoughts. These terms probably came to be applied to music *after* the period when compositions generally conformed to traditional patterns. As more and more composers broke with the past, they were said to be writing in certain idioms. In my view, an idiom is something that pertains to groups of people. As you well know, we have in the United States a great many idioms, some aboriginal, some springing from the people who came here from other lands. Someday probably the separate idioms in America may merge, or a composer will come along who will make an overall use of them and we will then have a distinctly native idiom, recognizable as such.

Undoubtedly the music which exemplifies a folk idiom was originally created by individuals, now nameless, but over a period of years, the people in general have accepted it as their own, often adding to it with the passage of time, so that it now speaks for *people*, rather than for individual creators.

Because an idiom stems from, and belongs to, the people, a composer who belongs to a particular group of people may have musical tendencies expressive of his people's idiom. He may consciously study that idiom and employ its characteristics, or he may simply write music, unconsciously expressing his heritage. In any event, "idiom" is rarely something that can be acquired or discarded at will. It should be an integral part of every composer, to such an extent that no one could argue him out of it even if he tried. There have been instances where composers have adopted, for specific purposes, the idioms of people foreign to them. Their successes or failures have been due entirely to the degree of their own sensitivity and adaptability.

A good example of the manner in which a composer can be influenced by a racial idiom and yet be able to develop an individual style is expressed in this obituary, written in Australia after the death of Sibelius: "It has been said that the art of Sibelius took its root in the soil of his country, but became individualized by contact with his experience of life. Thus, because of his strong personal bias, combined with his racial consciousness, he evolved an artistic code of his own, neither modern nor archaic; his music is simply unlike any other."

"Style" is quite a different matter. It is a personal thing dictated largely by personal taste and, because of that, can be shaped by the individual's conscious mind. In other words, a style can be acquired, and an idiom can play a part in influencing that style.

Nowadays, there are two common concepts of style. One is not far removed from conventional music. The other departs radically from what we have known in the past. I long ago decided not to limit myself to the ultra-modern style, but I have never failed to perceive its value, or to use it whenever its use seemed to be justified. That being the case, I don't criticize either mode of expression--I take issue only with those people who espouse one or the other style and refuse to accept or approve any other. They are comparable to a painter who decides to use only the cool colors, or vice versa.

Some people scorn consonance in writing contemporary music, yet loudly praise Bach and other classicists. This appears inconsistent and hypocritical to me. If they really like the old masters so well, why can't they enjoy a tonic triad when it appears in the music of today?

On the other hand, there are those who close their minds to even the slightest departures from consonance. These extremists also display a lack of balance.

Additionally, there are other elements in the music of today which, in my opinion, deserve discussion and clarification. For one instance, the matter of *tonality*. Absence of tonality distresses me, producing a feeling of having lost my sense of direction and struggling to reorientate myself.

And then, *harmony*, which means, according to Webster, an agreeable blending of tones. Probably there are some who are not too greatly concerned over it, while others may give it undue importance. Unfortunately, many claim that harmonic resources have been exhausted, so they have turned to cacophony. I have the feeling that earnest experimentation, unhampered by the restrictions imposed by isms, should reveal that there is much more to be discovered in this field.

There is very little to be said concerning the *counterpoint* of today other than that some composers seem to be so greatly absorbed in directing the horizontal progress of the various voices that the vertical results of this same progress are neglected. Incidentally, when counterpoint calls attention to itself, crying out loudly, "Listen to me! I'm counterpoint, and I'm important", then it isn't good counterpoint.

Rhythm is so often taken for granted that it is sometimes hard to realize that some composers don't consider it important--at least, in a recognizable form. One of my colleagues once remarked that there is a difference of opinion as to what constitutes a rhythm, and then he cited a rhythm so stagnant that it approached actual inertia. Though the example he offered was indeed a rhythm in the broadest sense of the word, it had little value. Any rhythm worthy of the name should be recognizable as such even by laymen. Incidentally, this is a field that composers would do well to explore further. Someone may discover eventually that there is such a thing as rhythmic counterpoint, if that discovery has not already been made.

Last of all, there is *inspiration*. How very important it is! True, the mechanical side of creative work is important, but it should never take precedence over inspiration.

All of these elements are vital to the development of the well-rounded composer, who can not afford to exclude *anything* that may be useful to him. In this connection, let me make a qualifying statement. In advocating the study and use of all available materials, all idioms, all traditions and all forms of musical expression, I am decidedly *not* endorsing the creation of musical hodge-podges. It would be wrong to construct compositions in which a conscious effort is made to employ a variety of styles. It would be equally wrong for us to deny ourselves the right to use a contrasting style when it seems to be needed, and the biggest mistake of all would be to deny ourselves the right to learn *all* there is to know about *all* musical elements available to us.

No, my suggestion is that everyone would profit by being able to know and use various styles if and when he wishes. Then, the innate character of each composition will itself dictate the treatment, the style and the form the music is going to take. No outsider should presume to tamper with a composer's conviction in that respect. No matter how sensitive and alert we are to outside influences, we should never allow them to throw us off balance. Criticism must be *evaluated* before it's accepted or rejected.

By all means, the young composer should learn from everything and everyone. He should realize that nothing is valueless or totally undesirable. He should listen to all his teachers, study his textbooks, absorb all the musical influences around him--but at the same time, reserve the right to disagree with anything he feels unable to accept.

There is no substitute for keeping an open mind and for analyzing both sides of a question. There is also no substitute for having the courage of one's convictions. No one really wants to be a carbon copy of anyone else, no matter how much he may admire the other person or his work.

I have always felt, when people have asked me to bow to their will, that I may indeed be wrong--but if I *am* wrong, let it be my own mistake, not one I have been led into. It may be that I am mistaken in having tried to establish my own mode of musical expression. But it more nearly expresses my true self than any mode I might have borrowed! In it I have sought to attain a degree of balance in the use of both dissonance and consonance, remembering that while the music that leans toward the dissonant style expands the musical horizon and is unquestionably an asset, it is not in itself the only, or the most desirable end--remembering too that consonance will never be outmoded.

Beethoven was said to have "freed" music because he had courage enough to investigate new horizons. Yet he did not discard what had gone before!

Our world is big enough for every idea. In it we all can enjoy freedom. Let us then develop in ourselves those qualities that will enable us to use these ideas and this freedom in opening the new horizons which *always* exist--only waiting for the magic touch of inspiration to release them for mankind.

William Grant Still

A COMPOSER'S VIEWPOINT

I would like to preface my remarks by stating what will soon be an obvious fact to all of you, namely that I am a composer, and not an orator. You may well decide that composers such as I ought to devote themselves to composing, not talking. However, I have been asked to speak in public so often in recent years that I have tried to accustom myself to what is expected, and I ask you to bear with me now through my ordeal.

Furthermore, although we are committed to an extensive discussion of Black music, I would like to emphasize that I speak not only as a Negro, but also as an American. For a long time we Afro-Americans needed something like the fact that Black can be beautiful to give us identity and pride in our racial heritage. Now that has been accomplished. Most of us have come to realize that Black is indeed beautiful, but only as White, Brown, or Yellow are beautiful: when we make it so. The term has served its purpose, so I hope from this time forward we will all want to emphasize our American ties, as well as our African heritage. Our parents and grandparents, I think, wanted us above all else to be good Americans and to get a substantial education, so that we could compete on an equal basis with all other Americans. And speaking about parents and grandparents, let's recapitulate for a few minutes and recall what it was like to be a Negro musician then, and how far we have progressed. Looking at the past may shed some light on the future.

To begin with, my father was one of those who endured all sorts of sacrifices in order to get an education and to become, on the side, a musician. Long before the turn of the century, he worked hard toward this end. He taught mathematics, had a half interest in a store, sang solos in church, and learned to play the cornet the hard way. Each lesson cost him a seventy-five mile trip from Woodville, Mississippi, to Baton Rouge, Louisiana, where the only competent teacher for miles around could be found. When he had absorbed enough of this training, he formed the only brass band in Woodville. People who knew him in those days said that he was admired by both Negroes and Whites. I can well believe it, for many Southern people have a feeling of genuine affection for Negro musicians--not enough, of course, to make them acceptable as equals, but enough to make them the objects of a certain amount of indulgence. W. C. Handy once elaborated on this by saying that if he needed money, he could get it if he pretended he wanted it to buy liquor or to gamble, but not if he said he wanted it to buy books for his children. I think this affection for Negro musicians has extended to the present day, when so many Southerners are truly interested in culture, and so many take pride in those Negro artists who have succeeded and who had their roots in the South.

My father may have been, as they said, the idol of the town, but he surely would have found it difficult to transform that worship into cash at that time and in that area. In fact, I wonder whether he ever was paid at all for his musical activities. Had he lived beyond his twenty-fourth year, he might have had enough drive to earn his living in music if he chose to do so, for he was an ambitious young man. But he didn't live, so we'll never know.

The earning capacity of Negro musicians was indeed limited in those days, and continued to be so for quite a while. I recall the serenaders, small groups of Negro musicians who, when I was a boy, would go from house to house at night, playing stringed instruments and singing. Residents would throw them coins. Yesterday that was a fitting reward. Today it would be less than a mere pittance.

When I was along in my school years, my mother engaged a teacher to give me violin lessons, and encouraged me to study music. However, I didn't want to be a performer. I wanted to compose, and no sooner did I learn to read music than I wanted to write it. This was fine, as far as my mother was concerned, until she learned that I wanted to make music my life's work. Then she opposed me. This seemed strange to me at the time, because my mother was herself a person of more than ordinary artistic ability. She taught English in the secondary school, wrote and directed plays, painted, and played the piano a little. Her own goals were high. She constantly urged me to make something of myself, and not to follow the path of least resistance. However, a career in music was outside the bounds of consideration for her and, as she persisted in her efforts to discourage me, I began to understand why. The Negro musicians of her day were not socially accepted into the better Negro homes. In fact, many Colored people considered them immoral. They disapproved of their drinking, and they certainly looked down on their earning capacity! My mother was very explicit on the latter count. She pictured me as wearing threadbare clothes, starving, and unable to provide the bare necessities of life. Her ridicule was

65

fairly constant and unwavering. She wanted me to become a doctor so I could make enough money to live on. Today I can see that she did what she did for my benefit, yet even today it is hard for me to realize that the structure of Negro society at that time was such that even a woman of her vision could not understand that the kind of composer I meant to be was far different from her concept, nor would she or others of that period have envisioned an Afro-American attaining a position of prominence in the symphonic or operatic fields! You can understand that when I tell you that not until I got to Oberlin and reached my majority did I ever hear a symphony orchestra! That would explain it. I wonder what the people of that day would say today, when so many American Negroes are seeking to reach such goals, with a reasonable number actually making the grade.

After I left college, economic and racial factors did indeed influence my way of life--to my ultimate advantage, however. I was determined to make a living in music, and the popular field was the commercial field open to me and others like me. I went into it with one thought uppermost in my mind: I intended to learn all I could from American popular music in order to put the knowledge to good use in my later career. In other words, I wanted to learn but not to make the popular field an end in itself. I still feel that this was a wise course of action, for what I learned there was not available anywhere else. It later balanced my conservatory training to give more facets to my musical personality.

When I went to work with W.C. Handy in Memphis in 1916, playing in his orchestra and arranging, I gained a first-hand contact with Negro folk music that was not available to me at home. I learned, for example, to appreciate the beauty of the blues, and to consider this the musical expression of the yearnings of a lowly people, instead of accepting it superficially as being immoral and sexy, as so many other people did.

Most of you are no doubt aware that there came a time in our musical history when American Negroes even looked down on spirituals, because they associated them with the days of slavery. Knowing this, you can well imagine the prejudice that existed against the blues which stemmed, supposedly, from the big city dives. I recall when I was a boy in Little Rock asking a pianist to play the *Memphis Blues* for me. She was afraid, because of the bad reputation of the music. Fortunately, both spirituals and blues have emerged from the period of ill repute, and are now generally recognized as very important contributions of the Negro to our American life.

Other aspects of my association with Handy will shed light on the social conditions of the Negro musician of that period. At home I had been sheltered, and had moved in what I would consider enlightened social circles, but on the road with Handy and his orchestra, I found that the indulgence many people felt for Negro musicians did not extend to giving them much consideration for their ordinary needs. Handy's orchestra played the length and breadth of the South. Larger cities had accommodations for us (segregated, of course) but in some of the smaller communities there were no places for Negroes to stay. I remember once in winter, in the mountainous section not far from Bristol, Tennessee (where we were playing), we stayed in a mountain home where the flooring consisted of rough pieces of wood and the openings were almost a half-inch apart. The wind blew through these openings, just as if we were outdoors. It was cold even in bed! And we had to eat grits and sow belly. I'll never forget that experience.

At another time, we were playing in a little town of Arkansas. It was very interesting there. A White man came and sat by me. He liked the 'cello, and he stayed right there and listened. He didn't get far away at all until it came time for us to quit playing. Handy went to collect his pay, which was given without question, but we discovered that no one had thought to make arrangements for our housing. There simply was no place to stay, so we walked back to the station. It was locked, and we were out in the cold. Handy took his cornet case, broke a window, and unlatched the door. We sat inside the station for the rest of the night, and Handy later paid for the broken window.

Our traveling was done in Jim Crow cars, which were usually only half cars. They offered very little that was comfortable or desirable: cinders, smoke, unpleasant odors, and the feeling of humiliation, being compelled to pay first-class fare for third-rate accommodations. One time in Alabama, a Negro prisoner was placed in our car. His captors relieved themselves of responsibility by locking him in the toilet which, by the way, was the only one on the train Negro passengers could use. Under these circumstances, we naturally could not use it, but the prisoner solved our problem by breaking the window and escaping.

Early one morning, our train made a short stop in Rome, Georgia. We had gone all night without food, and we were all hungry. Again there was no place for us to eat. We were told at one restaurant that if we went to the back, we would be served. We didn't want to do that, partly because of the humiliation, and partly because we were afraid of missing the train, so we got back on and rode until past noon without food.

My last incident has a brighter ending. One day in a Kentucky town, we went to the Negro restaurant, but it smelled like a privy. None of us wanted to eat there, so we went to a white restaurant right in town, across from the old court house. We described our predicament to the owner and he promptly invited us in, sat us by the front window, and served us a delicious meal. With our thoughts geared to the reality of segregation, we had expected him to put up a screen in front of us, but he didn't. He treated us just like his other customers.

In relating this, I've had another purpose in mind besides telling you about Negro musicians and their world over a half-century ago. I have heard reports of Negroes today who are trying to turn the clock back, and bring separation and segregation again into our lives. I say they can't know what they are talking about. They have certainly never experienced segregation and its inconveniences as some of us have. Even if they do understand what it is, and are willing to endure its humiliations for themselves, it is not fair to advocate it for the rest of us and for our children. Instead of all this big separatist talk, they should get down on their knees and thank God that the present laws in the United States have made segregation illegal.

One prominent White California educator, on reviewing the current separatist efforts, recently wrote: "Shades of the Ku Klux Klan! What ever happened to the wonderful idea of America as one united people, the great melting pot of all nations, all colors, and all races? Has it gone forever down the drain of history? All of us had better hope not." Make no mistake about it, segregation today is illegal because those of us who came before fought a legal battle against it, and struggled against it in our rights as American citizens. And this was during a period when our opportunities were so far less than those of today. We didn't waste any time and energy in returning hatred for hatred. Instead, we continued moving toward our goal, never forgetting that our progress was being hastened because of the help given us by many fine White Americans. We won the battle with their help. Now let's take a brief look at some of the conditions that existed before the battle was won.

Today there are several capable Negro orchestral conductors active in various parts of the world. But who remembers Alli Ross? He was a capable conductor in New York, not too long ago, who worked daily to prepare himself. Every morning he would have his coffee and toast, and then start reading scores. He couldn't get a real chance because of his color, and he died a frustrated man.

And when we look at the Negro players in some of our contemporary symphony orchestras, let's not forget the colored instrumentalists who tried so hard in the old days but were always rebuffed, and finally had to adopt different professions in order to make a living. By the time there came conductors and opportunities that would have given them a chance, they had grown rusty and could not qualify. But it was they, the seemingly unsuccessful, who by knocking at the doors so persistently, helped to open them for the Negro musicians who followed. We all owe them a great debt.[1] Many of the pioneers of Negro music were contemporaries and close friends of mine. Each took a step toward the development of our racial culture and toward its integration into American culture. I never knew Samuel Coleridge-Taylor personally, but the very fact of his success as a serious composer served as an inspiration. In college, I even tried to make my hair grow like his. That was something of a task, because his hair was bushy, and mine was fairly straight.

I did know Harry T. Burleigh. He was such a gentleman; he had beautiful manners, courtly. I knew Nathaniel Dett, and Edmund Jenkins. Jenkins was a very talented young man, who died early. He had done some symphonic writing, and was working on a symphony when he died. Had he finished it, he would have been the first. Clarence Cameron White, John Work, Florence Price--all of these are mentioned in Maud Cuney Hare's competently researched book, *Negro Musicians and Their Music*.

I also knew bandsmen like Frank Drye, instrumentalists like Joe Douglas, Louia Von Jones, and Hazel Harrison, singers like Sissieretta Jones (who was also known as the Black Patti), Roland Hayes and, later, Marian Anderson, as well as orchestrators like Will Vodery. All these and many others had individual contributions to make, and for

---

[1] James Baldwin, in *The Fire Next Time* (Middlesex: Penguin Books, 1965, p. 85) states: "I have great respect for that unsung army of black men and women who trudged down back lanes and entered back doors, saying 'Yes, sir' and 'No, ma'am' in order to acquire a new roof for the schoolhouse, new chemistry lab, more beds for the dormitories, more dormitories."

none of them was the path unfailingly easy.

Credit has been given me for being the first Negro to conduct a major symphony orchestra in the Deep South, for being the first to write a symphony which was performed, the first to have an opera produced by a major American company, and first to conduct a White radio orchestra in New York. I would like to say here that none of these accomplishments would have been possible if it had not been for the work done before by so many of our pioneers--those who were successful in their respective fields, and those who were unsuccessful too. They made tremendous efforts in their lifetimes, and thus made it easier for me and for the others who came after me. I can not conceive of any possible way in which I or anyone else could have come up absolutely alone, without any predecessors, and could have made the grade, because I believe every accomplishment has to be built on foundations established long before.

I am so well aware of these past accomplishments that when I came across the book entitled *Black Music*, published in 1967 by a reputable New York firm, I was affronted when I glanced inside and found mention of only a few contemporary jazz artists, with not one acknowledgment of progress in any other field of Negro music. I ascribe this in some measure to a bias on the part of the writer, and in some measure to ignorance and bad taste, for although no one holds authentic jazz in higher esteem than I, I still refuse to concede that it is the only or even the most important form of Negro musical expression. True, it has spread all over the world, but so have Negro spirituals, and so, I venture to guess, would a certain amount of Negro symphonic music if it had behind it the same commercial drive that has long activated jazz.

I am equally affronted by what I have been told of the new courses in our universities, purporting to be courses in Negro music but actually no more than courses in jazz. If they are solely jazz courses, let them be so labeled. If they intend to be courses in Negro music, then let them encompass the whole panorama of Negro music: the study of the development of Negro music from the songs of the African natives, on to the classic period when Negro music was represented by men like Bridgetower (who was the first to perform Beethoven's *Kreutzer* sonata) and the Chevalier de Saint-Georges (an esteemed composer), even Beethoven (who some observers believe had Negro blood). From there the course could move on through the folk music of Latin America, the

West Indies, the United States, and up to its individual creators and performers of today. What a fascinating area for research! It can't be dismissed lightly, but its true value can be assessed only in its relation to music as a whole and not as a separate entity.

One of my friends, Theodore Phillips, who inaugurated and taught a course in Afro-American music at one of the Southern California colleges, now stresses the need for a formal study in depth, and insists that courses in Negro music should be a necessary part of the overall study of music. Further, they should be made attractive to White as well as Colored students, for only in this way, he says, can Negro music be recognized for what it has already contributed to our culture, and I agree with this completely. It's my view that such a procedure would add a new dimension to our music, in that it would contribute to good public relations for the Negro, as it has so often in the past. Incidentally, in his initial days in the class, my friend was staggered to discover that only a few of his students had ever heard of a Negro spiritual, that none knew of the shouts or work songs! None were even aware of the advances in "serious" music!

Some of the students set themselves to challenging his every statement, no matter how simple or how obvious. Through the ages, students have been expected to inquire and to question. All of us have done it when we were forming our thoughts and planning our future actions. None of us accepted everything blindly. At the same time, it has generally been accepted that students are supposed to learn from their teachers, not to teach the teachers. It seems to me that our future might well depend on our willingness to receive instruction and to respect qualified instructors. No doubt some members of my friend's class shared the attitude of a seventeen-year-old Black Student Union member who was interviewed by the *Los Angeles Times* on March 14, 1969. He said that racist training involved teaching about Johann Sebastian Bach, whom he described as "that old, dead punk." He added that he wanted to learn about Ray Charles, The Supremes, and about Black composers. From one of my personal experiences which I plan to recount later, I'm wondering if he really meant that, or if he only wanted to know about those who fitted neatly into his concepts.

In the first place, I would suggest that students who want to learn about Negro music should undertake it in all sincerity, not with the idea that they will be taking a snap course, or that they will be permitted to sit and listen to jazz recordings during every class period. This may be enjoyable, but it is not genuine study. The latter in my opinion should be historical, analytical, comparative, and should be undertaken above all with an open mind. It should be studied and explored in all seriousness, not merely as a means of getting credits without working for them. Along with this, the Negro student of music should learn about Bach, "that old, dead punk," and all the other composers who have made valuable contributions to music. He should prepare himself from all angles.

Now that the doors are opening to us, it would be tragic to have them shut in our faces again because those who enter are not yet truly prepared. You see, I'm all for studying our racial heritage. Most people are. But I'm also with Roy Wilkins, Thurgood Marshall, and Bayard Rustin when they advise young Negro students to learn what the White students are learning *in addition*, or else they will be left out in the mad scramble for jobs. Justice Marshall declared that you're not going to compete in the world until you have training, just like everybody else, and hopefully better, because when you're a Negro, you've got to be better. Bayard Rustin even went so far as to question the advantages of the so-called soul courses in college, saying that in the real world all they want to know about is if you can do mathematics and write a correct sentence. I know that if I were an employer, I would hesitate to hire anyone who could not or would not do the work he has been hired to do. Moreover, as more and more Negroes do qualify, the day will soon be past when we can blame our failures on our color. In other words, racial studies can certainly be advocated, but they should be open to all who are interested. I wouldn't want anyone, Colored or White, to study music unless he feels he can not resist it as I felt, for the competition is intensely keen. One who adopts it as a profession should feel much like a potential minister when he gets his call to service. When the musical call comes, and the individual decides that he really does want to make music his ministry, I would suggest an exhaustive review of every aspect: harmony, harmonic analysis, form, counterpoint, fugue, musical history (including the history of Negro music), and so on.

Some years ago, one of my colleagues of the early jazz days came to me with a story of a Colored musician who had been engaged as an arranger because he was Colored, and, therefore, was assumed to have an original slant on the music. He did very well at it for several years, despite his limited training. One day he happened to get into a

72

discussion with someone who was quite able to talk about music in technical terms. He became quite enthusiastic during the conversation and exclaimed, "Say, this is great! I think I'll go and study harmony!" A little late in my opinion, but commendable, nonetheless.

One of my Negro friends who plays professionally in symphonic groups on the West Coast recently came to me with another problem. He had been trying to organize a Colored chamber music group, but had difficulty finding members willing to rehearse. Some wanted only to show up at the concert, sight-read the music, and collect the pay. Now this is something that not even the most famous and experienced artists dare to do; they all know the value of rehearsals. Jazz players often do it, of course, since improvisation has been one of their obligations, but in "serious" music one must stick to what is written, and the people who are so good they don't need to practice are rare indeed. In the end, my friend was forced to get an interracial group, which incidentally worked very well.

I am very pleased that I have become acquainted with the works of gifted younger composers like Hale Smith, Ulysses Kay, and others, but unfortunately for me and for the purposes of this discussion, I am not as yet familiar with the work being done by all of our young Negro composers. (So many composers never answer their mail!) Despite this, I have seen some scores and have heard some of their music, and much of this has been very encouraging, indeed! Several of the composers handle their material expertly from the viewpoint of craftsmanship and, creatively speaking, I think we can look forward to a bright future. In some instances, the younger men remind me of myself when I was their age, experimenting, learning from everything possible, and trying to develop an individual form of expression.

Some of you possibly know that, for me, the so-called avant-garde is now the rear guard, for I studied with its high priest, Edgar Varèse, in the 20's, and I was a devoted disciple. Some of my early compositions in that idiom were performed auspiciously in New York. I was amused recently when a writer heard one of my works and was upset because it was not in the avant-garde idiom. The writer said, "Time has passed Mr. Still by." Well, if this writer had done his homework, he would have known that it was I who recognized the handwriting on the wall many years ago, and voluntarily left the type of time he referred to, and I'm convinced I made the right decision.

I learned a great deal from the avant-garde idiom and from Mr.

Varese but, just as with jazz, I did not bow to its complete domination. I had chosen a definite goal, namely, to elevate Negro musical idioms to a position of dignity and effectiveness in the fields of symphonic and operatic music. This would have been extremely difficult, or even impossible, had I chosen the avant-garde idiom. Through experimentation, I discovered that Negro music tends to lose its identity when subjected to the avant-garde style of treatment. I made this decision of my own free will, knowing very well that pressures would be brought to bear to make me follow the leader, and compose as others do. I have stuck to this decision, and I've not been sorry. American music is a composite of all the idioms of all the people comprising this nation, just as most Afro-Americans who are "officially" classed as Negroes are products of the mingling of several bloods. This makes us *individuals*, and that is how we should function, musically and otherwise. My personal feeling is that the avant-garde idiom as it stands is not the idiom of the future, no matter how its adherents try to convince me that I'm unsophisticated to think so. I've watched its deleterious effect on audiences and have noted that the general public, for whom music is supposed to be written, couldn't care less. I would urge young Afro-American composers to think of the avant-garde as a phase, not an end in itself, and if not a phase, a facet of composition.

Negroes have long been known as spontaneous creators. One has only to study the wealth of artistic innovations they have given to the world. Not every Negro is a spontaneous creator naturally, nor is everything all of us do superlative. We can not lay claim to this distinction and neither can any other group of people, but we can evaluate the past, present and future in music, and begin again to write with heart instead of brains, with love instead of disdain, and with attention to spiritual as well as scientific values. Experimentation for the sake of experimentation can only produce a poor substitute for music, and we are now in need of *real* music, not contrived sounds. We need a new contemporary goal. I suggest that this goal be beauty, and I maintain that there is no substitute for inspiration. Every composer should work toward expressing his own personality in music. I shudder to think of the consequences if all of us were to start turning out music that is like the music of all the others. Such a trend has been observed in contemporary music. It is my hope that its end is near, and that sanity will assert itself.

Afro-American composers, incidentally, have a wonderful opportunity to influence a trend toward sanity if they will make up their minds to return to the originality for which Negroes have become famous.

I cannot close without commenting on the current riotous conditions on our college campuses. In case you think they have nothing to do with Negro music, you are wrong. If they are allowed to continue without restraint, there will be no future for any of us, in music or anywhere else. When white students riot and display their ugliness on TV, the public immediately speaks of anarchy, of communism, and the hampering of the silent majority's right to gain an education. When Negroes riot, the same thoughts are present, plus other conclusions not amicable to us as a racial group. The unfortunate result of Negro rioting is that so often those who are most ignorant, violent and unwholesome are constantly in the forefront of our TV screen. By whose wish: theirs or the TV medium? I cannot say. One thing is certain: their images create a climate of fear and distrust among their fellow Americans, White and Colored alike. Many White Americans know they are not typical, but there are some who are positive they *are* typical, and that they represent the Negro race. Without stopping to analyze the situation, they automatically cast all of us into the same mold. Of course, it affects Negro musicians and their music just as it adversely affects all decent Afro-Americans, including the children yet unborn. In the end it will probably affect the rioters themselves. It has been said that the Negro students have been influenced by the White dissidents, but that it is the Negro students who will go to prison, while the Whites go free, and this is not an impossible theory, I think you will agree. To me, one of the most significant factors in this current trouble is that it came when there seemed to be no need for it. Negroes were already getting ahead as they qualified. The situation was not yet perfect, but it was improving, and it gave every indication of continuing to do so. There was enough of a climate of good fellowship first to make outsiders see some merit in the demands that were made by campus militants. Then, as the demands escalated and became more and more ridiculous, and as it became evident that people were coming from off-campus to incite trouble, even our friends began to lose patience. When it was noted that the ignorant were insisting upon dictating to the educated, and the inexperienced were demanding the right to direct the experienced, many formerly well-disposed people were on the way to losing all their permissiveness. The picture was not an attractive one.

Only twice have I had encounters with the so-called Black militants, both times unpleasant ones. The first came during a general discussion of racial matters, when two young men found themselves in complete disagreement with me. Their displeasure came not in an orderly discussion, but in a rather belligerent verbal warfare. As I am now 74 years of age, and have been a Negro for all of the 74 years, I did not need people fifty years younger than I to tell me what it is, or what it should be, to be a Negro. The second encounter came when it was least suspected, college music class. I don't expect complete agreement with my views, though I do look for some respect. This I have received in every other student aggregation I have addressed, from elementary schools, even in deprived areas, to university audiences. Moreover, in this class there were only two belligerents. The rest were studious and appreciative. They did not seem to be in agreement with the militants on any count, although the militants seemed as if they were ready to do battle.

Those two should have known that they could do nothing to make me talk or compose differently, but perhaps they hoped to alter the good opinion of their classmates. Basically, they told me my music was not Negro music which, in their opinion, was the jungle-type sounds heard over a particular radio station in that city. All else was what they termed "Eur"-American music, rather than Afro-American. They also seemed disturbed because the clarinetists in the orchestras that played my music (one of them was the Royal Philharmonic of London) didn't play like Duke Ellington's clarinetist. Indeed, they seemed astonished that my compositions didn't sound like the Duke's! They were even a little sad when I told them they were not intended to sound that way. One of them prattled about the bourgeois and White man's music, while the other made it a point to let me know that he did not "identify" with my music, no doubt expecting me to be crushed by this verdict. He then made the separatist statement that we have grown up in America with only two different cultures, White and Black. This is a fallacious statement for, as you know, here in America, the melting pot, a large number of cultures may be found, gradually influencing each other. The Negro culture has definitely been influenced by Whites, just as White culture has been influenced by Negroes. In my opinion, we have both gained by the fusion, and who can define the exact line of demarcation?

The day after this second encounter, the Black Student Union asked for the resignation of their Negro instructor, despite the fact that students were then signing up for his next term course, and the enrollment had nearly doubled. The interesting angle was that the Black students themselves had requested the course with specifically a Negro instructor. The college had been fortunate enough to find a retired head of a music department from a eastern university, with a degree from the Oberlin Conservatory and almost forty years of teaching experience. The college and most of his students were pleased with his work. Only the two militants, they alone, wanted to drag his ideals down to their level, and thus limit the development of Negro music in general. This occurrence cast serious doubt on the sincerity, at least, of those militants. If they made a reasonable demand which was met by the college in good faith, shouldn't they have been properly receptive? Why should they, obviously the most unprepared in class, have assumed the task of dictating to their classmates? What actually were their motives? What were they trying to accomplish? Remembering that the two militants had almost succeeded in taking over the full discussion period, I wondered why they were so insistent on freedom of expression for themselves, while denying it to all the others. They did not hesitate to insult others, but made it appear that a crime had been committed when their ideas were questioned. I confess that in one short class period, I lost whatever sympathy I might have had for militants.

Noting that this one little experience has multiplied and expanded to the level of violence on so many college campuses, I cannot blame the public in general for being so impatient with such hypocrisy. It is good to take pride in one's race, but is *this* pride? When these people begin to appreciate the good things that are available within America, to respect the rights of others, to develop a sense of true values and to talk about civil responsibility along with civil rights, then everyone will be willing to listen. Our forebears were willing to assume a share of the burden, along with the blessings. Why can't we? If it is clear that our attitude is changing in a constructive way, then perhaps the violent backlash which Billy Graham has predicted will never appear. At the very least, we might say that the idea of letting unprepared students choose their studies, choose their teachers, and even indicate what they want to be taught within a given subject is certainly open to question.

To all those who talk of separation, I would say again that I am now and forever against it. I am for integration. We're all Americans in our hearts, in our music, in our very being. At this point in our history

77

we should begin to weigh, to analyze and to evaluate, all with a view to deciding whether or not we want to jump on bandwagons indiscriminately and to making up our minds as to what we actually do want. Of course many of us are frustrated! All of us are to some extent, and all of us probably will continue to be in some degree as long as we live. But, as Thurgood Marshall has so aptly remarked, we are not going to settle anything with guns, fire bombs or rocks. It appears now that many American Negroes feel that they are frustrated specifically because of White people and their attitudes, so it seems to me that we should take a long look at White people in general to see whether this is entirely correct.

In my opinion, there are three broad categories into which White people will fit. The first type has not been given enough credit, and yet it is they who have done the most to help us up the ladder to full citizenship and success. They are the sympathetic ones who try just as hard as we do to make brotherhood a reality. I know that I shall always be grateful to the many White friends who helped me. I could not have made it in a community solely of Negroes for the simple reason that Negroes did not have the facilities of the large orchestras, publishing houses and so on, which I needed in order to advance. White people made these facilities available to me in nearly every instance.

The second class of White persons is known to all of us as the uncompromising bigot. He is a difficult person to deal with, so he is best ignored.

He is still easier to take, however, than the third sort of person, the one who talks loudly about his commitment to brotherhood, enthusiastically welcomes you until you begin to measure arms with him. Then he surreptitiously opposes you while continuing to shout his love for his less fortunate brethren. He is the most frustrating, and least approachable of all. *Sneaky* would be the best word to describe him.

I've always found it wise to go on my own way, doing the best that I can, and trusting that God will eventually show people the errors of their ways, for I am convinced that we must all work together harmoniously. Only in this way can America's greatness reach its zenith. Make no mistake about it: the future of our music is tied immutably to that of the individual musician, and the future of the race as a whole is bound up in the future of America. What is good for our nation is good for the race. We must never let ourselves think otherwise, nor allow ourselves to be duped into a separatist philosophy, no matter how frustrated we may feel. We and our fellow Americans are in this together. As Americans with Negro blood, we are willing and able to contribute something of value to America. Those of us in the field of music know that our music has already proved to be a distinctive contribution. Our forebears contributed their sweat and their blood. Our sons have fought on foreign shores for the ideal of democracy. We have an investment in this nation. We own a share of it. Now is the time to decide: shall we protect that investment, or shall we destroy it?

William Grant Still

III

STILL'S WORK: AN OVERVIEW

WILLIAM GRANT STILL'S MUSICAL STYLE
A Monumental Contribution To American Music

One observation, arrived at by a study of Still's life and music, is unmistakable: the composer and the man were inseparably entwined. Still's music, the essence of his whole being, provided an underlying, spiritual framework from which to express himself, not only as a musician but as a humanitarian, one aspiring for the elevation of his entire race.

Still's substantial output of approximately 600 compositions includes ballets, operas, symphonies, choral works, instrumental solos, chamber music, songs, and miscellaneous incidental music. Before scoring he explored thoroughly the possibilities of each instrument, just as he researched details of scenario and character for his operas. Periodically he visited Negro churches and revival meetings, hoping to absorb first-hand the flavorful naturalness of their spirituals. He constantly jotted down musical ideas, many of which came from his methodically recorded dreams and from an interest in spiritualism. As he schemed out the formal structure of each work, he wisely allowed leeway.

Still virtually taught himself basic orchestration, instrumentation and conducting, determined to pull the desired sound from the orchestra and use it as a compositional tool. By constant experimentation with ranges, rhythms, doublings, unlikely combinations of instruments, and orchestral tonal colors, he found that the outmoded "rules" of composition could be bent to advantage. Opposed to orchestrating from his own piano score, he rather sought the immediate full orchestral sound. Fearing that hired copiers might make careless mistakes in his manuscripts, he trusted this chore only to himself.

Under the tutelage of both George Chadwick and Edgard Varèse, Still was given plenty of freedom. Though acknowledging the trendy *avant-guarde* technique as a useful idiom, he never wanted it as his own sound. Ultimately he was able to balance academic musical training with practical experience in several idioms to suit his own needs.

Still's works of the 1920's, particularly *Darker America*, a symphonic poem for chamber orchestra, reflect the struggle of his emerging style. By the later 1940's, his increasingly sure sense of classical construction had begun to mature in works less identifiably ethnic, though they were markedly indigenous to North America. Eileen Southern considers his

81

style neo-romantic, fully utilizing the Afro-American folk elements of spirituals, blues, worksongs, ragtime and jazz, one offering piquant harmonies and ingratiating melodies.

It is necessary to examine some of Still's better known compositions in order to define specific characteristics of his musical style. In none of these did he intentionally strive for an Afro-American musical sound for its own sake. He simply wanted his melodies to appeal emotionally to the listeners, and to elevate them by imparting some of the inspiration that he felt while composing. With this philosophy he achieved a high level of artistry. Still said himself: "The true function of the Negro musician in America is as an *American*."

ORCHESTRAL WORKS

Of his well-known and listenable *Afro-American Symphony* (1930), which sings and swings with tasty refinement, Still said: "I wanted to use music that would be recognizable as American Negro music . . . Now, in the blues, I saw this: a unique musical creation of Negroes . . . I created a theme in the blues idiom and used it as a basis for this symphony."

Still's compositional philosophy that melody should be foremost, intensified and supported by the employment of a logical and balanced formal scheme, is evident in the *Afro-American*. As he explained: "Once having decided upon which themes to use, I then go on to planning the form . . . My usual practice is to map out a plan which conforms loosely to the established rules of musical form and then to deviate from it as I see fit. This method serves as a stimulant to invention and inspiration."

Each movement is prefaced by one of Paul Laurence Dunbar's poems. "Longing," the first movement's subtitle, was well selected, as the opening twelve-measure blues theme in A-flat, played by the English horn, suggests just such a mood. Variations of the theme continue throughout the piece, through thematic transformation, i.e., the principal theme is altered each time by either rhythmic or orchestral treatment. A transitional passage, using this first theme, leads into the subordinate theme in G, one resembling a Negro spiritual in three-part song form, which is developed similarly and lastly presented in A-flat minor.

82

Basically the harmonic progression of this movement is that of standard blues: I, I^7, IV, V^7, I, with a few slight variations. Still frequently uses the embellished triad, such as the addition of a minor seventh or a ninth, but is sparing with the added sixth. He uses the tonic seventh as a chord of repose, or as an embellished I chord, rather than moving it to a IV chord. His textural techniques are chordal, contrapuntal, homophonic, and "give-and-take," with a careful mixture of dissonance. Duple meter, syncopation, and Still's explicit instructions to treat the dotted-eighth-followed-by-a-sixteenth pattern as the first and third of triplets further establish a blues feeling.

"Sorrow" or Adagio, the *Afro-American's* second movement, is in 4/4 time and built around tonal centers of F major and f minor. Except for the addition of a coda, Still's treatment of the themes in this movement is similar to that of the first movement. But unlike the first movement, there is extensive use of altered chords based on scale degrees II, IV, V and VII. Occasionally he introduces altered III and VI chords. An infinite variety of combinations may be found within a given chord, such as raising or lowering the root or fifth, flatting the ninth, or raising the seventh. Tonal color is enhanced by triads with added major sevenths, diminished triads, augmented triads (usually with major sevenths), diminished seventh chords, chords with added sixths, and chords having both the major and minor third.

Since Still rarely uses but one chord change per measure, the harmonic rhythm is moderately slow. Meticulously he works out the melodic line/harmonic structure relationship, to more clearly define each phrase. Delicately softened dissonances are detectable in this overall homophonic movement. The rather simple rhythms are kept interesting with syncopation. Still unifies this movement with the first one by presenting the original blues melody in the introduction and in the subordinate theme. A powerful element of pathos is sustained by clever use of melodic nuance and grace notes of half-step intervals to suggest a vocal sigh or sob.

The livelier, joyous third movement, a Scherzo ("Humor"), marked Animato, also has a coda. Blues progression chords are again evident, with some new usage of secondary dominants, such as the VI^7, II^7, and V^7, producing a "barbershop" effect. Still made extended use of the tonic with added sixth in this movement, introduced eleventh chords, and employed an unusual chord: root with added major third, plus two superimposed tritones. The last twenty-four measures of the Scherzo pick up in pace, though a brisk tempo is in order from its beginning. Two rhythmic motives found in accompanimental figures seem to unify the movement. (One of these may have been part of Still's orchestration for a soft shoe dance in the show, *Rain Or Shine*.) This multi-textured movement features, for the first time in a symphonic work, the tenor banjo, which not only accentuates the strong, dance-like rhythms, but lends humor as well.

The last movement of *Afro-American*, Lento ("Aspiration"), is the only one in 3/4 meter, later changing to 6/8 during the variation. Its tempo and key center constantly change. The opening theme, announced by the strings, is supported by chordal accompaniment from the clarinets, trombones, tuba and string bass. The subordinate theme derives from the blues theme of the first movement, again, a method of unification. Phrase beginnings and endings are less obvious, due to overlapping melodic figures. This is the most harmonically complex of all the movements, though the harmonic rhythm is not always rapid.

The *Sunday Symphony*, or *Symphony No. 3*, was written in 1958 to fill the void when the original third symphony became *Symphony No. 5*. In it, as in the first symphony, Still proves himself a master at scoring for the harp. *Sunday* opens with a bold announcement by the brass, which gives way to a bustling first section, filled with short, insistent motifs, tossed with good effect from one instrumental choir to another, and punctuated by percussion, ending suddenly on an up-beat. In the second movement, appropriately subtitled "Prayer," Still features the oboe, which weaves a plaintive theme in and out, unifying the movement. The use of lowered thirds and sevenths results in a Negro spiritual-like treatment.

Staccato figures suggest the third movement's name, "Gaily: Relaxation." In this up-tempo section, complemented by the tambourine's shimmer, the full orchestra is busy until the movement ends suddenly on an up-beat. Russian flavor is present in the last movement. After an introduction by full orchestra the strings have a legato, mellow vocal theme, counterpointed by the oboe. Like the previous movement, it ends on an up-beat. Nowhere in this symphony is dissonance pronounced, but the work has some unusual and unexpected modulations.

Still's fourth symphony, *Autochthonous* (1947), is similar to the *Afro-American* in style, though it contains more dissonance and tension. Described as "neo-romantic," it embraces several idioms, including popular and quasi-modern, and reflects the sophistication which Still inevitably absorbed and imparted as a seasoned composer.

84

In Memoriam, The Colored Soldiers Who Died For Democracy (1943), a forceful five-minute orchestral work, has been called by Verna Arvey, Still's wife and pianist, a "poignant requiem," and by Winthrop Sargeant "an essay in pure lyricism." Its spiritual-like melody is contrasted with a mournful motif, handled mainly by the brasses. The score is full-textured, thickening toward the close, when it rises to ffff in dynamics.

BALLETS AND OPERAS

Still's expertise in planning a total work is further evidenced in his ballets and operas. Most of them have been well received though infrequently performed, but their fabric was no less carefully designed, their authenticity no less carefully researched.

Of Still's four ballets, *Lenox Avenue* (1937), inspired by Harlem street scenes, may be remembered best for its piano "Blues" section, which was later arranged for violin and piano/orchestra and for small orchestra. It is in ABA form with improvisations. Still uses the chord progressions I, IV^7, V and I^7, stepwise movement in the inner voices, melody in left hand (or lower instruments), and a syncopated triplet pattern throughout. Dictated by its lazy tempo, this irresistible piece in the blues idiom has all the elements of a refined cabaret number, including a short tag or coda.

Lenox Avenue and two of Still's other ballets, *La Guiablesse* (1927), and *Sahdji* (1930), were scored for chorus and/or solo singers. (*Miss Sally's Party*, 1940, was not.) Such scoring further confirms the full scope of his thoughts and his all-seeing stage eye. *La Guiablesse*, based on a legend from the island of Martinique, expresses hypnotic rhythms of mysterious island peoples. A vivid, authentic atmosphere is conveyed in the piece, ending dramatically with comments from an unaccompanied chanter.

After poets Countee Cullen and Langston Hughes had failed Still as librettists, Verna Arvey became his chief collaborator. Though in a sense Still's music carried its own drama, Arvey's consummate skill at fitting words to melody was invaluable. In commenting on their "team," Eileen Southern asked Still in an interview "How does it work?"

He replied, "Fine! Our premise is that one writes a libretto in the same style as one talks. In preparing for an opera, I do the necessary research and outline the plot. Then my wife and I get together, and she writes the lines. We work closely together with the text and music. Sometimes we have spent hours or even days on a special vocal-diction problem."

Then Southern asked, "How do you go about writing an aria?"

Still said, "First comes the recitative. Then she (Arvey) writes the first line of the aria--so it will tie in with the plot. After that, the entire music for the aria is written and the words added later." Still preferred ABA form for an aria. In the Wagnerian manner he gave each character a musical motif.

An examination of three arias (piano/vocal score) is in order. In the closing scene of *Troubled Island* (premiere, 1949) contralto Azelia, wife of slain Haitian emperor Dessalines, reaffirms her undying love for him. The aria's range covers a ninth, from c^1 to d^2. Accompanimental movement is provided by an arpeggiated sixteenth-note figure, undoubtedly given to the harp in the orchestral score. Supported alternately by a contrapuntal bass line and broken altered seventh and ninth chords boldly reiterated, the aria is quite moving. The few meter changes from 4/4 to 3/4 and back work smoothly with the libretto.

Bob's contrite aria of love for his wife, Mary, in the first scene of *Highway #1* (1962) is a rather strenuous one for the baritone, for there are no relieving accompanimental interludes. A declamatory recitative over sparse accompaniment prefaces the pleading message which follows. The aria, encompassing the range of a tenth (from d to f^1) is as well conceived as an art song, a true ensemble between vocal line and accompaniment, with a minimum of awkward prosody. The harmonic structure is largely that of seventh and ninth chords. The score is romantic in style with a strong sense of musical characterization.

Costaso (1950), set in colonial Spanish America, allowed Still to use the Latin idiom he handled so well. In Manuel's aria in Act III, beginning "I deserve no praise for what I've done," triplet patterns, some broken, are sung against a duple rhythm in the accompaniment. It is short but makes a powerful statement. Again, the use of seventh and ninth chords predominate.

A *Bayou Legend* (premiere, 1974) and *Minette Fontaine* (premiere, 1984) have both been well-received by audiences. The first has been compared favorably with works by Delius, with its "misty orchestral hues," and to Puccini and Romberg in its melodic style. It has been commended for its powerful choral writing, the lilting, rag-like quality of the dances, and a Wagner-like love duet. Still used his own version of Creole themes and showed a thorough understanding of voodoo in *Minette*, set in New Orleans in 1845. One critic called the opera "unabashedly romantic."

Donald Dorr, designer and director for *Minette's* premiere by the Baton Rouge Opera, feels that as an operatic composer Still is far removed from the *verismo* process. A champion of Still's work, he calls his "visionary, yet down-to-earth method" a conscious decision. In these operas he attempts to explain the purpose of life, especially that of the Afro-American, as the "chosen image." "His mysticism is undeniable--as he dreamed and wrote his dreams, his characters evolved," Dorr writes.

VOCAL WORKS

Still's most ambitious and best known work for chorus and orchestra, *And They Lynched Him On A Tree* (1940), requires full orchestra, Negro chorus, White chorus, narrator and contralto soloist. It contains motivic rhythms, polyrhythms, antiphonal effects, and strong blues tonalities.

The following year, on a similar but smaller scale, Still composed *Plain-Chant For America* for orchestra and baritone soloist. Lower brass announces the main motif, which prefaces a heavily textured score. The introduction continues authoritatively, slightly faster, with accompanimental tremolos of diminished chords. A tremolo (a minor) invites the soloist in. After eight measures the key signature changes from the previous G to E. Massive chords occupy the accompaniment, well supporting the vocal line, for the next eleven measures. Then the tempo slows, the key signature is canceled, and the mood alters. At this point Still adroitly scored staccati and rests descriptive of the text, "We fear tyranny as our hidden enemy: the black shirt cruelty, the goose-step mind . . .. " The singer is spared during a majestic interlude of the theme. Following is a short recit-like passage, which segues into the piece's powerful end, again punctuated by the drama of rests and appropriate rhythmic figures in the accompaniment. A bravura twelve-measure postlude stunningly ends the piece.

Still composed many art songs, for he was especially fond of poetry and of setting it to music. The five *Songs Of Separation* (1949) for high voice, are set to texts of one Haitian and four American poets, purposefully selected to depict a logical cycle of lost love. Though each song is shorter than others of Still's, this eleven page cycle is exemplary. The mostly chordal accompaniments, full of seventh, ninth and eleventh sonorities, lie comfortably for the pianist. Introductions are brief and interludes are no longer than one measure. "Poéme," by Phillipe Thoby Marcelin, is set to its original French. All the cycle's poets are black, but there is no prevading "black sound." *Separation* is of sufficient difficulty to challenge a thoughtful, well trained singer.

Three of Still's longer songs, *Breath Of A Rose, Winter's Approach*, and *Song For The Valiant* bear mention. In *Rose*, set to words by Langston Hughes, two- and four-measure blocks of B-flat and E-flat tonalities suggestive of pedal point underlie most of the lush harmonies, some not particularly tonal to the vocal line. The accompaniment to *Winter's Approach* cleverly and humorously features repetitive, syncopated figures, spiced by snap rhythm in the vocal line. Still's stirring *Song For The Valiant* begins with a rather free four-measure vocal recitative over sustained accompanimental chords. The rest of the song in 6/8 time is martial in mood, systematically laid out in four-measure phrases using accented, staccato broken chords on the main beats. The chord progressions are fairly standard, with only two accidentals.

In 1937 Still's arrangements of twelve Negro spirituals were published. He left the melodies unembellished, choosing to enhance them with a more contemporary chordal accompaniment. Explicit dynamics and expression markings for each spiritual are indicated.

PIANO WORKS

Despite Still's lack of formal piano training, he wrote well for the instrument, a genre affording the utmost expression of his mystical ideas. Both *Three Visions* and *Seven Traceries* are worthy of programming as a recital group. Dominique René DeLerma, who urges piano teachers to use illustrations from the literature of Black composers, compares Still's skill in using seventh and ninth chords to Debussy's in *La Fille Aux Cheveux De Lin.*

DeLerma's reference is to "Summerland," a dreamy, expressive mood piece, the second of Still's *Three Visions* (1936). To the listener its sound is almost improvisatory. Pianist Natalie Hinderas describes it as the "relaxed timelessness one feels on a hot summer day," but Still's daughter says that it constitutes a description of Heaven, or, life-after death. Part of the melody is chordal, and part a single line, as if written for a violin or cello. Plenty of rhythmic interest is provided by subtle syncopation and fragments of arpeggiated figures in the left hand accompaniment. "Dark Horsemen" is a strong, tension-filled, dramatic contrast with its brusque rhythmic figures, which plainly say "Giddiyap, giddiyap!" Judith Anne Still, the composer's daughter, says "Horsemen" shows an image of death and divine judgment. Sixteenth notes pretty well carry the rhythm of "Radiant Pinnacle," the third of the *Visions*, an impressionistic piece of some interpretative difficulty, representing man's aspiration toward God. Nuance is natural within the rise and fall of each phrase.

Seven Traceries (1940), a second piano cycle, is a clever gem, as precious as the *Songs Of Separation*. Its seven parts are all in ABA form, and most of them have several key changes. The arched melodic line of "Cloud Cradles" suggests curly, fluffy clouds--as each phrase gets higher in range more clouds can be imagined--a picture interrupted by an arpeggiated, frolicsome run, as if the wind had rearranged them. The minor ninths and augmented chords never quite resolve in "Mystic Pool," a dissonant mood piece with overall dynamic markings of ppp. "Muted Laughter" is whimsically playful, like a game of children's tag. The simple rhythms which change every four measures give it a pleasant conversational quality.

The fourth of the *Traceries*, "Out Of The Silence," is introspective, dissonant and unresolved, though, oddly enough, its tempo is soothing. The B section is lyrical and expressive, a contrast to the improvisational style of the opening. It ends on an E major chord with an added tritone of F to B. "Woven Silver," mainly in triplet patterns, is another mood piece, with dynamics ranging subtly from p to pp. Anguish is created by augmented chords in the aptly named "Wailing Dawn." The B section really does wail, as if scored for a trumpet, climaxes stridently, then returns to the chordal A section. It ends ppp on a ninth chord. "A Bit Of Wit," is fanciful, with tricky alternating patterns of sixteenth notes, ending on ninth chords marked "as loud as possible." Its key center is identifiable throughout.

Bells (1944), a short suite for piano, includes two pieces in ABA form, "Phantom Chapel" and "Fairy Knoll." In "Chapel" right hand triads give an excellent effect of bells, added to by left hand dissonances and subtle pedaling which provide overtones peculiar to bells. Four different rhythmic figures, switched from hand to hand, in addition to snap rhythms, major sevenths, tritones, and a dynamic range of pp to ff keep "Knoll" interesting. As in "Chapel" Still effects more reverberation of spooky quality, as if the bells were played with soft mallets. The four-measure B section is built completely on the C major sixth chord in contrast to the more dissonant A sections.

Kaintuck' (1935) for piano and orchestra/two pianos is a hauntingly beautiful tonal piece, shimmering as it depicts misty sunlight on Kentucky blue grass. The entire work grows from two themes. Arvey, who premiered it, wrote: "The piano opens the poem quietly, then runs into a rhythmic accompaniment to the orchestral statement of the themes. Both the piano and the orchestra are heard in huge, authoritative chords just before the cadenza by the solo instrument. This cadenza, unlike most, does not aim toward the exploitation of the interpreter, but simply and colorfully enhances the thematic and harmonic material that has preceded it. The theme is restated, and the piano closes the poem as quietly as it opened it."

CHAMBER AND INSTRUMENTAL WORKS

In 1958 Still agreed to write a solo piece for harp at the request of harpist Lois Adele Craft. After thorough research, the result was *Ennanga* (named for the African harp). The piece is replete with a cadenza and original themes inspired by African music. To Still *Ennanga* represented his own spiritual journey through life's temptations and dangers. Craft has said of it: "For me the three movements speak of the development of life in the primitive world. In the first, with its percussive wildness, the listener gets a glimpse of the danger and rhythm of the jungle, the snakes and tigers, and dense, dark undergrowth. The second movement is more spiritual, bringing into view the green beauty of ferns and grasses, the calm and peaceful water. The final segment brings out the magnificence of the environment, and the joy."

In 1960 Still wrote two accordion solos, *Aria* and *Lilt*, for accordionist Elsie M. Bennett. In rondo form, *Aria's* two major themes recur throughout the nine-part piece, in which development, contrast and transition stand out as compositional devices. *Lilt*, less difficult, was commissioned by Bennett as a teaching piece for the American Accordionists' Association.

Suite For Violin And Piano (1943) and *Pastorela* (1945) were the only violin and piano works that Still composed. The suite was inspired by sculptures and a lithograph of Negro subjects. *Pastorela* gives an unserious, languorous picture of a California landscape.

Romance For Saxophone And Piano (1954) is simply what the name implies, an expressive bit of give-and-take between the two instruments.

It is tonal and straight forward. Of moderate difficulty, it makes an ideal teaching piece.

In a more familiar genre, Still's *Folk Suite No. 4 For Flute, Clarinet And Cello* (1962) affects in the first movement a gypsy atmosphere with its chordal piano accompaniment and a dance-like gaiety in the solo parts. The second movement, opening with a flute solo, is more sustained and romantic in contrast with the last segment, a festive Brazilian dance in rumba beat.

The themes in *Miniatures For Flute, Oboe And Piano* (1948) are all taken from folk melodies. A mixture of duple and triple meters and changing tempos in "I Ride An Old Paint" suggest the unevenness of a journey in unknown country. Its ending, on a I^7 chord, is a surprise. Mexican flavor in "Adolorido," in ballad style, is provided by the piano articulation imitative of a guitar. Still's rhythmic treatment in "Jesus is a Rock in a Weary Land" corresponds to that given similar spirituals in today's rural churches. The tune is in minor mode, supported by a rhapsodic piano part. In "Yaravi," derived from a Peruvian lament, the flute and oboe have conversational solos, later complemented by one for the piano. The old tune "Frog Went a Courtin'" captures the essence of the strutting frog through clever articulation in all three parts.

The foregoing essay concerning William Grant Still's musical style is intended to emphasize his creativity and expertise as a total musician. A full listing of his classical works may be found in the "Works And Performances" section of this book.

Anne K. Simpson

ESSAYS OF BIAS: BLESH, MELLERS AND "BLACK MUSIC"

Vieuxtemps, Ole Bull and Henry Russell--have made us all musical.
From the amateur organ grinder through the whole horned tribe,
sarpent, sackbut and all, Frenchman, Jewman, Dutchman, Miss at
her piano and Cuff, with his blade of grass, are all blowing it hard...
-- Franklin Soule, *Woodville Republican*, February 3, 1844

Back in 1985 I read a review by Bernard Holland in the *New York Times* that made me want to cry. "An afternoon of music by Black composers that says little about Black music seems an arbitrary kind of affair," he wrote on February 20. "Blind Tom Bethune's 'Sewing Machine' borrowed shamelessly from Liszt and Schumann . . .. William Grant Still's 'Seven Traceries' were a ponderous imitation of French impressionism . . .."

And one had thought that music was a universal language! (And even that Grieg's borrowing from Brahms--and vice versa--was rather fun!)

For some at least, evidently not. For however far we think we've come from "separate but equal," there are those in this "colorblind" society who will still assert the right to issue value judgements based on race alone, on the theory (itself arbitrary, perverse and cunning) that "Black composers" must incessantly and inevitably and *sui generis* be saying something about "Black music." Where, and this is the genius of the thing, does it stop? When all is said and done, how black is black *enough*? Kafka would be delighted.

Music historians, hurting to reduce jazz origins to the impossible irreducible point, have often called for a sort of parthenogenesis. This is the scenario: though initially limited to quills, jaw bones and the "hollow drums", blacks "with no formal training" but "extreme musicality" achieved "quick mastery" of "difficult instruments", surmounting "difficulties they did not even know existed"--or so, for instance, Rudi Blesh.[1]

---

[1] Rudi Blesh, *Shining Trumpets: A History of Jazz* (N.Y.: DaCapo reprint, 1976, of Alfred Knopf second edition, 1958), 160, who also assumes that marching bands preexisting jazz played in "self-taught and highly Negroid style." (156) In fact, trained black marching bands existed at least as far back as

Au contraire. Jazz music evolved as most other forms of music have, originating in the hands of well-trained, capable musicians.

Asked by Leonard Feather where he had acquired his "Jazz musicians" (Feather's term) for his 1896-97 band, W.C. Handy said simply, "from all over the country," but added that "you got your best musicians back in the '80s and '90s from Shreveport, Baton Rouge, Vicksburg, Jackson-- Mississippi and Louisiana.   Alabama had some, also Florida and Tennessee."[2] One explanation for this amazing pool of talent lies in a letter from Handy to Still in 1944: "The theatres all had Negro musicians that played the traveling shows, like Rembert Brooks at Vicksburg, Miss., the Wylers at Pensacola . . .." Their training had been under "Germans and Italians who came South . . . and had come to the colored homes; and taught some very fine musicians that were as good as any musicians at that time, but were held back."[3] J. Russel Robinson, manager for Handy's publishing firm (and composer of "Margie") had played silent movie theatres around the South and his "solid piano" is heard on Nick LaRocca's Dixieland Band recordings of 1917.[4] In other words, most of these supposed "untrained" musicians had both prior experience *and* training.

The Blesh school, of course, would say that neither Handy nor Feather knew what they were talking about, as they were both men who had denied their musical heritage. Case in point: Jelly Roll Morton, Blesh tells us, "retained for Handy and his pretenses the contempt a great creative personality might be forgiven for feeling," explaining:

Although a Negro, Handy is, and in sympathy always has been, rather remote from the racial wellspring from which blues and jazz emerged. He seems, from the time of his youth, to have been in the un-negroid tradition that goes back to the Fisk Jubilee Singers *or farther*, a tradition that always has aimed to "disinfect" Afro-American music by Europeanizing it.[5]

---

style." (156) In fact, trained black marching bands existed at least as far back as Chalmette, and were regularly attached to the Confederate army: Bell Irwin Wiley, *Southern Negroes, 1861-1865,* (New Haven, Yale, 1938), 136n.

[2] Leonard Feather, *The Book of Jazz* (Horizon Press/Paperback Library, 1961), 30.

[3] "In Retrospect: Letters from W.C. Handy to William Grant Still", in *Black Perspective* in Music, 7, No. 2, 1979.

[4] H.O. Brunn, *The Story of the Dixieland Jazz Band* (Baton Rouge, 1960), 122.

[5] Rudi Blesh, *Shining Trumpets*, 146, emphasis mine.

What exactly qualifies, in point of time, as an "un-Negroid tradition"? Eileen Southern indeed dates the Fisk style back to a white instructor in 1867[6], but this predates W.C. Handy's birth by only five years and post-dates Harry Burleigh's. But Blesh coyly fields an alternative in his "or farther", positing an "un-Negroid tradition" in what must have been the days of slavery--perhaps in the secular music of the black musicians of the *Intrepid* on the bay of Naples ca. 1800, or in "the sooty sons of Afric forgetting their bondage" William Bartram found, while touring Georgia in 1775 (who "in chorus sang the virtues and beneficence of their master in songs of their own composition")[7], or even in the "torrent of sacred psalmody" the Reverend Mr. Davies heard in 1756.[8] But never mind fact: what Blesh must have are "racial wellsprings" and the poisoning of these springs by "Europeanizing." In this he would certainly agree that ...

> the ability to sing the (Negro) folk song effectively is not prevalent among the educated Negroes, for it is considered bad musical taste by most of those who teach Negroes. This is because such teachers have no comprehension of the importance of race consciousness, or they have no understanding of the worth of the music. Some are, as yet, too thoroughly possessed by the classical idea, or too sensitive to the question of slavery . . . To assert that (there is) any greater resemblance between the Negro's music and European music than would naturally result from the oneness of human nature . . . is uninformed, misinformed, superficial, unscientific, or all of these.

Surely a thorough condemnation of "un-Negroid tradition"! And yet these are precisely the words of John Wesley Work, Jr., director of the Fisk Jubilee Singers from 1900 to 1916, and one Blesh accused of maintaining this tradition.

Work's chapter on "Characteristics and Peculiarities" in his 1915 *Folk Song of the American Negro* is a landmark; *this* is the Fisk tradition, but for Blesh, eager to stroke "The Originator of JAZZ," Morton's fervid dislike of Handy was enough to diametrically misrepresent it and read "the Father of the Blues" out of church. A wary investigator might have found instruction in Eubie Blake's smiling admission that what Whitey

---

[6] Eileen Southern, *The Music of Black Americans, A History* (N.Y.: W.W. Norton Co., 1971), 249.

[7] 257 Mark Van Doren, ed., *Travels of William Bartram* (1773-1778) (N.Y., Dover reprint of the 1928 Macy-Massius edition, 1955), 257.

[8] Letter from "Rev. Mr. Davies", in John Wesley Work, Jr., *Journal*, March 1, 1756.

wants whitey gets: "The people wanted to believe that Negroes couldn't learn to read music but had a natural talent for it ...'Isn't it wonderful,' they'd say, 'How those untrained musicians can pick up on all the latest songs instantly without being able to read music?' That William Grant Still who played oboe with us--I wonder if he could read music when he was arrangin' for Paul Whiteman?"[9]

William Grant Still certainly could read music and so could the multitudes of other Negro musicians who were performing at the time. Thus, the theory that jazz was born in a vacuum just won't wash, and even Blesh admits the formative influence of at least the "French Quadrille" on Jelly Roll Morton (probably since Jelly himself, rather famously, brought it up). Curiously, the German influence on Black musicians has been often overlooked in a search for "French quadrilles" in the jazz bloodline. Because more often than not, even in New Orleans, it was, as Handy wrote Still, the German musician--or the Italian, like Luigi Gabicci--who taught (and wrote) the quadrilles.

And not only, as Handy obliquely noted, in New Orleans.

In this regard, another piece of shallow thinking regarding the origins of popular music and the training of popular musicians--again on the white side--from John Tasker Howard, who in an essay on Stephen Foster quoted by Elie Siegmeister in *The Music Lover's Handbook*, opines that Stephen Foster, "born and raised in the interior, was little affected by the foreign immigration of the musicians that enslaved the seaboard in mid-century"--yet without missing a beat credits "Henry Kleber, a German resident musician in Pittsburgh" for Foster's "few rudimentary lessons"![10] The musical history of Woodville, Mississippi, where William Grant Still was born, is peppered with reports of European teachers who paused in the little inland town and--unless one is ignorant of the geography of the "interior"--Woodville can serve for Pittsburgh as well. Whether one counts the contributions of Philip Werlein, of the great New Orleans music house (or even an Audubon, who had more than one string to his bow) to American music as "enslavement" is, one supposes, subjective. Both taught in Woodville.

America was not isolated, and the American Black was not isolated. And in neither case was music held hostage to isolation.

---

[9] Al Rose, *Eubie Blake* (N.Y.: Schirmer/Macmillan, 1979), 59.

[10] Quoted in Elie Siegmeister, ed., *The Music Lover's Handbook* (N.Y., William Morrow, 1943), 741.

Scott Joplin, for example, "dreamed of writing a music which would be accepted with the piano works of Chopin, Schumann and Liszt but which would reveal the mind and soul of the Black man . . . Joplin always felt that 'ragtime' was a scurrilous term invented to discredit black music and musicians, and he only grudgingly accepted it in the titles of his compositions,"[11] which were often, at any event, "too complex to gain wide acceptance."[12] To even an amateur the kinship of Joplin's "Leola," say, with the Schumann of "Einsame Blumen" seems obvious. It may be worth remembering in this regard that late in his own lifetime and for a period thereafter Schumann was in eclipse, and only toward the latter part of the century was rediscovered; to him, nevertheless, and in W.S.B. Matthew's words, "the entire art of modern piano playing is indebted for some of its most impressive elements . . . the accompaniment upon the off beat . . ., chords which always come in upon the half beat or quarter beat, and rarely or never upon the full accented part of a measure."[13] Schumann was also to be credited with "a new style of composition, or of music thinking [in which] a single phrase or motive is repeated through nearly an entire movement, in a thousand different forms and transformations . . . with such mastery of rhythm and of harmony" as to preclude monotony and, of course, innovative use of pedal "for blending notes." Even Rudi Blesh must bank--albeit unfavorably--against Schumann's "syncopations" to find a comparison for "variety and complexity," the polyrhythmic, melodic variation" of a Jimmy Yancy.[14] At any event, Blesh's assertion that "Romantic nineteenth-century European music, particularly German"--which he identifies with "a cloying, sentimental sweetness"--"entered with the Wolverines", and in particular with Bix Beiderbecke and the "Jazz Me Blues" in 1923 or 1924,[15] is simply off-base, and lucid only in support of his undoubtedly well-meant thesis that "white men led most of the Negroes into deserting the music that had come from their hearts."[16] As is disconcertingly his

---

[11] William J. Schafer and Johannes Riedel, *The Art of Ragtime: Form and Meaning of an Original Black American Art* (Baton Rouge, LSU, 1974), 52.

[12] Albert McCarthy, *The Dance Band Era* (London: November Books, 1971), 9.

[13] W.S.B. Matthews, *A Popular History of Music from the Earliest Times to the Present* (N.Y.: John Church, 1915), 472.

[14] Rudi Blesh, *Shining Trumpets*, 307.

[15] *Ibid.*, 228.

[16] *Ibid.*, 238.

wont, Blesh attributes psychological ills to those he disagrees with: as to Beiderbecke, "weakness characterized his life."[17]   The Beiderbecke contagion reigns in Wilfrid Mellers as well, where Artie Shaw's rendition of his own "The Blues" is troubled by a "Beiderbecke-like frailty" that is "emotionally indulgent . . . wistfully nostalgic, even self-pitying."[18] In fact, Artie Shaw does remember "Traumerei" as a childhood hurdle; *there*--you see?[19]

What has all this to do with jazz (or *Jazz*) which, as the parthenogenicists would have us believe, sprang full-grown from the head of a cat?

The minimum that New Orleans Jazz can admittedly be reduced to ("the real creators of jazz," Herbert Asbury calls them,[20] the fabled 1895 Razzy Dazzy Spasm Band of Harry Gregson, Emile Lacoumb, Willey and Frank Bussey, Charley Stein, Emile Benrod, and the pseudonymous Chinee and Warm Gravy) is to point of comedy inextricably linked with the dreaded Teuton:

> We used to 'bump' the old German band quite a bit. We would wait for the band to start playing on a corner and attract a big crowd and then we would 'bump' it, taking over the audience and passing the hat. The German band most of the time would play for beer, and we would play for peanuts.
>
> Ragtime? No, we didn't play that stuff. Our stuff was something different. It was just an idea. *I doubt that we got it from Negro music.* We just started putting in this hot stuff all of a sudden.[21]

And then, said "Stale Bread" Lacoumb, they began to get "store-bought" instruments.

"Cuff with his blade of grass . . ." Or, in the case of the Razzy Dazzy Jazzy Band, a half-barrel bass fiddle, cheese box banjo, soap box guitar, cigar box violin, tin tray mandolin, and a harmonica, a kettle, a whistle, a

---

[17] *Ibid.*, 230.

[18] Wilfrid Mellers, *Music in a New Found Land: Themes and Developments in the History of American Music* (N.Y.: Oxford, 1987), 315.

[19] Artie Shaw, *The Trouble with Cinderella* (N.Y.: Farrar Strauss, 1952; Da Capo edition, 1979), 50.

[20] Herbert Asbury, *The French Quarter*, (N.Y.: Knopf, Cardinal Edition, 1966), 326.

[21] Orin Blackstone, "Hot Music Born Here, Says Blind Musician Who Played With Band that Started It", New Orleans *Times-Picayune*, Nov. 3, 1935. Italics mine.

cowbell, "various horns" and an enthusiastic and infectious "Hi-di-Hi, Hi-di-Ho!" "The human voice, feet, and hands are instruments common to the American and the African American Negro; the piano, trumpet, silver-plated banjo, and saxophone are not," wrote Winthrop Sargent.[22]

Take it or leave it.

So soon as you push it through the whiteman's whistle or brush it across the whiteman's washboard or spread it across the whiteman's ivory keys you, by definition, have not black music. And so if that's what you thought jazz was, you are wrong.

It's like the chicken and the egg.

It's like the problem of the irreducible point. An impossibility. *But if this be true*, then a whole lot of "experts"--a lot of professional reactionaries--are wrong, and William Grant Still, and all of the others who, like him, sought in all they did to blaze new trails with Afro-American music, were right on track. The question is not where jazz came from, but what to do with it: and that is the mission of art.

Donald Dorr

---

[22] Elie Siegmeister, ed., *The Music Lover's Handbook*, 695.

IV

THE SYMPHONIC WORKS

INTRODUCTORY NOTE

The purpose of this section is to present a comprehensive portrayal of William Grant Still, the man, his style of musical composition, his compositional philosophy, and his place in the historical style continuum of American music. The *First Symphony* (*The Afro-American*) and the *Fourth Symphony* (*Autochthonous*) have been chosen for study because they represent examples of Mr. Still's highest level of achievement in the field of musical composition. The *Afro-American Symphony* (1930) and *Autochthonous* (1947) will be submitted to analysis and comparison; comparisons will be made in the following areas:

1. Formal structure
2. Harmonic structure and vocabulary
3. Origin of themes and thematic development
4. Factors that unify the symphonies
5. Methods used to obtain variety of expression
6. Orchestration technique
7. Rhythmic devices employed
8. Accomplishment of the tension-release cycle
9. The basic compositional style of the symphonies

William Grant Still is recognized as one of the first Negro composers to obtain national and international recognition. His *Afro-American Symphony* has received world-wide acclaim and is considered one of his finest compositions; it is a favorite of the composer. The symphony subtitled *Autochthonous*, written some seventeen years after the *Afro-American*, is also highly regarded. A partial goal of this study is to examine these two symphonies and to point out how they are similar and how they differ.

The gathering and enumeration of a composer's ideas, attitudes, feelings, and compositional philosophy while he is still living can have special value to musicologists of the future, as well as to the interested student of music and music history.

Paul Harold Slattery

100

A COMPREHENSIVE STUDY OF THE
AFRO-AMERICAN SYMPHONY

William Grant Still has informed the writer that a comprehensive study of the *Afro-American Symphony*, which includes a detailed harmonic analysis, has not, to the best of his knowledge, been made. The aim of this chapter is to examine this symphony and to present a clear, concise, and complete picture of the musical devices involved in its composition.

I. GENERAL CONSIDERATIONS

The Creation of the Afro-American Symphony

The composer's intention. "I knew I wanted to write a symphony; I knew that it had to be an *American* work; and I wanted to demonstrate how the *Blues*, so often considered a lowly expression, could be elevated to the highest musical level." The above statement by William Grant Still was submitted to Karl Krueger to be included in the jacket notes for the Society for the Preservation of the American Musical Heritage's recording of the *Afro-American Symphony*.[1]

In the text of a speech given to a Composers' Workshop in 1967, Mr. Still gives us further clues concerning his precompositional thought:

> Long before writing this symphony I had recognized the musical value of the *Blues* and had decided to use a theme in the *Blues* idiom as the basis for a major symphonic composition. When I was ready to launch this project I did not want to use a theme some folk singer had already created, but decided to create my own theme in the *Blues* idiom.[2]

The collection of themes. The actual creation of material for the *Afro-American* was taking place for several years prior to 1930. The composer penciled themes in a sketch book over a period of years. These themes were listed in categories such as passionate, happy, dramatic, plaintive, and barbaric.

The compositional process. The themes had been collected and the inspiration and motivation for composing were vividly present in the

---

[1] See page 169.

[2] Speech to Composers' Workshop, annual convention of National Association of Negro Musicians, Los Angeles, CA, August 17, 1967.

mind and in the heart of the composer; the remaining necessary ingredients were the time and the place to begin the creative activity. Mr. Still describes this creation:

> It was not until the Depression struck that I went jobless long enough to let the Symphony take shape. In 1930, I rented a room in a quiet building not far from my home in New York, and began to work. I devised my own Blues theme (which appears in varied guises throughout the Symphony, as a unifying thread), planned the form, then wrote the entire melody. After that I worked out the harmonies, the various treatments of the theme, and the orchestration.[3]

The addition of program notes and poem fragments. At the time the *Symphony* was written, the composer states that no thought was given to program notes; these were added after the completion of the work, as were the verses from poems by Paul Laurence Dunbar. In 1939, Mr. Still made the following comments concerning these additions:

> I have regretted this step because in this particular instance a program is decidedly inadequate. The program devised at the time, stated that the music portrayed the "sons of the soil," that is, that it offered a composite musical portrait of those Afro-Americans who have not responded completely to the cultural influences of today. It is true that an interpretation of that sort may be read into the music. Nevertheless, one who hears it is quite sure to discover other meanings which are probably broader in their scope.[4]

Excerpts from the poems of Paul Laurence Dunbar precede each movement of the symphony. Each movement is designed to portray a specific emotion and the poetic excerpts serve as an extra-musical means of reinforcing this emotion. To this limited extent, the *Afro-American Symphony* may be described as being "programmatic" in nature.

Significant Data

Brief descriptive statement. The *Afro-American Symphony* is a tonal composition in four movements with emphasis placed on the free flow

---

[3] From jacket notes (Krueger), *op. cit.*

[4] Verna Arvey, *William Grant Still: Studies Of Contemporary American Composers* (New York: J. Fischer & Bro., 1939), pp. 23-24.

of the melodic line. The use of the *Blues* scale (a nine-tone mode which includes the flatted third and seventh degrees of the regular diatonic scale) permitted extensive usage of melodic nuance. The harmonies are basically simple, but differ from traditional European harmony in that they include an extensive use of added-tone cords. These added-tone chords include the root, third, and fifth along with the sixth, seventh, or ninth. The most used device, however, was the triad (major or minor) with the added minor seventh interval. The "blue" notes in the melodic line and the embellished, piquant harmonies are the major devices that accomplished uniqueness for this composition in 1930.

> . . . the *Afro-American Symphony,* was composed in 1930, dedicated to Irving Schwerke and performed by the Rochester Philharmonic Orchestra in Rochester in 1931 and 1932 and in part under the direction of Dr. Howard Hanson (who introduced it) in Berlin, Stuttgart and Leipzig in 1933. These dates show conclusively that Still's work preceeded that of another Negro composer who in 1934 was heralded as having written the *first* Negro symphony.[5]

It is important to note here that this is *probably* the first use of the banjo in a major symphonic work. None of the sources comment on this fact, but both Verna Arvey and William Grant Still are of the opinion that this is the first serious usage of this instrument. In the personal interview of February 12, 1969, both Mr. and Mrs. Still stated that they knew of no attempt to use the banjo in a major composition prior to 1930.[6]

Time breakdown. The following time breakdown is taken from page four of the score of the *Afro-American Symphony,* Fischer Edition No. 0318, with revisions by William Grant Still. (Revision dates impossible to establish.) It is of interest to note that the divisions of this symphony are referred to as Part I, Part II, Part III, and Part IV instead of being referred to as *movements*; also, Mr. Still does not use the terms exposition, development, and recapitulation, but rather the terms Division I, II, & III. This, in a sense, helps to demonstrate his desire to break away from a strict adherence to traditional practices. The time breakdown is as follows:

---

[5] Arvey, *op. cit.*, pp. 23-24.

[6] Personal Interview: Paul H. Slattery with Verna Arvey and William Grant Still.

Part I	7¼ minutes
Part II	5¼ minutes
Part III	4 minutes
Part IV	7¼ minutes
Total Performance Time	*23¾ minutes.*

II. SPECIFIC CONSIDERATIONS

The Formal Scheme

William Grant Still defends the somewhat unorthodox form that is employed in the *Afro-American Symphony* in the following statement:

> When judged by the laws of musical form the Symphony is somewhat irregular. This irregularity is in my estimation justified since it has no ill effect on the proportional balance of the composition. Moreover, when one considers that an architect is free to design new forms of buildings, and bears in mind the freedom permitted creators in other fields of art, he can hardly deny a composer the privilege of altering established forms as long as the sense of proportion is justified.[7]

In the compositional philosophy of Mr. Still, melody has the position of foremost concern; however, he feels that melody must be supported and intensified by the use of a formal scheme that is logical, balanced, and clear. Form is the next most important element of composition. In a speech given for a Composers' Workshop in 1967, Mr. Still comments further on the importance of form:

> Once having decided upon which themes to use, I then go on to planning the form of the new composition. My usual practice is to map out a plan which conforms loosely to the established rules of musical form, and then to deviate from it as I see fit. This method serves as a stimulant to invention and inspiration.[8]

---

[7] Arvey, *op. cit.*, p. 24.
[8] Speech to Composers' Workshop, annual convention of National Association of Negro Musicians, Los Angeles, CA, August 17, 1967.

FIRST MOVEMENT: MODERATO ASSAI

Outline of Form: First Movement

In Figures 1A to 1E following, the formal structure of the First Movement is presented in outline form. It is of interest to note that the rehearsal numbers assigned by the composer are placed to correspond with the sectional breakdown:

Figure 1A. Outline of Form -- *Afro-American Symphony*: First Movement

No	Pages	Section	No. Of Measures	Key	Tempo	Comments
1	5-6	Introduction	6	A Flat Major	♩ = 88	*Moderato assai*; mezzo-forte; common time; English horn solo in a rubato style; melody derived from the principal theme.
2	6-8	Principal Theme *Blues* Theme (First subject)	12	Same	Same	Follows the pattern of the "standard" twelve-measure *Blues*; may be termed a multi-phrase period; consists of 3 four-measure units: 1. Statement of theme 2. Imitation at the 2nd 3. Imitation at the 5th Melody in muted trumpet (Harmon mute); Contrapuntal texture.
3	8-11	Restatement Of *Blues* Theme	14	Same	Same	Clarinet on melody with contrapuntal texture in woodwinds; chordal texture in spiccato style; contains a two-measure extension.

Figure 1B. Outline of Form - *Afro-American Symphony*: First Movement

No	Pages	Section	No. Of Measures	Key	Tempo	Comments
4	11-13	Variation Of Principle Theme	12	A Flat Major	♩ = 112	*piu mosso* Rhythmic variation of the *Blues* theme carried in the violins against a rhythmic counterpoint in the woodwinds/horns. Thesis--4 measures Antithesis--4 measures Transition--4 measures
5	13-14	Subordinate Theme (Second subject)	8	G Major	♩ = 72	*andante cantabile* Second subject carried in the oboe; descant by the flute; counterpoint in low strings, plus arpeggiation in the harp. Multiple-textures. Masterful orchestration. Note the change to an unrelated key center: a nuance in 1930. Passage consists of a statement and a counter-statement both four measures in length.

105

Figure 1C. Outline of Form - *Afro-American Symphony*: First Movement

No	Pages	Section	No. Of Measures	Key	Tempo	Comments
6	14-16	Alteration Of Subordinate Theme	8	G		Slightly faster than 72, *poco piu mosso*; the subordinate theme is restated with a slight rhythmic alteration by the first violins, then by the flute.
7	16-17	Variation Of Subordinate Theme	7	Same	Same	Melody in celli. (4 Ms.) Melody in harp. (4 Ms.) Note special harp effects, "with nails close to sounding board."
8	17-18	Transitional Passage	6	G Minor		*piu mosso* *Accelerando poco a poco sin al allegro.* Transitional passage in the strings building up to division two, (Development); thin texture mainly chordal; ends in an E7 chord in the horns which prepares the key, Ab minor.

Figure 1D. Outline of Form - *Afro-American Symphony*: First Movement

No	Pages	Section	No. Of Measures	Key	Tempo	Comments
9	18-21	Division II (Development)	16	A Flat Minor	♩ = 160	*Allegro* Development of material from the principle theme, "Give-and-take" texture. Melodic line shifts from section to section every few measures.
10	21-23	Continuation Of Above	14	Same	Same	Richly orchestrated; much rhythmic counterpoint. First use of full orchestra.
11	24-25	Division III (Recapitulation)	10	A Flat Minor	♩ = 72	*Andante cantabile* Subordinate theme now appears in Ab minor: a radical departure. Melody in violins, ctpt. in low strings; complex texture used, both contrapuntal and chordal at once; solos by bass clarinet and bassoons on extensions of the theme.

Figure 1E. Outline of Form - *Afro-American Symphony*: First Movement

No	Pages	Section	No. Of Measures	Key	Tempo	Comments
12	25	Transition	2	Same	♩ = 88	*Tempo primo* A two-measure transitional passage, prepares new key (Ab major) and new, slower tempo.
12	26-28	Restatement Of Principle Theme	14	A Flat Minor	Same	Final appearance of the principal theme, chordal texture, melody in the muted trumpet, rhythmic counterpoint in woodwinds, return to the strict *Blues* harmonic pattern: I, I^7, IV, V^7, I.
13	28-29	Coda	7	Same	Slower	*Meno* Bass clarinet imitates the principal theme; complex harmony resolves to a "I^6" chord; a prelude to modern, popular harmonic cliché. End of first movement. Total measures = 136. Time--7 1/4 minutes.

Thematic Material: Introductory Theme

The introduction to the First Movement of the *Afro-American Symphony* is derived from the principal theme of that movement. The five-note melodic pattern shown under the bracket is taken directly from the first subject, note for note; the only change that occurs is in the rhythmic pattern. See Figures 2 and 3.

Figure 2. Introductory Theme: First Movement

The melody above is presented as a solo by the English horn--a favorite solo instrument of Mr. Still. The metronome marking for the introduction is eighty-eight for the quarter note. The plaintive sound of this solo creates a musical gesture which helps to reinforce the mood of the first movement--longing. The movement is prefaced by the following verse by Paul Laurence Dunbar which tends to enhance the extra-musical associations:

"All my life long twell de night has pas'
Let de wo'k come ez it will,
So dat I fin' you, my honey, at last'
Somewhaih des ovah de hill".[9]

The principal theme. Figure 3 below states the principal theme of the First Movement; the theme is also referred to as the first subject, but more often is described as the *Blues* theme.

Figure 3. Principal Theme (*Blues* theme)

---

[9] *The Life and Works of Paul Laurence Dunbar*, Dodd-Mead & Co., 1907 ed..

It is important to note that this theme adheres to the standard twelve-measure *Blues* pattern. Despite the fact that it is a typical *Blues* melody, it was not borrowed from existing folk music, but was a pure musical creation of the composer. Through the use of thematic transformation, variations of this theme are heard throughout the composition. These variations are musical gestures which serve as the factor of unification for the *Afro-American Symphony*.

Variation of Blues theme. Figure 4 below gives an example of Mr. Still's style of thematic transformation. The principal theme is repeated with certain alterations in the rhythmic and orchestral treatment.

Figure 4. Variation of the *Blues* Theme

Extended transition. An extended transitional passage occurs next. Figure 5 below shows yet another transformation of the *Blues* theme which is used in the transition. This is the fourth consecutive presentation of the principal theme. This transition leads to the subordinate theme.

Figure 5. Transition: Variation of *Blues* Theme

The subordinate theme. The composer describes the second subject as follows: "The Subordinate Theme in G Major is in the style of a Negro Spiritual and bears sort of a relationship to the *Blues* theme. The three-part song form is used here as follows: two measures of thesis, two measures of antithesis, and two measures of repetition of thesis."[10] Figures 6, 7 and 8 present the three elements of the subordinate theme.

---

[10] William Grant Still, Speech to Composers' Workshop, 1967.

Figure 6. Subordinate Theme: Thesis

Figure 7. Subordinate Theme: Antithesis

Figure 8. Restatement of Thesis

The development. After a short treatment of the subordinate theme, a transitional section leads to the development, or Division Two as it is listed in Verna Arvey's booklet. Figure 9 states the opening phrase of the development section; this melody is derived from the *Blues* theme.

Figure 9. Development: Opening Theme

109

The Recapitulation. To use Mr. Still's words:

> Division three is a Recapitulation, in which there is a radical departure. The subordinate theme reappears in A flat minor, instead of a repetition of the principal theme.[11]
> The music rises to a climax and then diminishes as it nears the recapitulation.[12]

The motive of the recapitulation is seen in Figure 10.

Figure 10. Recapitulation: Opening Theme

Harmonic Style Employed

Basically, the harmonies employed in the First Movement are relatively simple; the chords are largely dictated by the melodies. However, within this framework of simplicity, the composer devises harmonic nuance and variety.

Basic harmonic progression. The basic harmonic progression of the First Movement is the standard Blues progression: I, I^7, IV, V^7, I. The composer strays from this pattern many times, but the dominant-tonic relationship is always kept intact.

A prominent feature of *Blues* harmony is the tendency to move from the tonic toward the subdominant side of the key; in most cases, the tonic seventh is used rather than the simple tonic triad. This I^7 to IV progression strongly resembles the V^7 to I relationship, but we do not actually feel a modulation has occurred. Mr. Still occasionally uses a plagal relationship (IV to I), but there is a preponderance of the I^7 to IV and V^7 to I relationships in this movement.

Use of the embellished triad. In the First Movement, the embellished

---

[11] Arvey, *op. cit.*, p. 25.

[12] William Grant Still, Speech to Composers' Workshop, 1967.

110

triad occurs roughly twice as frequently as does the simple triad; the four-note chord far outnumbers all other chords. The most frequently used chord is the triad (major or minor) with the added minor seventh. The use of the added major seventh is rare in this entire symphony. The added ninth is used frequently with the dominant chord and occasionally with the subdominant. The triad with added sixth is used sparingly.

Tonic seventh as chord of repose. An interesting harmonic device is Mr. Still's use of the tonic seventh chord as a chord of repose. In many instances the I^7 does not move to the IV chord, but merely acts as an embellished I chord. This is an harmonic nuance and suggests the use of this device by jazz bands that traveled the Mississippi River in earlier years. In the jazz idiom, the added-seventh chord used as a chord of repose was used prior to the chord with added sixth.[13]

Tonic chord with added sixth. The final chord of the First Movement is a tonic chord with added sixth. This device had been used by earlier classical composers, especially in the late Romantic Period, but in 1930 the device was relatively new and fresh and added harmonic interest. Unfortunately, in the two decades that followed, this style of chord was grossly overused and became trite. Still's use of the chord, however, was in good taste and served, in a way, as a preview of things to come.

Texture of the orchestration. Four styles of texture are used by the composer; these styles may be referred to as chordal, contrapuntal, homophonic, and "give-and-take." The First Movement is multi-textured; however, the give-and-take texture predominates. Chordal texture is not used alone, but in conjunction with one of the other texture styles. Through the careful use of voicings and balance, Mr. Still is able to use dissonances that would normally be considered quite harsh, without creating a high degree of tension. The composer uses harsh dissonances, but they are softened through clever orchestration devices. Mr. Still looks upon dissonance as a "spice" that should be carefully mixed in, but certainly not overdone.[14]

Rhythmic considerations. The rhythmic patterns employed in the First Movement are basically simple; duple meter is used throughout the movement. In keeping with the traditions of the *Blues* idiom, the rhythmic style is characterized by the free and extensive use of syncopation. The *Blues* theme employs syncopation and the melodic use of the *blue* note. These two devices combine to form the basic musical gesture used to unite the entire symphony. Rhythmic alterations play an

---

[13] Gunther Schuller, *Early Jazz: Its Roots and Musical Development* (New York: Oxford University Press, 1968), pp. 38-43.
[14] Personal Interview: Slattery-Still, 12 Feb. 1969.

important role in Mr. Still's technique of thematic transformation.

It is important to note that the composer did not want the dotted eighth followed by the sixteenth note to be played in strict time. Explicit instructions are given on the score that the unit of beat should be thought of as being divided into three parts rather than into four. The above rhythmic figure should be mentally pictured as a quarter note and an eight placed under a triplet ligature.[15] This is another example of the composer being true to the *Blues* idiom. This bastard form of beat division is an integral part of the *Blues*, jazz, and American popular music in general; it is autochthonous to American music.

SECOND MOVEMENT: ADAGIO

The Second Movement of the *Afro-American Symphony* is entitled *Adagio*. It is written in common time with a metronome marking of sixty-three for the quarter note. The key center is F (major or minor) throughout. The underlying mood reflected is that of sorrow.[16] The movement is prefaced by the following excerpt by Paul Laurence Dunbar:

> "It's moughty tiahsome layin' 'roun'
> Dis sorrer-laden earfly groun'
> An' oftentimes I thinks, thinks I
> 'Twould be a sweet t'ing des to die
> An' go 'long home."

Outline of Form: Second Movement

An outline of the form of the Second Movement along with pertinent comments is given on the following pages in Figures 11A, 11B, and 11C.

---

15 William Grant Still, *Afro-American Symphony* (New York: J. Fischer and Brother, 1935), p. 26.

16 Arvey, *op. cit.*, p. 24.

Figure 11A. Outline of Form - *Afro-American Symphony*: Second Movement

N	Pages	Section	No. Of Measures	Key	Tempo	Comments
14	30	Introduction	6	F	♩ = 63	Solo violin on melody; chordal accompaniment in strings plus muffled tympani. Melody derived from last half of the 2nd measure of the *Blues* theme.
15	30-31	Principal Theme	8	F	Same	*Doloroso*: melody in the oboe with obligato by flute (contrapuntal); chordal accompanied by strings; multi-textured; *Blue* note used as a grace note.
16	31-32	Restatement Of Principal Theme	8	F Major and Minor	Same	*Doloroso*; viola section on melody; countermelody in flutes, clarinets and muted trumpets (Harmon mutes); *Blue* grace note appears in flute countermelody.
--	32	Extension	1	Same	*poco riten.*	A miniature codetta; helps to prepare the forthcoming transition.

Figure 11B. Outline Form - *Afro-American Symphony*: Second Movement

N	Pages	Section	No. Of Measures	Key	Tempo	Comments
16	32-33	Transition	4	F	*rit. poco a poco*	Transition section; English horn solo set against chordal accompaniment in strings; solo derived from introduction to second movement.
17	33	Subordinate Theme	4	F Major and Minor	*a tempo* M. M. 63	Melody starts in the fl. and continued in first violin. Melody derived from the *Blues* theme (1st movement).
--	34	Restatement Of Subordinate Theme	4	F	Same	Melody in solo clarinet; chordal accompaniment by muted trombones. (Harmon mutes.)
18	34-35	Development Of Principal Theme	6	Same	*piu mosso non tanto*	Rhythmic alternation of principal theme; melody in first violin; chordal accompaniment in strings; ends with harp arpeggios and a *fermata*.
--	35-36	Development (Cont.)	6	Same	*poco piu mosso*	Melody in first violin four measures; melody in bass clarinet for two measure extension.

Figure 11C. Outline Form - *Afro-American Symphony*: Second Movement

N	Pages	Section	No. Of Measures	Key	Tempo	Comments
19	36-37	Development (Cont.)	8	F Minor	*a tempo* M. M. 63	A continuation of the development of the principal theme; melodic line is passed around; some use of the full orchestra.
--	38	Extension	2	Same	*ritard. poco a poco*	Transition leads back to the principal theme; melody in the st. bass.
20	38-39	Final Statement Principal Theme	9	F Major and Minor	*a tempo*	*Doloroso*; melody shared by flute and bassoon; chordal accompaniment in harp and low strings; counterpoint in violins; ritard and fermata.
21	39	Coda	8	F	M. M. 63	Introductory motive restated by first violin over a contrapuntal then chordal accompaniment by strings. Ends on a simple triad; constantly diminishing to *il piu piano possibile*. Total performance time in 5 1/4 minutes.

Thematic Material: Second Movement

The principal theme. The principal theme of the Second Movement is first stated by the solo oboe accompanied by violas and *'celli divisi* and by a flute obligato. This theme is stated in Figure 12 below.

Figure 12. Principal Theme: Second Movement

The subordinate theme. The subordinate theme of the Second Movement is an alteration of the *Blues* theme. In its initial presentation, the theme is given to the flute. The theme is depicted in Figure 13 below.

Figure 13. Subordinate Theme: Second Movement

Alteration of principal theme. The section that follows the subordinate theme is described by Mr. Still: "Then comes an alteration of the principal theme of the Second Movement that represents the fervent prayers of a burdened people rising upward to God."[17] The rising of the prayers to God is depicted musically by ascending *arpeggios* on the harp.[18] In his speech to the Composers' Workshop in 1967, the composer further stated: "Finally, a variation of the *Blues* theme, followed by a return to the principal theme of the Second Movement, leads to a coda built on the same material as that of the Introduction to this movement." The above-mentioned variation of the *Blues* theme is stated in Figure 14 below.

---

[17] Speech to Composers' Workshop, 1967.

[18] *Afro-American Symphony*, p. 34.

Figure 14. Variation of *Blues* Theme

Important Features of Second Movement

Harmonic considerations. The harmonic vocabulary of the Second Movement is more complex than that of the First Movement; there is an extensive use of chords of addition and chords of omission. Altered chords based on scale degrees II, IV, V and VII are plentiful; on two occasions altered III and VI chords are introduced. Some of the alterations that may occur in a given chord are:

1. Raising or lowering the root
2. Raising or lowering the fifth
3. Flatting the ninth
4. Raising the seventh

The above alterations occur in an infinite variety of combinations. Other colorful chords that appear in this movement are:

1. Triad with added major seventh
2. Diminished triad
3. Augmented triad (usually with seventh)
4. Diminished seventh chord
5. Chords with added sixth
6. Chords containing both the major and minor third

The harmonic speed is moderate; there is rarely more than one chord change per measure. The standard *Blues* progression is not utilized in this movement. The plagal move (I, IV, I) using complex alterations is given much usage. The modified dominant is the preponderant harmonic device used in this movement. Points of departure and arrival are clear and well-defined; this feature is accomplished through the careful handling of the melodic line in conjunction with the harmonic structure.

Texture. The texture of the Second Movement is basically homophonic. The last five measures of the coda display a purely

115

chordal texture. As in the First Movement, normally harsh dissonances are softened through careful voicing of the chords and through a delicate balance in the orchestration.

Rhythmic considerations. The rhythmic figures are simple, direct, and held in bounds by the bar lines. The use of syncopation is again much in evidence.

Unification factor. By means of masterful thematic transformation, elements of the *Blues* theme are presented in the introduction and in the subordinate theme. A variation of the *Blues* theme also occurs after the subordinate theme. These musical gestures serve as a strong factor of unification throughout the composition.

Elements of pathos. The sob and the sigh are vocal gestures that may suggest sorrow, frustration, or despair. In the Second Movement, these vocal gestures are imitated by the composer through the use of melodic nuance. The half steps and the "blue notes" used as grace notes in the melodic line strongly suggest the slight vocal inflection involved in the sigh or the sob. The listener is led toward this type of interpretation by the title of the movement, *Sorrow*, and by the verse of Dunbar which is used as a Preface.

The combination of the title, the verse, and the imitation of vocal gestures can readily bring about a strong spiritual enactment on the part of the listener and the performer. Probably the most important feature of the Second Movement is the powerful element of pathos involved therein.

THIRD MOVEMENT: ANIMATO

The Third Movement of the *Afro-American Symphony* is entitled *Animato*. It is written in common time with a metronome marking of 116 for the quarter note. The key center is A flat (major and minor) throughout. The underlying mood reflected is that of humor. The following verse by Paul Laurence Dunbar prefaces the movement:

> "An' we'll shout ouah halleluyahs,
> On dat mighty reck'nin' day."

Outline of Form: Third Movement

An outline of the form of the Third Movement along with pertinent comments is given on the following pages in Figures 15A, 15B, and 15C.

Figure 15A. Outline of Form - *Afro-American Symphony*: Third Movement

N	Pages	Section	No. Of Measures	Key	Tempo	Comments
22	40-41	Introduction	7	A Flat	♩ = 116	*Animato*; melodic material derived from principal theme (first subject). Melody in clarinet, bassoon, two horns, and 'cello.
23	41-42	Principal Theme (First Subject)	8	Same	Same	Melody in strings; horns carry rhythmic counterpoint; standard *Blues* progression used; thesis: four measures; antithesis: four measures. Banjo is used on afterbeats as a chordal accompaniment.
24	43-46	Principal Theme (Second Subject)	8	Same	Same	Woodwinds and violins on unison melody: brass on chordal accompaniment; thesis and antithesis form used again. Harmonic speed quickens: four chords per measure. Series of secondary dominants used for the first time . . . marked *tutta forza*.

Figure 15B. Outline of Form - *Afro-American Symphony*: Third Movement

N	Pages	Section	No. Of Measures	Key	Tempo	Comments
25	44-46	Restatement Of Principal Theme (First Subject)	8	A Flat	Same (116)	Thesis (mm5) oboe solo with rhythmic counterpoint in clarinet, harp and strings. Antithesis (mm5): clarinet and flute on melody ending with bass clarinet solo. Give-and-take texture is predominant.
26	46-48	Transition Section (Theme I)	7	A Flat Minor	Same	Theme I is derived from second subject (principal theme). Melody first in trombone then in unison with horn, woodwinds, viola and cello; then passes to first violin.
--	49	Theme II	8	Same	Same	Woodwinds and first violin on melody; rhythmic countermelody in trumpets and trombones.

Figure 15C. Outline of Form - *Afro-American Symphony*: Third Movement

N	Pages	Section	No. Of Measures	Key	Tempo	Comments
27 & 28	49-52	Development	22	A Flat Major	Same (116)	Development of principal theme: first subject: marked *graziosamente*. Give-and-take texture is predominant; melodic line passes through flutes, oboe and clarinets; strings; English horn and bassoon; and finally trumpets, trombones, tuba, 'celli and string bass.
29	52-54	Recapitulation (First Subject)	8	Same	Same	Thesis and antithesis form used again; melody in woodwinds and strings; Banjo re-enters.
30 --	54-55 56	Recapitulation (Second Subject) Extension	8 3	Same	Same	Thesis and antithesis; strings and woodwinds carry the melodic line.
31	56-58	Coda	13	Same	Same	Alteration of principal theme: (first subject) in strings, piccolo, oboe and clarinet; *Blues* theme is played by trumpet and trombone; full orchestra; richly textured; high tension.

117

Thematic Material: Third Movement

The introduction. The introductory theme of the Third Movement of the *Afro-American Symphony* is presented in Figure 16 below. This melodic material is derived from the first subject of the principal theme.

Figure 16. Introduction: Third Movement

The principal theme. The introductory material is followed by the principal theme, first subject. This first subject is divided into a thesis and an antithesis. This pattern of thesis and antithesis is used throughout the Third Movement. The thesis of the first subject is stated in Figure 17 below; the thesis of the second subject is shown in Figure 18 on the following page.

Figure 17. Principal Theme: First Subject

118

Figure 18. Principal Theme: Second Subject

Variation of the first subject. Following the statement of the second subject, the first subject is repeated in a slightly different form. This variation is seen in Figure 19 below.

Figure 19. Variation of First Subject

Figure 20. Transition Section: Theme I

Transitional themes. The transitional material is divided into Themes I and II. Figure 20 above presents Theme I which is derived from the second subject of the principal theme. Theme II is introduced by the woodwinds and the first violins while the trumpets and trombones play a countermelody. Theme II is stated in Figure 21 below.

119

Figure 21. Transitional Section: Theme II

The development. The development section elaborates on the thematic material of the first subject of the principal theme. Figures 22 and 23 demonstrate the orchestration technique of William Grant Still.

Figure 22. Development of First Subject: Principal Theme

Figure 23. Continuation of Development

The recapitulation. Figure 24 presents the recapitulation of the first subject of the principal theme.

Figure 24. Recapitulation of First Subject

The coda. Figure 25 presents the first four measures from the closing passage of the Third Movement. The upper score displays an alteration of the first subject of the principal theme carried by piccolo, oboe, clarinets and strings. The lower score shows a restatement of the *Blues* theme from the First Movement taken by trumpets and trombones.

121

Figure 25. The Coda

Important Features of the Third Movement

Harmonic considerations. The points of arrival and departure are again clearly marked by the harmonic progressions. The standard *Blues* progression is frequently used.

The composer uses a series of secondary dominants for the first time in this composition: this series runs: I, VI^7, II^7, V^7, I (see page 43 of score). This device has been referred to as a "Barbershop progression." In later years this progression became a standard jazz effect.

Other points of harmonic interest are:
1. First use of II^7, III, VI, and VI^7 chords
2. Extended use of tonic with added sixth
3. First use of chord with added fourth (this is actually an added eleventh). (page 47 of score)
4. Continued use of major/minor sonorities
5. Continued use of chords of addition and chords of omission
6. Use of unusual chord: root plus major third plus two superimposed tritones (see page 48 of score)

The harmonic speed is moderate until the last section. From page fifty-four onward (the final twenty-four measures), the harmonic speed increases greatly with four separate chords per measure. This results in a heightening of tension which carries through to the end of the movement.

122

Although some complex sonorities are used for purposes of coloration, the basic harmonic progressions remain relatively simple. Only tertial sonorities are used in this movement and throughout the entire composition.

Rhythmic considerations. A steady, brisk tempo is maintained throughout the movement. This contributes to the "happy-go-lucky" mood that the composer wishes to reflect.

The Scherzo is characterized by the use of two rhythmic motives which are utilized in almost every section. The rhythmic motives are:

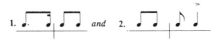

These motives serve as a unifying factor for the entire movement.

Texture. "Give-and-take" texture is predominant throughout most of the Scherzo. The coda section, however, is multi-textured, containing a combination of contrapuntal and homophonic styles.

Other features. The tenor banjo is used in this movement to accentuate the strong, dance-like rhythms. The cheerful "twang" of this instrument on the chordal afterbeat suggests the occasional fun session of the southern Negro of earlier years; one can readily picture a plantation party or a Saturday night dance. There is a strong possibility that this is the first use of the banjo in a composition of symphonic magnitude.

The Scherzo, as the third Movement is commonly referred to, won immediate and enthusiastic response from audiences. For a period of time it stood out as a separate entity from the rest of the composition. This is demonstrated by the fact that the first recordings were made of the Scherzo only. Howard Hanson directed for a Victor recording and Leopold Stokowski conducted for a Columbia recording, neither of which is available commercially at this time.

Verna Arvey comments on the first Berlin performance of the *Afro-American Symphony* in 1933:

> An audience in Berlin broke a twenty-year tradition to encore the Scherzo from this Symphony when Dr. Howard Hanson conducted it there; several years later, when Karl Krueger conducted it in Budapest, his audience did the same thing.[19]

---

[19] Arvey, *op. cit.*, p. 23.

FOURTH MOVEMENT: LENTO, CON RISOLUZIONE

The Fourth Movement of the *Afro-American Symphony* is entitled
Lento, con risoluzione. The movement opens in three quarter time with
a metronome marking of sixty-six for the quarter note; the opening key
center is E major. However, both the tempo and the key center are
altered frequently. The suggestive title given to this movement is
Sincerity.[20] The movement is prefaced by the following poetic excerpt
by Paul Laurence Dunbar:

> "Be proud, my Race, in mind and soul.
> Thy name is writ on Glory's scroll
> In characters of fire.
> High mid the clouds of Fame's bright sky
> Thy banner's blazoned folds now fly,
> And truth shall lift them higher."

Outline of the Form: Fourth Movement

An outline of the form of the Fourth Movement along with pertinent
comments is given on the following pages in Figures 26A, 26B, and
26C.

Figure 26A. Outline of Form -- *Afro-American Symphony*: Fourth Movement

N	Pages	Section	No. Of Measures	Key	Tempo	Comments
32	59	Principal Theme	16	E Major	♩ = 66	Thesis and antithesis: 8 measures each; melody in violins, violas, and 'celli; countermelody in string bass and bass clarinet.
33	60	Principal Theme (Altered and Extended)	12	Same	Same	Strings same as above; woodwinds and brass play a chordal accompaniment.
34	61	Subordinate Theme	4	A Major	♩ = 88	*Piu mosso*; three-measure theme plus one measure extension; soli by oboe and flute with chordal accompaniment in strings; material derived from *Blues* theme (first movement).
--	62	Restatement (Subordinate Theme)	4	C Major	Same	Flute and clarinet soli; strings on chordal accompaniment.
35	62-63	Variation (Subordinate Theme)	10	F Major	Same	Thesis: 4 measures; antithesis: 4 measures; plus a two-measure extension. Melody passed around; English horn, solo in the extension (*piu lento*); multi-textured.

---

[20] Ibid, p. 22.

Figure 26B. Outline of Form -- *Afro-American Symphony*: Fourth Movement

N	Pages	Section	No. Of Measures	Key	Tempo	Comments
36	63-64	Development Subordinate Theme	14	E Major	♩ = 112	Oboe, clarinet and first violin on unisonal melody; multi-textured background; melody passes to flutes then to woodwinds horns and trumpets.
37	65-67	Development Subordinate Theme	28	F Minor	♩ = 72	*Andante, molto expressivo*; Section opens with a melody in strings; obligato for bassoon. Melody in flute, flute and bassoon; then strings and woodwinds; *stringendo*.
38	66-67	(Continuation)	--	--	--	
39	67	Extension	3	--	--	
39	67-68	Transition Section	8	Not Fixed	Same	Key center uncertain; modulatory passage; oboe solo with accompaniment in clarinet family; chordal accompaniment. Complex harmonies.
40	68-69	Variation Of Principal Theme	16	C Sharp Major	♩ = 66	*Lento, con risoluzione*; Soli in 'celli. *cantabile*, countermelody in flutes; melody next to first violin; homophonic texture; unusual chord progression (see harmonic coverage).

Figure 26C. Outline of Form -- *Afro-American Symphony*: Fourth Movement

N	Pages	Section	No. Of Measures	Key	Tempo	Comments
41	69	Variation Of Principal Theme	8	E Major	Same (66)	Melody in 'celli; harp carries countermelody; ends on III chord; G sharp minor.
42	70	Transition Introductory	6	Not Fixed	♩ = 112	*Vivace*; 6/8 time; prepares for a scherzo-like resume of several themes; colorful chord progression.
43	71-73	Variation Of Principal Theme	16	A Flat Major	Same	Extensive use of give-and-take texture; many complex sonorities.
44 to 47	74-82	Variation Of Principal Theme	45	C Minor	Same	Mostly give-and-take texture; melody passed throughout orchestra; simpler sonorities now.
48	82-85	Closing Theme	17	F Minor	♩ = 72	*Maestoso*; brasses play a variation of principal theme, altered and extended; remainder of orchestra plays a continuous "multiple-ostinato." Continuous ostinato based on F minor chord; no ritard; full orchestra.
--	86-88	Coda	9	Same	Same	

Thematic Material: Fourth Movement

The principal theme. The principal theme of the Fourth Movement is initially stated by the strings with chordal accompaniment by clarinets, trombones, tuba, and string bass. The principal theme is presented in Figure 27 below.

125

Figure 27. Principal Theme: Fourth Movement

Figure 28. Subordinate Theme: Fourth Movement

The subordinate theme.   The subordinate theme of the Fourth
Movement is derived from the *Blues* theme of the First Movement. This
is a further example of how the composer used the technique of thematic
transformation as a factor of unification. The subordinate theme is shown
in Figure 28.

Important Features of the Fourth Movement

Harmonic considerations. The sonorities of the Fourth Movement are
the most complex of the entire composition.   Mr. Still exhausts the
possibilities of tertial sonority.   There is a marked increase in chords
which contain both the major and the minor third.   The chord of the

diminished seventh is used frequently (see pages 64 and 65 of the score). Despite the increase in complexity of the chords, there are sections where the harmonic speed is extremely slow.

The points of arrival are not as clear as they are in other movements; this is partially caused by the overlapping or extension of melodic figures into new sections. The standard *Blues* progression is not a significant factor in this movement.

Rhythmic considerations. The manner in which the composer handles the rhythmic variations in six-eight time is the most prominent rhythmic feature of this movement. The use of *ritardando* and *accelerando* is greatly increased.

The composer's description. In his speech to a Composers' Workshop in 1967, Mr. Still describes the Fourth Movement thus:

> The Fourth Movement is largely a retrospective viewing of the earlier movements with the exception of its principal theme. It is intended to give musical expression to the lines from Paul Laurence Dunbar which appear on the score: "Be proud, my race, in mind and soul . . ."

A summarization of the important features of *Afro-American Symphony* will be presented in the next section.

Paul Harold Slattery

A DISCUSSION OF THE *FOURTH SYMPHONY*
INCLUDING COMPARISONS WITH THE *FIRST SYMPHONY*

The purpose of this chapter is twofold: (1) important background information on *Autochthonous* is presented along with an enumeration of the important features of this Symphony, and (2) a comparison of the pertinent features of *Autochthonous* and *Afro-American* is drawn. Comparisons are drawn with reference to the nine specific areas listed in the Introductory Note.

GENERAL CONSIDERATIONS

The Creation of Autochthonous

The composer's intention. *Autochthonous* was not intended as a programmatic work. Mr. Still comments on this: "Both the *Afro-American* and the *Autochthonous* were similar in the sense that both were written as pure music--and a program, or descriptive notes, added after the completion of the music."[1] The composer further states: "The *Afro-American*, however, was intended to describe the American Negro from the outset, while *Autochthonous* was intended to be descriptive of the American spirit, as the subtitle implies."[2]

The compositional process. The composer has supplied the following detailed information concerning the actual writing of *Autochthonous*:

> I began the *Autochthonous* on July 22, 1947, decided to subtitle it "*Autochthonous*" on July 31st, and completed the sketch on September 4th. I had been composing (i.e., working on the sketch) steadily, and as soon as the sketch of a movement was completed, I had started to score it, going on to the composition of the next movement meanwhile. On September 8th, the entire Symphony was completed and I took the master sheets to the blueprint company, after which I started to extract the parts and to proofread what I had already done.[3]

---

[1] Slattery-Still correspondence, April 25, 1969.
[2] *Ibid.*
[3] *Ibid.*

The addition of program notes. The program notes that were devised by Mr. and Mrs. Still read as follows:

> The *Autochthonous* was written in Los Angeles, in the house where we lived for twenty years, and where our children were born: 3670 Cimarron Street. The Symphony was copyrighted October 20, 1947.[4]
>
> This Symphony, dedicated to the composer's old friend and teacher at Oberlin, Maurice Kessler, is subtitled "Autochthonous" to explain that the music has its roots in our own soil, and portrays--in a sense--the spirit of the American people. The First Movement exemplifies the feeling of optimism and energy: The American ability to "get things done." The Second Movement is more pensive, then, in the "second subject," animated in a folky way. The Third Movement is humorous and unmistakably typical of our country and its rhythms. The final movement depicts the warmth and the spiritual side of the American people--their love of mankind.
>
> It may also be said that the music speaks of the fusion of musical cultures in North America.[5]

Significant Data

Brief descriptive statement. The *Fourth Symphony* is a multi-textured, tonal composition in four movements. There is much emphasis placed upon the free flow of the melodic line. The form is generally free with a vague reference to traditional patterns. The harmonic vocabulary includes both tertial and nontertial sonorities. The points of departure and arrival are generally clear and well-defined. Although two or more style idioms are used, the overall impression of the compositional style is that of Neoromanticism.

First performance. The *Fourth Symphony* was first performed in Oklahoma City on March 18, 1951. This performance was broadcast over the Mutual Radio Network with Victor Alessandro conducting the Oklahoma Symphony Orchestra.[6]

---

[4] The Still family lived at this address from 1939 until 1959. They then moved to their 1972 location: 1262 Victoria Avenue, Los Angeles. The two children mentioned are Duncan and Judith.

[5] Slattery-Still correspondence.

[6] *Ibid.*

Instrumental requirements.   Woodwinds: three flutes (third interchangeable with piccolo), two oboes, English horn, two clarinets in B flat, bass clarinet in B flat, and two bassoons (second interchangeable with contra bassoon).

Brass: four horns in F, three trumpets in B flat, three trombones, and one tuba.

Percussion: timpani, glockenspiel, resonator bell in G, triangle, wire brushes, small cymbal (suspended), large cymbal (suspended), cymbals, small snare drum, military drum, bass drum, and celesta.

Strings: normal string section plus the harp.

Time breakdown:	
First Movement	7' 5"
Second Movement	7' 37"
Third Movement	3' 25"
Fourth Movement	<u>10' 50"</u>
Total Performance Time	28' 57"

SPECIFIC CONSIDERATIONS

FIRST MOVEMENT: MODERATELY

Synopsis of the Form

The form of the First Movement of *Autochthonous* is best described as "free." However, there is a suggested reference to *sonata allegro* form. The basic sections of the First Movement consist of an introduction, a statement of the principal theme with elaboration, and a statement of the second subject with elaboration.   This is followed by a series of alternating variations on the two main themes, ending in a short coda.

The pattern of key centers is as follows: D major, D minor, D major, C major, D minor, and D major. The basic tempo of the movement is 126 for the quarter note; this remains steady throughout. There are no *caesuras*. There is a short section where the metric pattern alternates between two-four and four-four time.

130

Thematic Material

The introduction. The introduction is stated by the bassoon, bass trombone, tuba, 'celli, and the string basses. The thematic material is derived from the second subject of this movement. The introductory motive is stated in Figure 29.

Figure 29. Introductory Theme: First Movement

The principal theme. The principal theme of the First Movement is initially stated by the strings in chordal texture. A counter-melody is heard first in the clarinet, then in the bassoon. This theme has a significant role in this composition; it acts as the factor of unification much the same as the *Blues* theme serves in the *Afro-American Symphony*. In various altered forms, this theme is used as the second subject of the next three Movements. The principal theme is presented in Figure 30.

Figure 30. Principal Theme: First Movement

The second subject. The second subject is introduced by the trumpets in chordal texture. The composer calls for mutes and supplies the following directions: "Preferably mutes with which a more delicate and less piercing tone may be obtained."[7] The *legato* chords of the trumpets are accompanied by *staccato* chords in the strings. The distant relationships of the chords involved, E flat major and G major, produces a polychordal effect. The polychordal sonorities are extended for a section of four measures.

---

[7] Score of *Autochthonous Symphony*, No. 4, p. 4.

The second subject of this Movement is presented in Figure 31.

Figure 31. Second Subject: First Movement

Important Features of the First Movement

Harmonic considerations. In this Movement, there is an extended use of chords of addition. The most prominent added notes are the major second, sixth, seventh, and ninth scale degrees. A moderately harsh dissonance is created by the use of "cluster" chords. These "cluster" chords are formed by placing the root, major second, and major or minor third in a closed position; this produces a reasonably high degree of tension. Quartal-quintal chords and tritone chords are used in juxtaposition with tertial sonorities. Polychordal sonorities are used to some degree, but these sections are of short duration. The harmonic speed of the Movement is relatively fast. The points of arrival and departure are clear and well-defined. The overall harmonic style moves away from Neo-romanticism in the direction of Modernism.

Texture. The First Movement contains a wide variety of textural styles ranging from unisons to polychordality. Chordal and "give-and-take" styles are the most prominent.

Rhythmic considerations. Except for a short section of alternating two-four and four-four measures, the basic meter is kept intact. The meter is held within bounds by the bar lines. The use of syncopation is prominent.

Comparison with First Movement of Afro-American

Areas of similarity. The First Movements of the *Afro-American* and *Autochthonous* are similar in the following areas:

1. Formal structure
2. Use of thematic transformation
3. Factors of unification

4. Orchestration technique
5. Limited rhythmic complexity
6. Strong emphasis on a tonal center

Areas of contrast.   The greatest area of contrast is found in the harmonic vocabulary employed.   The vocabulary of the *Afro-American* is basically limited to tertial sonorities with added-tone chords.   The sonorities used in *Autochthonous* are much more complex, involving quartal-quintal chords, tritone chords, and polychordality.   The use of an extended harmonic vocabulary enlarges the possibilities for creating higher levels of tension and for attaining a greater variety of expression. The basic style of the *Afro-American* is Neoromantic, while the First Movement of *Autochthonous* leans more toward the Modern idiom.   A summarization of the areas of similarity and of contrast will be given at the end of this chapter.

SECOND MOVEMENT: SLOWLY

Thematic Material

The introduction.   The introduction to the Second Movement is derived from the principal theme of the First Movement.   The opening melody is stated by the flute with chordal accompaniment by the woodwinds; it is then repeated by the string section.   The introduction to the Second Movement is presented in Figure 32.[8]

Figure 32. Introduction: Second Movement

The principal theme.   The principal theme of the Second Movement is first stated as an oboe solo with a contrapuntal accompaniment first in

---

[8] Score of *Autochthonous Symphony*, No. 19, p. 24.

133

the violas and 'celli and then in the horns.[9] This theme is seen in Figure 33.

Figure 33. Principal Theme: Second Movement

The second subject. The second subject is a variation of the principal theme of the First Movement. The melody is carried by the first violins with a chordal accompaniment by the other strings.[10] Figure 34 shows the second subject.

Figure 34. Second Subject: Second Movement

Important Features of the Second Movement

The Second Movement is characterized by vivid contrasts in dynamics, texture, tempo, and the level of tension. The harmonic vocabulary includes chords with the highest level of tension that is possible to attain such as tritone sonorities and chords with an added minor second, major seventh, or minor ninth. Other highly dissonant chords the composer used are chords which contain both the major and the minor third, or both the major and the minor seventh, and chords that contain both the augmented and the diminished fifth. On the other hand, the vocabulary also includes unisons which are placed at the other end of the tension cycle.

The form of the Second Movement bears a vague relationship to *sonata allegro* form. Points of departure and of arrival are well-defined and correspond with the changes in the tension-release cycle. This cycle

---

[9] *Ibid.*, No. 20, p. 24.
[10] *Ibid.*, No. 23, p. 28.

is accomplished mainly through harmonic means. The principal building device of this Movement is thematic transformation, which also serves as the factor of unification.

Comparison with Second Movement of Afro-American

Areas of similarity. The strongest point of similarity between the Second Movements of the two Symphonies is the element of pathos involved. The six areas of similarity listed above for the First Movements apply to the Second Movements also.

Areas of contrast. The Second Movement of *Autochthonous* uses more dissonances and the dissonances are more extreme in terms of producing harmonic tension. As a result, the tension-release cycle has a wider range. In general, the contrasts are more vivid than in the Second Movement of the *Afro-American Symphony*.

THIRD MOVEMENT: MODERATELY FAST

Thematic Material

The principal theme. The principal theme of the Third Movement is presented by flutes and oboe in octaves. The cello section provides a "walking bass" accompaniment. This theme is presented in Figure 35.

Figure 35. Principal Theme: Third Movement

The principal theme is preceded by a humorous introduction stated by a clarinet and a bassoon accompanied by wire brushes on a military drum.[11]

The second subject. After a series of variations which alternate between the principal theme and the introductory material, the second

---

[11] Score of *Autochthonous Symphony*, No. 29, p. 34.

subject is presented by three flutes in chordal texture. A contrapuntal accompaniment appears in the clarinet and bassoons.[12] The second subject is presented in Figure 36. It is derived from the principal theme of the First Movement; this is another example of the process of unification.

Figure 36. Second Subject: Third Movement

Important Features of the Third Movement

Harmonic considerations. The extent of the harmonic vocabulary is greatly reduced in this movement; the chords are basically less complex. As a result, the range of the tension-release cycle is not as extreme as it was in the First and Second Movements. The harmonic speed is relatively slow. The harmonic progressions are similar to those used in the popular style of the 1940's known as "boogie-woogie." Much use is made of the "walking bass," an ostinato which outlines the chord. Extensive use is made of the triad with added sixth.

Rhythmic considerations. The pulse remains steady throughout at a tempo of 104 for the quarter note. Extensive use is made of the dotted eighth followed by a sixteenth rhythmic figure. Syncopated figures are also abundant.

Texture. The texture is mostly "give-and-take." Certain sections, however, imitate the chordal texture of the "big band sound" of the 1940's. The melodic lead is passed around to a wide variety of instruments, each solo instrument retaining the melody for just a few measures.

The general feeling suggested by this Movement is one of gaiety. The melodic line is playful and witty. The mood is one of Americans in a carefree frame of mind, perhaps attending a dance.

Similarity to the Scherzo of Afro-American. As he does in the Scherzo of the First Symphony, Mr. Still again takes a large step away from the

---

12 *Ibid.*, No. 35, p. 40.

clichés of traditional symphonic compositions by introducing strikingly new elements into his Scherzos. Both of these Scherzos are witty, carefree, humorous, and dancelike in nature; both are basically simple.

FOURTH MOVEMENT: SLOWLY AND REVERENTLY

Thematic Material

The principal theme. The principal theme of the Fourth Movement is initially stated by the first violins. The other strings and the bassoons provide a chordal accompaniment.[13] The principal theme is shown in Figure 37.

Figure 37. Principal Theme: Fourth Movement

Episodic material. The Fourth Movement is composed in one of the higher Rondo forms. The principal theme alternates with an episode derived from the principal theme of the First Movement and with an episode based on the principal theme of this Movement.[14] The latter is shown in Figure 38.

Figure 38. Episodic Material: Fourth Movement

---

[13] *Ibid.*, No. 42, p. 50.
[14] *Ibid.*, No. 43, p. 50.

Important Features of the Fourth Movement

Harmonic considerations. Harsh dissonances are used in abundance, but their "biting" effect is softened somewhat by clever orchestration technique. The most severe dissonances are obtained by the use of added tones, polychordality, and major/minor sonorities. Frequently used added tones are the major second and the major seventh. The limits of the tension-release cycle are not as extreme as in the First and Second Movements. The harmonic speed varies between moderately fast and moderately slow. The triad with added sixth is used extensively and is treated as a chord of repose.

Texture. The Fourth Movement is multi-textured; a wide range of textural schemes is employed. Much emphasis is placed on chordal texture with the separate sections of the orchestra being used as blocks of tone color. The prominent textural styles employed are chordal, polychordal, and "give-and-take." The Movement is characterized by frequent, vivid changes in tone color and texture. The masterful skill in the art of orchestration possessed by Mr. Still is fully demonstrated in this Movement.

Other features. The Fourth Movement is marked by frequent changes in the tonal center and the tempo. The level of tension builds moderately rapidly to a peak and then drops off instantly. Free-flowing, *cantabile* melodies predominate.

Comparison with Fourth Movement of Afro-American

Areas of similarity. The two Fourth Movements are similar in formal structure, the use of thematic transformation, the factors of unification, orchestration technique, limited rhythmic complexity, and strong tonal emphasis. The mood of each is meditative and reverent. The basic style of composition is the same--Neoromantic.

Areas of contrast. The harmonic vocabulary of the *Autochthonous* Movement is more extensive than that of the *Afro-American* Movement. Accordingly, the tension-release cycle has a greater range of extremes. In the former, there are frequent changes in key, tempo, and texture; this is done to a greater degree than in the latter. The vividness of contrasts is more extreme in the *Autochthonous* Movement.

SUMMARY OF COMPARISONS

The following comparisons are drawn with reference to the nine specific areas listed in the Introductory Note.

Formal structure. The principals of formal structure are the same in both Symphonies. Mr. Still retains a limited reference to traditional forms, but alters and extends these forms to suit the needs of a given composition. The composer places his emphasis on balance, unity and variety of expression.

Harmonic structure and vocabulary. In the *Afro-American Symphony*, the harmonic structure is dictated mainly by the standard *Blues* progression. *Autochthonous* is not limited by any set progression except in the Third Movement where the chord progressions of popular music are followed loosely. Although there is an extensive use of modified dominant sonorities, the basic dominant-tonic relationship is kept intact in both compositions.

The harmonic vocabulary of the *First Symphony* is basically limited to tertial sonorities which is in keeping with the stated intent of the composition. The *Fourth Symphony* utilizes all of the harmonic devices of the *First Symphony* and goes beyond this to include tritone sonorities, quartel-quintal chords, and polytonality. Probably the most striking area of contrast between the two compositions is in the harmonic styles employed.

Origin of themes and thematic development. Mr. Still borrowed nothing from other composers or from folk music. All of the themes of both works are creations of the composer.

Mr. Still feels that the ability to develop and transform a theme is one of the most important assets that a composer should cultivate. His remarkable ability in this area is clearly manifested in both works. This is probably the strongest point of similarity between the two Symphonies.

Variety of expression. The methods that Mr. Still used to obtain variety of expression are much the same in both compositions. A listing of these devices could be quite extensive. A few of the more important devices are thematic transformation, melodic nuances, harmonic nuances, both subtle and abrupt changes in tone color, rhythmic variations, key changes, tempo changes, caesuras, and special instrumental effects.

Orchestration technique. The composer is a masterful orchestrator. This fact is amply manifested in both works. In the first two movements of *Autochthonous*, there is little attempt made to soften the harshness of dissonances through orchestration technique.

Rhythmic devices employed. The composer remained rather on the conservative side in his use of rhythmic patterns and in the sub-division of the beat. The meter is always held within bounds by the barlines. Syncopation and dotted rhythms are used extensively in both compositions. Mr. Still avoided the highly complex subdivision of the beat that is prominent in much of the music of the Modern idiom. The rhythmic devices employed in both Symphonies are markedly similar. One slight area of contrast would be the 6/8 variation in the Fourth Movement of the *Afro-American*.

Tension-release cycle. The tension-release cycle of the two Symphonies is accomplished through the following means: (1) harmonic vocabulary, (2) harmonic speed, (3) level of dynamics, and (4) texture. The points of departure generally coincide with a low level of tension. The points of arrival coincide with the *extremes* of the tension cycle. The main point of contrast is that *Autochthonous* contains extreme points of tension in comparison to those of the *Afro-American*.

Basic compositional style. The basic compositional style of the *Afro-American Symphony* is similar to the style of *Autochthonous*. The *Afro-American* remains basically in the *Blues* idiom. It may be termed a neoromantic composition. *Autochthonous* cannot be described as containing one basic style idiom; it is a combination of quasi-modern, popular, and neoromantic styles.

Paul Harold Slattery

SYMPHONIC WORKS
Summary

The following paragraphs summarize the comprehensive portrayal of William Grant Still:

Still's compositional philosophy. To Mr. Still, melody is the factor of primary importance. Next in priority comes harmony, form, rhythm, and dynamics. In music the exotic is desirable, but one should not lose sight of the conventional in seeking new effects. Dissonance does have a value and can be used with pleasing effects; it is a spice that should be used in careful proportions. Our contemporary music can be, and should be, an expression of a world that is not necessarily ugly. Music should be an enriching factor in our lives. Mr. Still strives to create music that people will understand, appreciate, and enjoy. The public is the final judge of what will live and what will not live.

Style of composition. In 1931, John Tasker Howard commented on Still's individuality: "He has established himself as a serious composer who utilizes the Negroid elements of jazz. Quasi-modern, he is seeking an individual idiom halfway between the ultra-modernists and the conservatives." [1] Mr. Still's compositional style is many-faceted. His well-defined forms and use of "give-and-take" texture are derived from eighteenth century Neoclassicism. The richness of his harmonies and texture along with the high level of emotional content in his works tend to mark him as a Neoromanticist. The harmonic vocabulary employed in some of his compositions is derived from the Modern idiom. Mr. Still possesses the rare ability to synthesize the best elements of the old and of the new into compositions that are fresh, meaningful, and expressive.

Historical style continuum. In the historical style continuum of American music, William Grant Still may be placed as a Neoromantic composer who displays tendencies to move in the direction of the Modern idiom.

---

[1] John Tasker Howard, *Our American Music* (3rd ed.; New York: Thomas Y. Crowell Co., 1947), p. 455.

William Grant Still, the man. William Grant Still is a musician's musician and a composer's composer. He is a highly self-demanding individual who seeks to obtain perfection in his compositions. In this regard he feels that "nothing ever is; it is always becoming."[2] He is a tireless worker, a tender father, and a devoted husband. He is a totally dedicated composer and yet he does not take himself too seriously. Mr. Still possesses a quick wit and a keen sense of humor; he will quite readily poke fun at himself in a good-natured way. Socially, he is without dissonance. He feels that he can improve race relations by doing the best job possible in his chosen field--the creation of beautiful music for all men to enjoy. Mr. Still is blessed with a balanced and well-rounded personality, a trait which is not always found in men of genius calibre. The prime motivator in the life of William Grant Still is his love of God, his people, and humanity. The genuine humbleness of this gifted composer is expressed by the phrase which he attaches to every composition, large or small:

"With humble thanks to God, the source of inspiration."

Paul Harold Slattery

---

[2] Personal interview, Slattery-Still, 1969.

V

THE OPERAS

CHOSEN IMAGE
The Afro-American Vision
in the Operas of William Grant Still

Ladies and gentlemen: come with me to
Mike's Harlem Saloon and share with me a
lover's tragedy, enacted in operatic style --
and, like the white man's opera, the theme
will be love, hate, passion, jealousy.

- Buddy De Sylva/George Gershwin
Blue Monday (1922)

I grew up knowing about William Grant Still. Lest you think that was
unusual in the East Tennessee bluegrass and gospel belt, let me remind
you those were other days. We had, when I grew up in the 1940's, our
Mozart Music Club; we played songs and recitals for each other there and
learned how to be proper concert goers at the university concert series,
and later we would all be members of the "Three B's," which met in the
Church Street Methodist Church downtown. That's how it was in those
days. For perfect attendance one year I won Helen Kaufmann's little
Story of One Hundred Great Composers,[1] and it became reading of choice
on long Sunday afternoons. And that was where I met William Grant
Still. He was one of the Hundred Greats. This was not an unshared
opinion; he was "the outstanding Afro-American composer of our day,"
according to the *Gramophone Shop Encyclopedia* of 1942; and two years
later John Briggs of the *New York Post* ventured that Still "may become
the American Tchaikovsky."[2]

This was pretty heady stuff for one born black, on a Mississippi farm, in

---

[1] Helen L. Kaufmann, *The Story of One Hundred Great Composers* (New
York: Grosset and Dunlap, 1943).
[2] George Clark Leslie, ed., *The Gramophone Shop Encyclopedia of Recorded
Music* (New York: Simon and Schuster, 1942), p. 414; John Briggs, "Rodzinski
and the Philharmonic Perform Two New Compositions," *New York Post*, 6
January 1944.

1895. It was also ironic, for his death in 1978 would be in a city--Los Angeles--where "most residents knew neither his name nor his music."[3] And few anywhere would know that at least fifty of his eighty-three years had found him locked in battle for opera--his opera, American opera: "Another bit of shame," wrote Knight-Ridder's Joe Saltzman in 1983, "for an America that ignores black composers and whose idea of the great American opera about Negroes is one composed by a white man."[4] Indeed for all that has passed it seemed that William Grant Still might instead have qualified for Kaufmann's ultimate sketch, "The Unknown Composer."

"Eventually," declared Alain Locke in 1924, "all people exhibit the homing instinct and turn back physically or mentally, hopefully and helpfully, to the land of their origin. And we American Negroes in this respect will not be an exception."[5] Black Americans, landlocked for generations in a nation of immigrants, looked within to see if there might remain, in the core, something ancestral not bred out, something uncontaminated by the Middle Passage of space and time. To some it lay in the music of America, as Locke said; to others it was a dream--of homecoming, as Locke also said. With white composers usurping the native black idiom (and Still, as the pseudonymous Willy M. Grant of the early 1920's, was not himself above the tinsel allure of Tin Pan Alley), it might be that Africa--the *ideal* Africa--would open a vista that would shatter forever the blackface stereotype of *Blue Monday*.

In 1927, Still began a serious collaboration with poet Countee Cullen, who within the year would publish an anthology of black poetry,*Caroling Dusk*, as well as his own *Copper Sun*, dedicated to Yolande Du Bois, daughter of W.E.B. Du Bois, educator, author, and a founder of the NAACP. Cullen evidently agreed to contribute the libretto for an opera based on an unpublished "African" novel of Still's wife, Grace Bundy Still. Although the collaboration was promptly interrupted by Cullen's marriage to Yolande Du Bois, in a wedding featuring sixteen bridesmaids and uncounted caged canaries, an agreement was drawn up for equal

---

[3] Joe Saltzman, "Life of 'Dean of Afro-American Composers' Little Known in U.S.," *Sunday Oregonian* (Portland), 6 November 1983.
[4] Ibid.
[5] Alain Locke, "Apropos of Africa," *Opportunity* 2 (February 1924): 37. Quoted in Russel J. Linnemann, ed., *Alain Locke: Reflections on a Modern Renaissance Man* (Baton Rouge, LA, Louisiana State University Press, 1982), 104.

division of profits. "I am delighted with it [the story outline]," Still wrote Cullen in 1928, "realizing that it now affords me the opportunity to write music that I can best write. I know that God is with us, and that we will have *tremendous success*."

What little can be gleaned suggests a typical operatic love triangle. Roshana (later changed to "Rashana") is loved by Sebande (later "Kalane") and Mokone. The names had no special derivation. Musicality was enough; for Cullen might, if he wished, "give the hunters any musical sounding names that occur to you." Grace Still wrote Cullen on 28 February 1928, "yet there are times in the lives of persons when life rather than death is tragedy. Such would have been the case with Rashana in our operatic version. To marry the object of one's deepest hatred is worse than the most terrible death."

In March the Stills moved, at Grace's insistence, from Saint Nicholas Place to 172nd Street, Jamaica, New York, where Cullen sent a section of the duet for Rashana and Mokone that Still found "beautiful" and "musical of itself." In return, the composer promised a piano reduction of the prelude, a "tone picture of the forest," sketched in Boston between work sessions on J.P. McEvoy's second *Americana*.

Whatever his satisfaction with the piecemeal text he was receiving, Still was laying out the course he would follow with future librettists. Though Cullen's verse was eminently suitable--"[It] possesses quiet dignity and strong emotional qualities. Moreover it is not over-polished"--Still firmly maintained that "dialogue should always be as short as possible without losing sense." That caveat also extended to the scenario. "I have other librettos and vocal operatic scores which I will gladly lend you . . . One is the libretto of *Turandot*, Puccini's last opera. There are examples in it of things that should not be done. Notably introducing characters who in no way help the development of the story." In another letter to Cullen, Still wrote, "Have determined all of the principal motifs. These are RASHANA, KALANE, MOKONE (a portion of this motif will be used to represent Mokone's regard for Rashana), KALANE'S REGARD FOR RASHANA, THE FOREST (The Call of the Spirits of the Forest is built on this motif), LOVE, RESIGNATION, HOPE, FATE, TRAGEDY and PREMONITION. Have discovered many interesting ways to present these motifs."

In part, the thematic outline Still sent to Cullen would serve to guarantee the inevitability between words and music, with the latter supreme: "Portions of the musical themes I wish to employ in Scene 3 are enclosed. The rhythm, being apparent, will need no explanation. The important thing will be, as far as possible, to use words whose inflections are in accord with the rising and falling of the melody." And in another letter Still wrote, "Everything must be timed as accurately as possible to avoid cuts after the work has been completed. I have seen so many beautiful compositions weakened by cuts that had to be made after the work had been done. Hope to avoid this in our opera." As an afterthought in yet another letter he added, "When I look at the above it impresses me as if I am trying to dictate. That is the trouble of a letter. It so often gives the wrong impression. These things are offered merely in the sense of suggestions based on what I have learned from study of the stage and dramatic technique. I know you will understand."

Some comment here: In *From the Land of Dreams* (a three-movement "fantasy" premiered under Vladimir Shavitch at a Composers' Guild concert on 8 February 1925), Still had experimented with "the instrumental use of human voices."[6] Other composers had similarly experimented--for instance Verdi, in the storm music for *Rigoletto*, a Red Seal favorite from Still's Little Rock boyhood. The *Rashana* motif, "Call of the Spirits of the Forest," was likely to allow some experimentation; later wordless choruses would heighten the mystery of the Mississippi coast in *A Bayou Legend* and the mood of isolation at Belle Foret, the plantation setting of *Minette Fontaine's* final tragedy. The use of motifs also would continue, as with the "Nemesis" theme of *Minette Fontaine*.

The need for concision would not be without peril. Although critic John Briggs would praise *Troubled Island*--yet years away--for the "strength and technical surety" of the score, he would blame the libretto for a nagging lack of effectiveness; the libretto of *Minette* (to a more recent critic) "leaps forward without an informative or credible development of character or plot."[7] In these cases two entirely different librettists were at work, respectively Langston Hughes and Verna Arvey, who in 1939 became the composer's second wife. Limp librettos (if such these be) are neither unknown nor insurmountable, surely, but Still's requirement that the text be "in accord" with the music creates tensions rife with foreshortenings and ambiguities. Still was his own dramaturge,

---

[6] Undated and unattributed review of the International Composers' Guild concert of 8 February 1925, found among the Still mementos.

[7] John Briggs, "'Troubled Island' Has City Center Premiere," *New York Post*, 1 April 1949; David Foil, "'Minette' Bare Romantic Opera Sketch," *Morning Advocate* (Baton Rouge, LA), 24 October 1984.

and his drama lies as much in the conflict and resolution of thematic material as in a superstructure of verbal communication: it is the music, not the word, that signifies.

In June 1928, having received a Guggenheim Fellowship, Cullen embarked for France; his marriage under stress, he was evidently (and understandably) less than enthusiastic about the opera in progress, and that is where the project ended. Early the next year Still left for California to orchestrate Paul Whiteman's "Old Gold Show," returning to New York for the premiere of his own orchestral suite *Africa* with Georges Barrere's orchestra. Subsequently heard to a "thunderous ovation" in Paris,[8] *Africa* would be the making of Still's international reputation. One suspects that the impetus, if not the inspiration of material for Africa, may well have derived from the aborted Rashana.

But whatever the success of *Africa*, Still's diary for 1930 reflects a growing disjointedness:

> Sept. 20 - Last night I dreamed that Dr. Boynton and some men (who seemed to be white) had me confined. I managed eventually to escape and went to the Metropolitan Opera House. There, as I stood in the entrance, I heard a work of mine being sung inside, and expressed my disappointment at not having known of it. . .
> Some other work was presented on the same bill. Later in the same dream a tall white man in evening clothes (a friend) and I were walking on the upper floors of the same theatre. At one spot a pit was covered with paper. This man stepped on the paper and fell to his death.

The crisis was in part emotional. Grace Still had not accompanied her husband to California. The marriage was breaking up. But the crisis may also have been cognitive; in those years, as Nathan Irvin Huggins would later demonstrate, "the Negro intellectual's fascination with primitivism was filled with ironies. Contrary to assertions of the soul community of Blacks, the American Negroes had to *learn* to appreciate the value of African art and culture." Pursuit of primitivism rested on "a very superficial knowledge of African life," and, in the midst of twentieth-century demands, represented an "escape in exotica" via "fancy of Timbuktoo."[9] *Rashana* had issued from--as Grace put it--"the

---

[8] Louis Schneider, in a 1933 review of a concert of the Pasdeloup Orchestra, included among Still's press clippings.

[9] Nathan Irvin Huggins, *Harlem Renaissance* (New York: Oxford University

148

immeasurable realm of fancy and imagination."[10]   Like the Harlem Renaissance itself, the artifice of an ideal Africa could not survive the Great Depression.

A month after his despairing dream, Still started his diary again. "Oct. 30--Start working on Afro-American Symphony. Things look dark. I pray for strength that I may do just as God would have me . . . I must not lose faith--I must not complain." Then, on 11 November, the mood of sorrow and resignation begins to change. "I am conscious of development musically. But this development has gone hand in hand with spiritual development.   Since I have been looking to Him for inspiration composing has become easy.   So much so that at times ideas come as rapidly as I can use them."   On 17 December the page brims with religious and creative exhilaration: "For years I labored in vain to master scoring for the orchestra. Then, one day, God showed me that I must turn to Him and rely solely on the Hand that knows no failure. Immediately, upon so doing, that I could not do before became easy.   My Lord showered his blessings of inspiration upon me."

Thus, with the *Afro-American Symphony* Still's creative powers woke with an urgency that made all before seem stale and unprofitable. The reason must lie in his subject--the American Negro, not the African. Paul Laurence Dunbar's exultant cry "Be proud, my Race" would be his motto, the superscription to his score.   Demeaned by blackface comedians, pilloried by film stereotypes, betrayed--as was the Harlem Renaissance-- by power brokers, and plundered of his music, the Black American could yet affirm that his name was "writ on Glory's scroll / In characters of fire."[11] "Home" was not Africa. It was America. And he could regain his birthright. Less than a decade from the charcoaled parodies of *Blue Monday*, such an affirmation took guts.

"Don't you think the next move now should be an opera?" It was Alain Locke writing--Locke, who as early as 1925 (in *The New Negro*) had seen in Still a star above the horizon. "Already I have a wonderful scenario idea, with an African and American background. I started to work it out . . . with a local musician and we have registered the title and outline scenario, under the name *Atlantis*."[12] Bruce Forsythe, Locke thought,

Press, 1971), 187, 189.

[10] Grace B. Still to Countee Cullen, 28 February, 1928.

[11] Lida Keck Wiggins, *The Life and Works of Paul Laurence Dunbar* (Chicago, IL, Wilmore Book and Bible Company, n.d.), 145.

[12] Undated letter from Alain Locke to William Grant Still.

might do the libretto, if Howard Hanson could provide an Eastman subsidy. *Atlantis* may have had too many cooks to please Still; at any event, nothing came of it, though *From A Lost Continent* (with "instrumental use" of voices again) a decade later suggests a continued interest. By then Still had begun orchestrating for the "Deep River Hour" on WOR. He would eventually take over the podium, but when the orchestra moved to NBC, "I couldn't conduct . . . because of my race."[13]

Things reached a nadir at home with Grace's departure, with the children, for Canada. As she later wrote: "My place is not in this U.S. No self-respecting person's, who has any strain of colored blood, is."[14]

In 1933 Still received a Guggenheim, enabling him to devote quality time to an opera: *Blue Steel*, with a libretto by Bruce Forsythe and story by Carleton Moss, Harlem playwright and actor. "Reticent" was a reporter's word for Still when asked about his new opera;[15] but his counsels to Moss were as forthright as they had been to Cullen. "He lived and breathed melody," Moss would tell Still's daughter Judith Anne years later. "When he was selecting names and situations . . . he said, 'Give me a name with music in it . Think of a conflict that fits this phrase. Give me a situation I can hear music against.'"[16]

The job at hand was to extrapolate an experience, a drama, a scenario that would be specifically Afro-American. The collaborators chose voodoo as their theme and its contrast with "city" values as their conflict. The scene is a settlement of cultists "in the deep of an inaccessible swamp" somewhere in an obviously mythical Alabama; we are told that it has been a sanctuary "for generations." Placed in this city boy's vision of the rural South is Neola, a "beautiful mulatto," soprano. Blue Steel, the eponymous baritone hero (or perhaps antihero), is "a boastful Negro from Birmingham" who chances on the locale and attempts to abduct Neola--much against the objections of the cultists, whose contralto spokesperson is Doshy, "an aged, toothless, and very black Negress," whose "utterances are often uncanny, and always shrouded in mystery." Steel takes Neola from the camp in a flurry of gunfire (his) that kills her father; inexorably pursued, his "barge" snags in the swamp. A momentary appeal to "a

---

[13] Eileen Southern, "Conversations with William Grant Still," ASCAP *Today* 7, no. 2 (Winter 1975): 21.

[14] Grace B. Still to William Grant Still, 15 April 1935.

[15] Undated and unattributed clipping announcing the Guggenheim Fellowship.

[16] Carleton Moss, quoted in a letter of 10 August 1983 from Judith Anne Still to the author.

Personal God" ends with a curse, and he falls into quicksand, "which draws him downward. As he madly tries to extricate himself, Neola screams, the drums cease, and Doshy voices the Chant of the Drums, again triumphant, again proclaiming the Voice of Dumballah."[17]

The Guggenheim Fellowship was renewed, and in late 1934 Still sent the score of *Blue Steel* to Chicago, where the "jazz opera" *A Light from St. Agnes* had been heard in 1925; Ruth Page had premiered Still's ballet *La Guiablesse* with Katherine Dunham; and in 1933 Still's old colleague from *Shuffle Along*, Caterina Jarboro, had become the first black to sing *Aida* with a major American company. Issac Van Grove of the Chicago Musical College responded enthusiastically to *Blue Steel*, calling it "a fine work, both as music and as theatre . . . I am going to suggest your opera as a good one for us." But, after a summer of delay, Van Grove was less sanguine. "Everything is so uncertain in the Chicago Opera Co. Will there be one or not? Will they produce a novelty or not? At present the answer is more 'no' than 'yes.'" Two weeks later, on 20 August, Henry Allen Moe of the Guggenheim Foundation wired that the Met had requested the score, but Met general manager Edward Johnson sent regrets on 9 September 1935: "We cannot see our way clear to accept this work."[18]

Still was undismayed. "I do not believe that any honors which have failed to come to me have done so because I am a colored man," he stated in *The Baton* in November 1937. "Nor do I believe that leading symphony orchestras the world over play my music because I am a Negro . . . My music is played because it is liked, because it says something to those who hear it . . . To me the crowning achievement is the fact that so many people . . . regard it as being truly, sincerely, American. Could any composer ask for more?"[19]

In 1938 Still began work on *Troubled Island*. Originally offered to Clarence Cameron White, Langston Hughes' libretto on Dessalines' tragic rule in Haiti had immediate appeal. It was broadly panoramic, firmly rooted in history, and posed a fine dramatic triangle. Dessalines is the Black former slave, firebrand, and dictator whose mulatto queen uses and

---

[17] William Grant Still, *Blue Steel*, story by Carleton Moss, libretto by Bruce Forsythe. William Grant Still Music.
[18] Issac Van Grove to William Grant Still, 4 January 1935 and 5 August 1935; Edward Johnson to William Grant Still, 9 September 1935.
[19] William Grant Still, "Are Negro Composers Handicapped?" *The Baton I*, No. 2 (November 1937), 3.

betrays him; Azelia, his Black and spurned first wife, is faithful to the end. Here at last was a ripe and strongly plotted text on Afro-Americans who played a part in the great world, nobly striving and yielding only to star-crossed destiny and all-too-human weakness.

July and August were spent in New York, where Still had been chosen in a blind competition to originate the theme music for the next year's World's Fair. Back in California as the year turned, he queried Juilliard about *Blue Steel*, now beginning to gather dust after a single performance at Hollywood Bowl in 1936. In April he finished the percussion parts for *Troubled Island* ("Thank God!") and bundled the manuscript off to the Met. It was rejected. Though Still later ascribed the rejection to the Met's unwillingness to accept a work "racial in theme,"[20] in fact Edward Johnson appears to have eschewed any and all American composers' operas until *The Warrior* (Norman Corwin and Bernard Rogers) premiered in January 1947. Whatever the reason for the rejection, it was for Still a crucial issue. "Made up my mind to fight," he wrote in his diary on 5 June 1939. "It shall be produced. Prepared list of people to write."

In late 1939, again at Locke's behest, Still began scoring *And They Lynched Him On A Tree*, for orchestra, biracial choruses, and contralto solo; the text, decrying race violence, was by Katharine Chapin Biddle. Successfully premiered at New York's Lewisohn Stadium on the eve of Independence Day 1940, the work drew applause from Locke in *Opportunity*: The ballad "universalizes its particular theme and expands a Negro tragedy into a purging and inspiring plea for justice and a fuller democracy. When, on occasion, art rises to this level, it fuses truth with beauty, and in addition to being a sword for the times it is likely to remain, as a thing of beauty, a joy forever."[21]

Spurred by the Met's apparent snub, Still was proceeding on his own with another opera, also turning on a hanging, but decidedly nonracial. The scenario--this time by Verna Arvey--calls for "a primitive community near a bayou . . . The production may be a fanciful one, as though the characters had stepped forth from a book of fairy tales, unlimited by either definite time or locale." Into this bayou-side dreamscape comes Bazile, an orphaned lad enwrapped in Wordsworthian longings for a "spirit lady,"

---

[20] T. Douglass Cook, "Visits to the Homes of Famous Composers, No. 3 -- William Grant Still," *Opera, Concert and Symphony 2*, no. 11 (November 1946), 9.
[21] Alain Locke, "Ballad for Democracy," *Opportunity 18* (August 1946), 228.

the soprano Aurore--whom for some arcane reason he encounters, despite her name, only at sunset. An earthy seductress, Clothilde--like the formidable Doshy, dark timbred--lies that he has brought about her (faked) pregnancy and entraps him into a promise of marriage. Clothilde identifies herself as an "artist." Bazile will "worship the artist" in her soul, "revere the poetry" that falls from her lips, and meanwhile, give her everything she wants: "prestige--and other worldly things." (That the hardheaded and career-minded Grace Bundy comes to mind here is probably no accident.) Bazile meets with an untimely end at the hands of a lynch mob informed by superstitious dread of the unknown and egged on by the jealous and unbelieving Clothilde; a heavenly rapture unites Bazile and Aurore. *A Bayou Legend* does touch ground here and there: a trio of mocking vagabonds--the script's "three gay blades"--provides a kind of demonic counterpoint not unrelated to the Ping/Pang/Pong trio Still had excoriated in *Turandot*, and by way of "local color" there are both a moving church scene that sets the stage for the town's uproar over "witchcraft" and a rousing *fais-do-do* in the last act.[22]

Still's powerful choral writing and his lilting, ragging dance sequence are wings to the centerpiece--a love duet of *Tristan*-like proportion and radiance. ("I often think of the days when you first came here and how you used to like *Tristan*," reminisced famed choral director Hall Johnson in a 1934 letter.) "I cannot think of where one might go short of Wagner to find so extended and so demanding a duet," wrote Jackson, Mississippi, music critic Frank Hains when *Bayou* was later premiered in 1974. "That this opera could have been neglected for so many years testifies to the cruel, often mindless vagaries of musical fashion," *Time's* William Bender observed. A second production at East Los Angeles College under Calvin Simmons elicited similar praise from *Los Angeles Times* critic Daniel Cariaga for its "utter simplicity and utter, direct naturalness . . . Beauties abound in the score."[23]

Such praise was, unfortunately, far in the future. Still again approached the Met, but before sending the manuscript "took pains to outline the plot

---

[22] William Grant Still, *A Bayou Legend*, libretto by Verna Arvey. William Grant Still Music. In Cajun usage *fais-do-do* refers to night dances that last long enough for the children to fall asleep while their elders dance on.

[23] Hall Johnson to William Grant Still, 13 April 1934; Frank Hains, "'Legend' Marvelous," *Jackson Daily News* (Jackson, Miss.), 25 November 1974; William Bender, "Opera in Mississippi," *Time*, 25 November 1974, 84; Daniel Cariaga, "Still's 'Bayou Legend' at ELAC," *Los Angeles Times*, 16 February 1976.

and explain the manner in which the music was handled. Shortly thereafter my letter was returned with an injunction not to bother sending the manuscript, nor any other for that matter."[24]

Whatever befell *A Bayou Legend*, the fight for *Troubled Island* was still paramount in Still's mind. On 3 June 1945 the *New York Times* announced that an effort to secure thirty thousand dollars for "an opera with an all Negro cast" had opened with a reception hosted by Mayor LaGuardia. "If sufficient funds are raised the opera will be first produced at the City Music Center, under the direction of Leopold Stokowski, after which it will tour the principal cities of the country." Mrs. Roosevelt would be honorary chairman of a committee formed under the direction of Newbold Morris.[25]

Less than a year later, in April 1946, the New York Philharmonic premiered Still's *Poem For Orchestra*. Olin Downes, who had covered Still's work for two decades, reacted forcefully--and in the negative. "The composer's expression is diluted in a way that deprives it of racial essence, or any strongly individual note. Years ago we heard music by Mr. Still, of an exoticism and imagination that recompensed considerably for the immaturity of its workmanship . . . In the piece heard last night he appears to have smoothed out as a composer--conventionalized . . . It is to be hoped that in later scores Mr. Still will return to what hide-bound academicians might call the original error of his ways."[26]

With the drive to mount the yet-unheard *Troubled Island* still in progress, Downes's criticism was ill-timed at best. Still's November statement to *Opera, Concert and Symphony* seems an obvious response to the charge that the *Poem* was "deprived" of what Downes considered to be "racial essence." "Why should not a composer be permitted to compose the kind of music he wants to compose?" Still asked. "Does it mean because I am a Negro that I should stick to racial themes? Music is bigger than that!"[27] The grim dichotomy was there for all to see: Still could, if he wished, assert himself in "racial themes" and win critical approval in the limited sphere available to the "race" musician; or he could storm the gates of academe and be damned in advance for a fruitless charade.

---

[24] Cook, "Visits to the Homes of Famous Composers," 9.

[25] Unsigned article, "$30,000 is Sought for All-Negro Opera," *New York Times*, 3 June 1945.

[26] Olin Downes, "Music of Negroes Concert Feature." *New York Times*, 5 April 1946.

[27] Cook, "Visits to the Homes of Famous Composers," 29.

The drive for *Troubled Island* stalled. In June 1947 the *Times* reported that Still had requested all contributions be refunded.

And then the miracle occurred: maverick producer Laszlo Halasz took *Island* up for his New York City Center Opera, premiering it on 31 March 1949 with, among others, Robert Weede and Marie Powers, a decade after its creation. As Judith Anne Still tells it, "Applause brought the composer to the stage for twenty curtain calls, alone and with the cast. The reception was unprecedented, almost ecstatic. It was a mystical height for my father, whose greatest love was opera." Julius Rudel, who conducted the third performance, fired off a note in response to Still's congratulations: "It was a very good performance, and at the end the entire orchestra cheered me, which made me feel very good."[28]

Incredibly, and unknown, during the twenty years of the 1940's and 1950's, Still was in fact writing and shelving away three major operas; *Costaso,* set in the American Southwest; *The Pillar*, inspired by American Indian themes; and *Mota*, set in "ancestral Africa."

Costaso, the earliest of the three, is purportedly linked to an old California legend: the hero, Costaso, is sent on a bogus search for Eldorado and, on the verge of exhaustion, is providentially rescued through the intercession of the Virgin. The ambiguity of the search, in which the dream of the "golden city" seems only an illusion masking certain death, is poetic and striking; the eponymous hero is again an "outsider" (though in this case supported by the warmly human Carmela),[29] and the happy ending is flawed because, as in *A Bayou Legend*, it is so patently contrived. But as an elaboration of what Robert Graves might call "the poetic theme," it moves in harmony with its predecessor.

The Pillar also deals with magic. As evil gains the upper hand in an Indian community, the beneficent guardian of the community, a "shining being" inhabiting a mystic stone, forsakes the land with predictably calamitous results.[30]

Mota returns to the "outsider" theme. The warrior Mota is "always one to depart from tradition;" in the denouement, "the only crime of which he

---

[28] Judith Anne Still, "In My Father's House," *The Black Perspective in Music* 3, no.2 (May 1975); 203; Julius Rudel to William Grant Still, 4 May 1949.

[29] William Grant Still, *Costaso*, libretto by Verna Arvey, William Grant Still Music.

[30] William Grant Still, *The Pillar*, libretto by Verna Arvey. William Grant Still Music.

is guilty in actuality is that of thinking independently and boldly; yet he refuses to compromise"--the central issue in *A Bayou Legend* as well. Mota dies a criminal's death together with Monase, daughter of the tribe's Nanga.[31]

In *Costaso*, *The Pillar*, and *Mota* there seems no doubt that the philosophical basis is Locke's "value relativism": reality is "a white light broken up by the prism of human nature into a spectrum of values."[32] In Still's poetic metaphor, the "shining being," the beloved Aurore, is at one with Locke's reality. And in all three operas the protagonist vibrates to Still's own proud self-assurance in the face of "arbitrary absolutes;" each is, no less than Wagner's Dutchman, a romantic hero.

In 1958, at age sixty-three, William Grant Still forged ahead on his ultimate opera, *Minette Fontaine*, turning again, as in *Blue Steel* and *A Bayou Legend*, to the South. Other composers had, of course, toyed with Creole idiom--Auber, as early as 1856, gives a curious account of the old popular ballad "Mam'zelle Zizi" in his *Manon Lescaut*. Still specifies (prejazz) 1845 as his time frame. Minette is a visiting diva who, slighted by the city's Creole gentry, avenges herself by enlisting the aid of voodoo "High Priestess" Marie Portier to steal handsome, wealthy Diron Hachard from the daughter of aristocratic Madame de Noyan. Once the charms have worked and the wedding has been accomplished, "the ritual spell wears off. Diron is seized with a severe headache (worse than he has had before) on the wedding night." A friend, Dr. Claude Dupre, presents a black servant who spills the beans on Minette's dealings with Marie Portier. "Diron works himself into a raging temper which brings on a stroke. Claude diagnoses this as one which will leave Diron paralyzed for life." The upshot is that "Minette has gotten what she wanted, but her triumph is bitter because, as Diron's wife, she is tied to a living corpse until God chooses to release them both.[33]

Two preliminary sketches deserve note. In the first, two women, a white and a quadroon, are daughters of the same father and are in love with the same man. The white succeeds in having the governor decree that quadroon women must wear, as a mark of shame, the distinguishing

---

[31] William Grant Still, *Mota*, libretto by Verna Arvey. William Grant Still Music.

[32] Ernest D. Mason, "Alain Locke's Philosophy of Value," in Linnemann, *Alain Locke*, 13.

[33] William Grant Still, *Minette Fontaine*, libretto by Verna Arvey. William Grant Still Music.

"tignon" and be subject to flogging at whim. Still asks, parenthetically, "How may this be manipulated to make a story that would be accepted in the United States?"[34] A second sketch presents an unhappily married composer who is writing an opera for a singer with whom he is having an affair. The singer, fatally ill, dies just on completing (at his behest) a first reading of the aria intended to be her showpiece. In the first sketch the question of caste is prime importance. As *Minette Fontaine* would stand, it would be Minette's caste as an opera singer that would bar her from Creole society and marriage with Diron. Having entertained Madame de Noyan's guests at a soiree, Minette is dismissed with instructions to eat in the dining room rather than among Madame's guests in the garden.

> *Minette*: I am an artist; a great one. Everyone admits it, yet she treats me like a servant.
> *Lucien*: Ah, well . . . . These old families won't accept us socially.[35]

Curiously enough, on 4 April 1938 Still recorded a dream in which he was "the hungry guest of honor at a banquet where all ate except me," possibly the genesis of the scene of two decades later. The artist/Clothilde persona based on his first wife, Grace Bundy, whom racial barriers had estranged from the American scene, is admittedly also the artist/Minette figure.

On 3 February 1959 Still could finally write Rudel, now general director of the New York City Opera: "During this past year, I have completed a new opera, set in New Orleans in the 19th century, in three acts. It does not have a tremendously large cast, but does require both white and colored singers and a small chorus. The story, which is original with us, deals with a prima donna of the New Orleans opera of that period, and is quite colorful." The score for *Minette Fontaine* evidently went to New York. On 5 January 1961, two years later, Rudel returned it: "I am afraid that I do not see any possibility . . . ."

One ray did break the horizon in 1960, with the premiere of Still's opera *Highway I, U.S.A.* at the University of Miami under Fabien Sevitzky; it would be repeated at Morgan State under Leon Thompson in 1967. Wrongly dated 1962 in some catalogues, it may represent a rewrite of at least some material from a discarded work called *A Southern Interlude.*

---

[34] William Grant Still, preliminary sketch for *Minette Fontaine.*
[35] *Minette Fontaine* piano-vocal score, 31.

In one act (two scenes) *Highway 1* presents a somewhat lurid story of a college-educated youth who, unemployed and rebellious, attacks his self-effacing brother's wife while the brother attends a church conference. Revived in 1973, by the Mississippi-based, predominantly black company called Opera/South, it drew praise from *Opera News* critic C. William Durrett for its "lushly romantic score" and "strong sense of musical characterization."[36]   The performance, under Margaret Harris, was recorded for Voice of America.

The Opera/South production of *Highway 1* was my working introduction (as stage director) to the Still operas. During a subsequent Central Opera Service meeting in Washington D.C., I squirreled myself away in the Library of Congress reading the scores--from *Blue Steel* on. The next year Opera/South produced the world premiere of *A Bayou Legend* to critical acclaim, and in 1979 the company produced it for television through the Corporation for Public Broadcasting.   It was another first for Still, the first of his race to have his work seen nationally as well as internationally over European networks. Gratefully, Still had lived to attend the premiere and garner the tumultuous applause that met his poetic masterwork; already in ill health, his mind gently failing, he died in 1978.

It remained for Baton Rouge Opera, which I had helped organize in 1981, to bring *Minette Fontaine* to the stage. Opening our third season on 24 October 1984, it was to be the company's most popular endeavor to date, beating out at the box office such staples as *Aida, Bohème, Lucia,* and *Tosca*.   The *Morning Advocate* found the piece "unabashedly romantic," though--forseeably--voodoo dances (borrowed from Still's *Archaic Ritual*) were "not as wild and orgiastic" as might be. The *State Times* found that "understanding and sympathy for the traditions and haunting moods of New Orleans come through in almost every passage of the opera. The libretto, written by Still's wife, Verna Arvey, ties in with the score and rounds out the imagery with skillful detail."[37]

"Today," wrote *Time's* William Bender after the premiere of *A Bayou Legend*, "being up to date does not seem quite as important as it once did. The reason lies partly in the same craving for nostalgia that in the pop

---

[36] C. William Durrett, "Reports: U.S.; Jackson," *Opera News* (13 January 1973), 23.

[37] Foil, "Minette' Bare Romantic Opera Sketch;" Helen Deermont, "'Minette Fontaine' Meets Audience's Expectations," *State Times* (Baton rouge, LA) 25 October 1984.

world has brought back Scott Joplin and the 1950's rock'n'roll. Mostly it seems to stem from a foundering of the musical avant-garde and a desire on the part of performers and audiences alike to reassess what was going on while the twelve-tone and electronic boys were holding sway in the academies."[38] This perception is partly right, but also--where William Grant Still is concerned--partly wrong. For Still was, in fact, numbered among the avant-garde in his formative years: in 1926 the New York *Journal* placed him "much nearer Schoenbergian Vienna than Mississippi."[39] In the following years, in the words of Louise Varèse, he "repented and repudiated."[40] In Bender's well-meant assertion that Still's work "does not introduce any innovations in musical or dramatic style,"[41] there is another misperception: For consciously and defiantly in the face of the avant-garde establishment, Still introduced his own visionary yet down-to-earth method. Still's career was one of conscious decision and moved to its own poetic lights.

What Still set out to elucidate--and the point is made best by the operas that form such a major portion of his work--was the meaning and purpose of life, specifically his life and the lives of his people: the Afro-American, the chosen image. His hero is , inevitably, the outsider at odds with established authority: tribe in *Mota* or *The Pillar*, the church-ridden community in *A Bayou Legend*, or caste and society in *Minette Fontaine*. His sanctuary is "that dreamlike state in which the ear reveals the inmost essence of all the eye beholds in scattered show, and tells him that his inmost being is one there with."[42] Still resets, for his own time, the vision of the arch-romantic, Richard Wagner. The dreamer and the dream are one.

From beginning to end, Still is in fact Wagner's disciple. The second score Still ever owned as a teenager was *The Flying Dutchman*; the first, not insignificantly, Weber's *Oberon*. For Still, to whom the voice of inspiration was the voice of God, the end of art would be--as with

---

[38] Bender, "Opera in Mississippi," 84.

[39] Undated and unattributed review of the International Composers' Guild concert of 24 January 1926. *"Journal"* is written across the text in Still's hand.

[40] Louise Varèse, *Varèse: A Looking-Glass Diary* (New York: Norton, 1972), I:226.

[41] Bender, "Opera in Mississippi," 84.

[42] Richard Wagner, "Artwork of the Future," in Albert Goldman and Evert Sprinchorn, eds., *Wagner on Music and Drama: A Compendium of Richard Wagner's Prose Works* (New York: Dutton, 1964), 186.

Wagner--"to assist the indefinite force of fancy to a sure, intelligent operation through the senses."[43] Thus the importance of the Stills' "dream books." "January 6, 1959," Verna Arvey writes, "Billy dreamed of the voice part of 'Minette Fontaine' with a reiterated G and D--he was looking at the music and hearing the sound . . . . The tenor was singing it, and Billy was writing out the parts." Nothing could more clearly distinguish Still from the *verismo* process. And nothing could more clearly distinguish just what it is that Still brings of "innovations in musical or dramatic style" to American opera: it is mysticism, veiled in the spell of Oberon. Frustrated attempts to pinpoint "blackness" in Still's later works (its absence is usually blamed on the "intentional" interference of Verna Arvey) fail to take into account a historic transcendentalism informing much Afro-American thought--in the New Orleans poets of *Les Cenelles*, for instance--predating the Harlem Renaissance by a hundred years. As scholar and student of his people, there seems little doubt that Still drew on the mystical resources of *les gens de couleur libres* centering around Joanni Questy: the "shining being" of *A Bayou Legend* is one with the "Sylphide a l'oeil d'azur" in Questy's *Vision* of 1841

> L'âme d'une âme,
> Le lucide rayon
> D'un beau globe de flamme
> Eteint à l'horizon[44]

for whom Still's name, in his opera, is "Aurore," and who shares a love that "has always been, and always will be."[45] Examples could be multiplied. To deny that such a strain is relevant to the black experience seems willful indeed, especially in the case of Still, who never tired of submitting that he had "been a Negro all my life."[46]

---

[43] Richard Wagner, "Origins of Modern Opera, Drama and Music," ibid, 129.

[44] Joanni Questy, *Vision*, 41, in *Les Cenelles* (*The Hawthornes*), first published in 1845 and reproduced in Edward Maceo Coleman, *Creole Voices: Poems in French by Free Men of Color* (Washington D.C.: Associated Publishers, 1945).

[45] *A Bayou Legend* piano-vocal score, 97.

[46] A Still family saying. Compare William Grant Still, "A Composer's Viewpoint," in Robert Bartlett Haas, ed., *William Grant Still and the Fusion of Cultures in American Music* (Los Angeles, CA.: Black Sparrow Press, 1972), 136: "As I am now 74 years, I did not need people fifty years younger than I to tell me what it is, or what it should be, to be a Negro."

What Still "firmly believes," wrote Louie Robinson in 1964, "is that if a composer has faith in himself, and sticks to his convictions--even to the point of being willing to starve for them--he will triumph in the end."[47] Still's is the striver's conviction, inherited from those who left the plantation to pursue and enrich the American dream--a dream for which his operas serve as metaphor and memoir. The pity of it is that with his friend Locke's death in 1954 Still had lost the last, as it were, of his contemporaries who held the key, who knew that opera precisely *not* "like the white man's" (in De Sylva's words) nor "Negroid" but of a "new race" --his, the Afro-American's--was the lure that had drawn him for a half century.

With the final notes of *Minette Fontaine*, at the end of the decade of the 1950s, Still could rest at last. It was at once his greatest work and his most self-revealing, his most harrowing and his most complete.

Donald Dorr

---

[47] Louie Robinson, "38 Years of Serious Music," *Ebony* 9, no.4 (February 1964), 106.

VI

THE STRING WORKS

THE VIOLIN MUSIC OF WILLIAM GRANT STILL

While living and studying in New York City in the 1930's, we had often heard with great pleasure an evening broadcast of the WOR Mutual Broadcasting System entitled "Deep River." The very original, effective and beautiful orchestrations of Negro Spirituals and semi-popular music which made up the repertoire of these programs deeply impressed us. Later on, when we had moved to Los Angeles, we happened to discuss these remarkable broadcasts with our good friend, the noted American composer, Robert Russell Bennett, and he told us that it was well known "in the trade" that the orchestrator for "Deep River" was William Grant Still, the composer of the "Afro-American Symphony" and other major symphonic works. He also mentioned that Mr. Still was a fellow member of his in the American Society for Composers, Authors and Publishers (ASCAP) and lived in Los Angeles.

We looked up Mr. Still's telephone number and introduced ourselves soon after at his home. To our dismay we learned that he had almost always composed with a specific performance or performer in mind, and that since he had not chanced to meet solo violinists, he had not yet written in that form. However, his resourceful and gifted wife Verna suggested that some piano pieces that she had played might well suit the violin.

One in particular, the "Blues" from the "Lenox Avenue Suite" (a piano interlude of an orchestral work commissioned by CBS) interested us both, and Louis Kaufman made a version of this piece for violin and piano which pleased the composer and his wife, and which the Kaufmans later played in countless concerts in the United States, South America and Europe. It has always received an enthusiastic response from audiences and critics. Later Mr. Still orchestrated an accompaniment for this violin piece for performances on Columbia Broadcasting Systems' "Invitation to Music" (conducted by Bernard Herrmann) and with the National Orchestral Association at Carnegie Hall (conducted by Leon Barzin). The critic, Robert Simon, of the *New Yorker* magazine wrote on February 26, 1944: "Mr. Kaufman and the orchestra added the 'Blues' movement from William Grant Still's 'Lenox Avenue Suite' to the great approval of the audience", and Henry Simon, the critic of *PM* noted on February 15, 1944: "As an encore Mr. Kaufman played the 'Blues' movement from 'Lenox Avenue Suite', which was the most typically American music of all in this evening of 'recognition'." The "Blues" seemed to naturally attract radio performances. Louis Kaufman broadcast it with conductor Lou Bring on September 30, 1943 over NBC's coast-to-coast RCA program, "What's New." He also played it with Leigh Harline conducting the Ford Summer Hour program for the ABC Network. It has always been puzzling to us that Mr. Still's publisher would not publish this violin arrangement so that many other violinists who have asked us and the Stills for the music, could have it. But in spite of the joint Kaufman-Still efforts over many years--this enchanting work is still in manuscript.

Other works Mr. Still composed for violin have had quicker publication. The "Suite for Violin and Piano" (or orchestra) was published almost before performance by Delkas. This major work was written for and dedicated to us both, and is based on three works of art by noted Negro artists. The first movement was inspired by "African Dancer" (a large bronze female figure) by Richard Barthe, which is in the collection of the Whitney Museum in New York City; the second movement was suggested by Sargent Johnson's handsome colored lithograph in the collection of the San Francisco Museum of Art; the third movement refers to "Gamin" (the bronze head of a small Negro boy) by Augusta Savage (the Rosenwald Fund). Incidentally, all these art works are reproduced in Alain Locke's fascinating book, *The Negro In Art*, which was published in Washington, D.C. in 1940 by the Associates in Negro Folk Education.

Louis Kaufman premiered this Suite in Boston's Jordan Hall with pianist Vladimir Padwa on March 15, 1944, and on March 17th of the same year with the same pianist in New York's Town Hall. He played the premiere of the 'orchestral version' in New York on March 25, 1946 with the WOR Symphony, conducted by Emerson Buckley. We also played this Suite at the Annual Festival of Modern Music at the First Congregational Church in Los Angeles organized by Arthur Leslie Jacobs in May of 1944. Another orchestral performance was broadcast by the Standard Symphony program conducted by Henry Svedrofsky on September 23, 1945.

Other Still compositions which we have consistently performed since 1943 are the "Pastorela" (a tone-poem inspired by California) which was written for us, and the two shorter compositions, "Summerland" and "Here's One" (an effective arrangement of the Negro Spiritual of the same name). Louis premiered the 'orchestral version' with the CBS Symphony, conducted by Bernard Herrmann, over the Columbia Broadcasting System. He has also played the quartet version of "Danzas de Panama" which was written for the violinist, Elizabeth Waldo.

Some of these programmed Still compositions have had an unlooked for 'social significance' that had never occurred to us working

164

musicians!

The *New York Times* and *Newsweek* magazine published photographs of Louis Kaufman and Mr. Still looking over music together. We were told by reliable reporters that this was the first time these publications had printed pictures of a "White" musician and a "Negro" musician together. Evidently each category had always been "solo only" photographs. Helping to end that barrier seemed a good (although unexpected) result of our pleasure in working with the Stills.

One more dramatic change for 1945. For seven years before we had played in Jefferson City, Missouri, the nearby (Negro) Lincoln University had been requesting permission to buy tickets to the Civic Concerts. No reserved seats! For seven years the answer had been, "No." Then the Negro press announced our forthcoming recital and the fact that we regularly programmed the works of William Grant Still. The University again sent in a request to buy tickets for the Kaufman program adding they were especially interested in Mr. Still's music. To our delight the President of the Civic Music Association of Jefferson City, Mr. Richard Arens, replied, "They're going to Heaven with us. There's no reason why they shouldn't hear music with us!" So about 85 Negroes came to our concert, and they all came backstage to tell us this interesting tale, and to shake our hands and congratulate us. So did many of the White members of this now happily unsegregated audience, who said such normal behavior would make the city a better place to live in.

We had long hoped to record these compositions, so we were very pleased to meet Mr. Giveon Cornfield, the director of Orion Records in the summer of 1971. He thought it was a most worthwhile project to commemorate our friend's 76th year with a long-playing record devoted to all these "major and minor" compositions for violin and piano, with the addition of another work, an arrangement of a folk-song of North America--"Carmela". This is a brief "serenade", which nostalgically recalls the charm of Spanish California. It was most gratifying for us to have this recording, which was made in Los Angeles and produced by Giveon Cornfield, with the best of modern technical equipment for Orion Stereo Records.

To our great delight Melody Peterson wrote in the *Los Angeles Times*, "The homespun warmth and bounding energy of Still's compositional style are conveyed in an extremely forthright manner by the Kaufmans." This inspired our friends (and life-long Still admirers) Mrs. Joan Palevsky and Dr. Robert Haas to ask whether we could "put together" yet another record of Still's works. We did: the very remarkable work for harp, piano and strings, entitled *Ennanga*; the *Danzas de Panama* for string quartet; and a very fine group of songs, *Songs of Separation*, based on texts by notable Negro poets, and *Song for the Lonely*, which Still wrote to the poetic text of his gifted wife, Verna Arvey. We had the great good fortune to obtain the cooperation of the splendid French mezzo-soprano, Claudine Carlson for this recording, and the excellent pianist-accompanist Georgia Akst. So, in March, 1972, the wishes of Mrs. Palevsky and Dr. Haas became realities, and the above works were recorded for Orion.

Both public and critical response to these records has been gratifying. William Grant Still's violin music has proven to be a significant contribution to the violin literature and has had an ever widening influence in furthering national and international communication.

[Addendum to the above article, Fall 1993: In honor of Dr. Still's approaching 100th anniversary on May 11, 1995, we wish to pay homage to the work of his daughter Judith Anne, who has been responsible for the steadily increasing awareness of the important work and influence of William Grant Still's compositions. Still successfully avoided the perils of Scylla and Charybdis, i.e. music of boring scholasticism or the facile path of folksy popular elements. His personal poetic music can be compared to the charm of flowing melody and rhythmic elements that endear the music of Franz Schubert and Frederick Deluis to us.]

Louis Kaufman and Annette Kaufman

WILLIAM GRANT STILL: THE FOLK SUITES AND OTHER COMPOSITIONS IN THE EDUCATIONAL SETTING

Strangely enough, even after the social uproar of the Sixties, most musicians still consider the music of Afro-Americans to be an entity external to the general history of American music. Music teachers devote a week or even a month each year, generally in February, to the discussion of Afro-American composers and minority music, rather than integrating those discussions into the general music curriculum throughout the year. However, whenever educational discussions of minority composers occur, the name of William Grant Still is raised. This despite the fact that Dr. Still never wanted to be identified as an "Afro-American" composer. To his mind, there was no minority music, there was only music. He was not a colored composer, he was an American composer. This concept was put to practical purpose in his use of folk material from all over the Western Hemisphere in many of his compositions.

The year 1995 is the one-hundredth anniversary of Still's birth, as well as the sixty-fifth anniversary of his celebrated *Afro-American Symphony*. Since its debut, hundreds of orchestras around the world have performed the *Afro-American Symphony* and in 1994 almost 1,800 presentations of the work occurred in the United States. Young musicians everywhere can understand and appreciate this great music, as it is based on an original Blues theme written by Dr. Still and portrayed in a truly American style. Most notable is the Scherzo, which introduces a banjo into the lilting rhythm. This was, in fact, the first time the banjo had been incorporated into a serious symphonic work. Young listeners immediately appreciate the tuneful, melodic quality of this work.

Author of over 200 pieces, Still wrote music for all ages and levels of development, including numerous symphonies, operas, ballets, chamber works, solo works and arrangements of spirituals and songs. Despite the recognition that much of his music has received, some of his compositions are not frequently performed, and many of them are well within the playing ability of high school students, such as *Serenade* and *Patterns*. Among the most gratifying of these compositions are the *Little Folk Suites* for string quartet. There are five of these suites in all, with each suite containing two pieces. They are intended to represent folk styles of the Western Hemisphere, and are superb in their clarity and rhythmic variety. These suites are both challenging and enjoyable, and have unlimited potential as educational tools.

The first piece in *Little Folk Suite #1*, "Salangadou," is based on a

plaintive folk melody from Louisiana.   It is enriched with Blues
harmonies and full strings.

The second piece, entitled "El Capotin," is based on a swinging
syncopated folk tune from California.

Little Folk Suite #2 begins with a composition called "EL Nido," which
is based on a rhythmic folk dance from Argentina. It features a lengthy
solo line on the cello which greatly enhances the ensemble sound, and
which is excerpted below:

The second piece in this suite is "Sweet Betsy From Pike," a well-
known and popular folk tune. Dr. Still has arranged it appropriately, with
moving rhythmic lines in the viola and cello, and a humorous dance
ending.

168

The *Little Folk Suite #3* begins with a combination of folk songs: "Aurore Pradere" from Louisiana and "Tant Sirop Est Doux" from Martinique. The two melodies blend gracefully in 2/4 time with moving counterpoint in the lower strings.

In the second piece, "Wade in the Water," a familiar and moving American spiritual is played over pizzicato strings.

In the *Little Folk Suite #4,* "Los Indios," an Indian chant from Brazil is combined with one from Peru. It is a syncopated dance featuring a solo part in the cello.

The second piece is the light and humorous "Crawdad Song." Still's arrangement is a continuous flow of moving notes, echoing the style of American fiddle music.

"Tutu Maramba," the first piece in *Little Folk Suite #5*, begins with a flowing folk tune from Brazil. The legato melody alternates with playful staccato strings.

In "La Varsoviana," we have a graceful 9/8 folk tune from New Mexico with a middle section which features pizzicato strings.

a)

170

b)

All of the *Little Folk Suites* are fun and challenging for high school students, with an average playing time of two minutes each. These pieces can also be used to introduce the student to the folk music of various cultures in the Western Hemisphere. Because of their use of melodies from all over North and South America, they can help to broaden young students' musical horizons.

Dr. Still used folk material, especially material from the Western Hemisphere, in a large number of his compositions. He found this music to be a rich and valuable resource, one which was unrecognized by most of his contemporaries. He comments on this:

> As we go from country to country in the Western Hemisphere, we find a tremendous amount of variety in the music--probably more than anywhere else on earth. This is due to the merging of the various indigenous cultures with those of the foreigners who came to settle here. The foreigners were English, Spanish, French, Portuguese, Danish and Negro, among others. In the different countries to which they went, they blended their own distinctive musical idioms with those already in existence, producing a new music just as the blend of nationalities produced--in many instances--a new race. *(Unpublished notes from a lecture given by the composer in 1935.)*

Still composed many arrangements of Negro spirituals for various combined instruments which high school conductors will find very useful and playable. In *Songs: A Medley*, Still arranged eight melodies for strings, piano, saxophones, clarinet, trumpet, drums, guitar and banjo. These songs have definite jazz and Blues elements and include: a) "Song of the Rivermen," b) "Slave Chant," c) "Oh, Dem Golden Slippers," d) "I'm Goin' Where Nobody Knows My Name," e) Medley of "Ain't Misbehavin'," and "Sweet Georgia Brown," f) "Some of These Days," g) "Love Will Find a Way," and h) "St. Louis Blues." Young musicians will find these compositions to be enjoyable and challenging. Still was very sensitive to the needs of performers, and was frequently seen asking individual players if they liked playing their parts. If the musicians had any special requests, he would frequently rewrite an individual part during the rehearsal.

The *Little Folk Suite from the Western Hemisphere* is written for brass quintet and includes the two tunes, "Where Shall I Be When the Great Trumpet Sounds?" and "En Roulant Ma Boule." This is an exciting arrangement for brass which has rarely been heard.

Among Still's works for band are *The American Scene* including three sections: a) "Tomb of the Unknown Soldier," b) "New Orleans Street," c) "Berkshire Night," and d) "Tribal Dance." *The Fanfare for American Heroes* is an outstanding piece for marching band as well as concert band.

There are a large number of pieces for voice ensemble as well as arrangements for S.A.T.B. choir which are well within the capabilities of high school groups. Especially enjoyable are *Sinner, Please Don't Let This Harvest Pass*, *The Blind Man*, *All That I Am* and the *Three Rhythmic Spirituals*. These pieces are stimulating and inspiring. Most importantly, William Grant Still Music encourages teachers to arrange Still works for their students, as long as permission is obtained and copies of arrangements are sent to William Grant Still Music for copyright.

Ultimately, all of our efforts toward equality and understanding between the races will be useless until Afro-American history, including the history of Afro-American music, is taught as part of the regular curriculum in the schools. And certainly, the works of William Grant Still must be included in any course on American music. Hopefully, the Still Centennial in 1995 will provide a platform for the introduction of Still to the youth of America.

Jean F. Matthew

VII

THE PIANO WORKS

FUSION OF STYLES IN THE PIANO WORKS
OF WILLIAM GRANT STILL

Earning a living as a composer in twentieth-century America is a remarkable accomplishment. Doing so from roughly 1925 until 1978 is even more noteworthy. Being African-American and writing primarily "classical" music, while earning a living composing, make the feat even more spectacular. William Grant Still, a Mississippi-born, Arkansas-raised composer, who happened to have decided upon a career in "serious music," as he referred to it, did just that.

Still often attributed his early recognition of his heritage to his grandmother's singing of Negro spirituals in their home. His mother was a highly respected, well-educated graduate of Atlanta University who taught English and established a Shakespeare circle. His father, who died when Still was a baby, was a graduate of Alcorn College (now Alcorn State University) in Lorman, Mississippi, and a trumpeter who founded a brass band after his graduation.

The social structures in Little Rock, Arkansas, were more open to interracial interaction than Wilkinson County, the rural Mississippi county where Still was born. As a young African-American child with a highly educated mother, Still enjoyed the freedom of the more cosmopolitan atmosphere and the luxury of opportunities in Little Rock. Still studied violin and, as an adolescent, he listened to recordings of opera with his stepfather.

When he prepared to go to college, his mother insisted that he enter the pre-medical program at Wilberforce University, which he did, while playing in the string quartet, organizing a recital of his own compositions, and teaching himself to play all the instruments of the band. When Still heard of the Afro-British composer, Samuel Coleridge-Taylor, who toured the United States early in this century, he decided absolutely to make music his career.

While Still's first compositions were written during his time at Wilberforce, his serious study of music composition was at Oberlin Conservatory and later in Boston with George Chadwick. Several years later in New York, he studied privately for two years with Edgar Varèse. When he was in New York during the 1920's, he did arrangements for a number of jazz bands, including Paul Whiteman's and Eubie Blake's, while continuing his serious composing. After several trips to California during the 1930's, he finally settled there to work as a composer for the rest of his life. Still's active career spanned over fifty years.

Infinitely pragmatic and remarkably self-sufficient, Still often wrote piano pieces for specific performers or "on order" from publishers for textbooks and anthologies. Still's second wife, Verna Arvey, was a concert pianist and the motivation behind Still's first attempts at writing for solo piano. At Miss Arvey's urging, he composed the first significant works for solo piano about 1936, the set called *Three Visions*.

It is difficult to pinpoint exact dates of the compositions for solo piano. The dates indicated on the list below are publication dates, which usually coincide with copyright dates. Still mentions some of his piano works by title in his diaries, where he indicates that he is working on a specific work or that he has finished the work. Since the diaries are not complete and do not exist for every year, they cannot be used solely as a systematic source for the dates of all of his compositions.

Of the sixteen separate entries in the current William Grant Still Music Catalog, ten are for solo piano, two are for two pianos, two are piano parts that accompany chamber groups, and two are duplications of works from other entries. Contained in the ten entries for solo piano are a total of thirty single compositions which have stylistic variety as well as a wide range of technical demands.

A complete list of the works originally written for solo piano by William Grant Still follows:

Piano Music	Publisher	Date

1. *Bells:*
  1) Phantom Chapel
  2) Fairy Knoll
	MCA	1944

2. *A Deserted Plantation**
  1) The Black Man Dances
  2) Spiritual
  3) Young Missy
  4) Dance
	Robbins	1936

Piano Music	Publisher	Date

3. [Five] Animal Sketches
  1) Camel
  2) Bear
  3) Horse
  4) Lamb
  5) Elephant
	Silver Burdett	1951

4. Marionette	MCA	1946
5. Preludes (1 - 5)	WGSM	
6. Quit Dat Fool'nish	WGSM	1938
7. Ring Play	WGSM	1964

8. Seven Traceries
  1) Cloud Cradles
  2) Mystic Pool
  3) Muted Laughter
  4) Out Of The Silence
  5) Woven Silver
  6) Wailing Dawn
  7) A Bit Of Wit
	J. Fischer & Bro.
	
	WGSM-SMC
		1940

9. Swanee River (Arrangement of Stephen Foster tune for piano solo by WGS)	WGSM	

10. Three Visions
  1) Dark Horsemen
  2) Summerland
  3) Radiant Pinnacle
	J. Fischer & Bro.
	
	WGSM Edition
		1936

* *A Deserted Plantation* is an arrangement for piano by the composer of the suite that Paul Whiteman commissioned for his orchestra. Other listings from the WGS Music catalog under "piano music" are either for two pianos or they are piano parts to larger works.

The pieces fall into three distinctly recognizable styles that could be labeled: (1) mystic/academic, (2) Afro-American; and (3) the neo-romantic, film music style. The largest number of pieces would be classified as being in the mystic/academic style, including *Cloud Cradles* and *Dark Horsemen*. The Afro-American style comes through clearly in the *Preludes, Ring Play,* and *Quit Dat Fool'nish,* as well as in the complete *Deserted Plantation* set, which were the only piano pieces written during Still's Harlem Renaissance period. *Summerland,* by far the most widely played and known of the piano works and the most frequently arranged by the composer for other combinations of instruments, is representative of the neo-romantic, film music category with its impressionistic parallel chords and floating rhythms.

On April 14, 1938, a diary entry notes that the composer wrote *Quit Dat Fool'nish,* a playful piece, which was dedicated to the composer's dog, Shep, in the published version. Anecdotal evidence suggests that it was actually dedicated to Still's friend, Bruce Forsythe, who was an alcoholic, and that it was an attempt to get him to give up his "foolish ways," most notably his drinking. The dedication to Shep was to protect the reputation of Bruce Forsythe, a fellow African-American and a composer.

The *Seven Traceries* were completed on May 11, 1939, according to another entry in Still's diary. On December 26, 1943, the composer noted that he started on "Phantom Chapel" from *Bells.* On New Year's day (six days later) in 1944, he indicates that the sketch was completed. The next day he started on "Fairy Knoll," which he finished fourteen days later. Four days after that, he started orchestrating both pieces. Rarely did Still ever date a manuscript, but the autograph of *Bells* in the William Grant Still-Verna Arvey Papers at the University of Arkansas Libraries, Fayetteville is dated December, 1943, the month Still actually began his work on *Bells.* The completion date is not given on the manuscript.

The piano works were not put aside once they were completed. In the spirit of Baroque performance practices, as well as of experiments in timbre often found in jazz, Still frequently arranged pieces for another medium. He continued his lifelong practice of fusing European musical traditions with characteristics of music of other styles, and he sought performances in every venue possible by whatever combination of instruments that might be available.

177

Several of the piano pieces exist in orchestral or chamber group arrangements and in versions for solo instrument accompanied by piano made by the composer. As a composer whose point of departure was usually melody and rhythm, his focus was on the theme first. Timbre could be adjusted to make a new setting effective. Still thoroughly enjoyed exploring the possibilities of combinations of sonorities. He relished the unique sounds of individual instruments of the orchestra while serving his pragmatic interests in gaining more performances. Throughout his career, he was less concerned with preserving the integrity of specific timbres than he was with communicating the music to listeners in performances.

For example, "Summerland" from *Three Visions* exists in at least nine arrangements, in addition to the solo piano version. It was arranged by the composer for small orchestra, full orchestra, and as a solo with piano accompaniment for flute, violin, viola, and cello. The composer set "Summerland" for solo harp and organ, and even expanded it into a two-piano arrangement.

His compositional process centered on his creation of melodies from the beginning. Since Still used melodies recorded in his sketchbooks when a need arose for a work because of a commission or an upcoming performance, the chronological dating of Still's compositions has little to do with observing a stylistic evolution. This is especially true in the piano works. Early he mastered the art of incorporating specific elements into his writings and took great care to identify those melodies in his sketchbooks with names like "Negroid," "Love," and "Mystic." Some of the melodies were recorded in extant sketch books that date back at least to 1926. Most of them were numbered and labeled with a descriptive word or phrase for reference. Still called some of these "motifs," and he wrote of the transformation of themes. "Tone painting" also appeared in his numerous published articles to describe the way he worked with materials. His diaries reinforce the notion that he started with a melody and, frequently, with a descriptive title, before he actually composed the work. Finally, he determined the form "more or less" [Still's own words] and harmonized the melody.

Still recognized and relied heavily on the mystery of inspiration, a nebulous, undefined area of his compositional process. Still once said:

He [the composer] must reach beneath what his objective faculties disclose to him to contact there the spirit of that he wishes to portray

178

. . . he receives the motive or germ he needs . . . usually when I seek new harmonies I sit at the piano expecting them to come, and awaiting their coming. Then it feels as though some external force attracts my fingers to the right keys. Under its guidance not only is the discovery of new chords made possible but also discovery of the proper way to resolve them to other new chords . . . the composer finds himself facing the problem of recurring special themes to depict some subject he has chosen. If his notebook contains no suitable material, he must search for it in the invisible world.

Still considered the orchestra "his instrument." He said, "I compose for it from the beginning. I do not first write for the piano and then orchestrate the material." His early years as a musician in W. C. Handy's Memphis blues band and later as oboist in the pit orchestra of the longest-running all-Black musical of the time, *Shuffle Along*, influenced his compositional process and strengthened for him the importance of melodic design.

Through his involvement with the creation of art and literature during the Harlem Renaissance of the 1920's, Still expressed his heritage in his music as did his contemporaries, Langston Hughes, W. E. B. DuBois, and Zora Neale Hurston, in their literature. For the first fifteen years of his career, he expressed his African-American nationalism in his music. He wrote operas, ballets, symphonies, and chamber pieces about Afro-American, African, and Caribbean cultures. He used descriptive titles that clearly identified his points of reference and inspiration. These early works bore titles such as, *Dismal Swamp* (reference to land in the South on which many poor Blacks lived), *The Black Man Dances, Levee Land* (a familiar area to residents of Mississippi and Arkansas on both sides of the Mississippi River), *The Deserted Plantation* (descriptive scenes of life on the plantation), *Lenox Avenue* (the center of Afro-American life in New York during the Harlem Renaissance), and the culminating work of 1930, the *Afro-American Symphony*. In these works, Still clearly expressed his desire to "uplift the Negro race" by using folk scenes and the melodic and rhythmic aspects of musical folk materials in European structures, such as suites, ballets, operas, and symphonies.

When he finally settled in California, his titles gradually changed. Many of the early works were listed as "discarded" by the composer as his compositions began to reflect more and more his assimilation into conservative classical composition. As his interest in spiritualism grew,

179

titles reflecting abstract concepts became more frequent. However, on close examination, one notes that even some of the later works, which are not identified with nationalistic titles, contain elements of Still's Afro-American nationalistic style.

The problem with attempting to label any portion of William Grant Still's music as "Black music," however, is a complex one tied closely to traditions. Still grew up in Arkansas in the early 1900's where Blacks were referred to as "Negroes" by a certain class of whites and, more frequently, as a derogatory bastardization of that word by others. As Still grew older, the more commonly used term was "colored people." "Black," during most of Still's lifetime, was a designation for a lower class of music and the nighttime activities of persons who were not part of cultivated society.

When he reached manhood, his generation called themselves "The New Negro," and later, the "Afro-American." Still spoke frequently of his desire to "elevate" the lowly blues, the music of his people, to loftier heights by using its essence in symphonic music. He felt that the blues, jazz, spirituals, and folk melodies of his people could contribute to the development of an American tradition in "classical" music that could break away from the European imitations still rampant in this country in the 1920's and '30's.

Still often referred to his Black music style as his "racial" style, a term typical of the days when big record companies marketed records to African-Americans under the designation, "Race" records. By the time of the 1960's civil rights movement when "Black is Beautiful" was the byword, Still was almost 70 years old. He never adapted to the positive implications of the sixties use of the word "Black" for his own race, nor did he want his music referred to as "Black music." To him the connotation meant street music, bar music, nightclubs, or the music of a lower class.

Still always thought of himself as an American. He would, no doubt, be quite comfortable having his music referred to as "African-American," because he was proud of his African heritage. He sought out accurate information on the music and customs of Africa, a task which was difficult even in the best of libraries at the time.

Still summed up the attitudes of his contemporaries when in 1964, he said,

180

. . . it has always been my belief that the Blues is one of the most important musical forms developed by American Negroes . . . when I was a boy the Blues were considered immoral.

He goes on to say,

I disagree with that idea [that the Blues were . . . immoral], because in 1916, when I worked with W. C. Handy in Memphis, on Beale Street, I was able to have a more intimate contact with the Blues . . . they usually do represent the yearnings of a lowly people who are trying to find a better life. [Notes from a speech in 1964, files of William Grant Still Music.]

As a member of the Afro-American intelligentsia of the Harlem Renaissance of the Twenties, Still believed throughout his life that art had the power to make the world racially better. He saw his heritage and his music as a bridge by which to communicate with all people. It is, therefore, difficult to attach a label, particularly the term, "Black music," to any of Still's works.

Judith Anne Still says in the talks she frequently gives on her father, "His primary goal was to say something melodic to which people in all walks of life would respond." Orin Moe, author of a probing article on Still's song cycle, supports Judith's belief that, "Of central concern to William Grant Still was not the composition of an aggressively Black music, but a music which would fuse the cultures both within his own and his country's backgrounds."

Still himself wrote in a speech on June 5, 1964:

Shortly after World War I, I began to feel that music with in the academic limitations of that day was not entirely satisfactory. And so, when a chance to study with Edgar Varèse, the French modernist composer, came along, I gladly accepted it . . . Sometimes I use polytonality in my music . . . [then later] I discovered that if I wanted to write music that was recognizable as Negro music . . . I could not use that [ultra-modern] idiom [referring to the style he was taught by Varèse] because the identity was lost . . . I did not want to confine myself to that particular idiom because I think that here in America we have so many idioms . . . the Indian music, the Creole music, and so on.

181

William Grant Still defined his own music as ethnically identified, whether one chooses to use the term "Black music," African or Afro-American, or, as he did, Negro Music. He said always very proudly, "My desire to write, when I wish to, in a Negroid idiom is prompted not only by the fact that I am colored . . . the Negro musical idiom itself has great value, and. . .Negro music can help build good race relationships."

Defining Still's style in terms of Black music scholarship is in itself quite distinct from just calling it "Black music" because a Black man wrote it or labelling it "Black music" because it received its inspiration from the music of persons of African descent. Samuel Floyd, in his 1980 pivotal article dealing with "Black American Music and Aesthetic Communication" in the *Black Music Research Journal*, said "*Black music* is that which expresses essentials of the Afro-American experience in the United States . . . [It] is a broader category that includes concert and recital music."

Still consciously and purposely used the materials of Afro-American music as part of the elements of his compositional language. He specifically used musical elements that are readily identified with Black music as defined by Floyd: blue notes (the lowered 3rd, 7th, or 5th of a major scale), inflections of all types, African-type antiphonal effects, as well as repetitions and contrasts. The composer used elements of melody, harmony, and rhythm in each of the three styles identified in this essay that could place any of these piano pieces within the broader definitions of Black music scholarships. In all three styles, he uses minor thirds frequently, he vacillates between major and minor tonalities, focuses on one motivic element throughout, and uses syncopation.

In analyzing Still's *Songs of Separation* for voice and piano in the *Black Music Research Journal*, 1980, Orin Moe points to a "strong affirmation of a Black aesthetic" in subtler ways. According to Moe, "[Still's] harmonic language is compatible with blues or jazz because he uses 7th and 9th chords." Moe points out, additionally, in the songs an alternation between major and minor thirds, syncopation, and the strong movement toward the final poem, "I Am A Black Pierrot," with the music in blues style with elements of jazz.

William Grant Still's mystic/academic style dominates his better-known piano works, because he used it frequently in the three major groups of pieces, *Bells, Seven Traceries,* and *Three Visions*, which comprise 12 of the 30 solo piano pieces. According to notes made in a thematic catalog of the composer's works compiled by Still and his wife, the composer's purpose in writing *Bells* in 1943 and 1944 was to "write some music descriptive of the sounds of different bells . . . primarily to appeal to children." *Seven Traceries*, on the other hand, published earlier in 1940, is described by his wife, Verna Arvey, as "abstractions bearing the imprint of mysticism."

Judith Anne Still, daughter of Verna Arvey and William Grant Still, wrote about the importance of mystical inspiration to her father's works. She emphasized the importance of understanding her father's involvement with numerology and his intellectual concern with dream interpretation and visions. She was highly correct in stating that her father's works are not easily categorized. Diary entries of the composer show his consistent use of numerology to reflect on the type of day he had or on future events.

In his mystic/academic style, Still used bitonality, frequent changes of key, chromaticism, and repetitive motives, as in "Cloud Cradles" from *Seven Traceries*. The ambiguity of the tonal center heightens the effectiveness of the rhythmic motive and emphasizes the intervallic structure of the melody. The first two measures set the tone with the prominent two-note motive, an ascending major third:

Example 1. Still, "Cloud Cradles," measures 1-2

While the rhythmic integrity of the motive is maintained throughout the piece, the melodic structure varies from a descending perfect fifth to an ascending major second, followed by a descending minor third. In this piece of only seventy-four measures, the key signature changes five times, vacillating between two flats and two sharps except for one eleven measure section where there is no key signature.

The tonal center is the pitch B-flat throughout the first six measures. The next six measures center around B natural while the succeeding twenty measures emphasize B-flat/E-flat. A G-sharp diminished seventh chord dominates measures 33-54, which includes the section with no key

183

signature. The descriptive title, "Cloud Cradles," quite accurately projects the instability of the final chord, an e-flat minor triad with a major 7th, minor 9th, and a suspended 4th.

The formal structure would best be described as organic, i.e., growing out of the motive, and arranged more or less loosely into brief sections which focus mostly by repetition on a specific pitch. There is no exact repetition of any idea beyond a measure or two. Use of repetitions and use of a single motive for an entire work have been cited as characteristics of scholarly "Black music," as well.

Still used his Afro-American style in the *Preludes, Ring Play,* and *Quit Dat Fool'nish*, piano works that obviously utilize jazz harmonies, modal scales, and syncopation. In an early work, *A Deserted Plantation*, Still used programmatic titles and nineteenth century musical idioms to suggest scenes on a plantation.

Ring Play, written in 1964, is perhaps the most obvious piece that displays characteristics of Still's Afro-American style in miniature. The title alerts the performer to the fact that the material comes from a dance of folk origins from the Caribbean.

In 1941, Zora Neale Hurston, the first African-American from the South to collect folk materials of her people as an anthropologist, demonstrated for William Grant Still the ring dances she had learned while on a field trip in the West Indies. Still's title indicates his deliberate use of African folk materials and African retentions in the Caribbean as the basis for the composition. The pentatonic melody disguises an F major/d minor key frame that is suggested by the initial F 6/4 chord and implied by the closing d minor triad. The form closely approximates the 32-bar pop song form often used in jazz with an AAA', expanded B, A' outline. The cadential II-V7-I at the end of each section further hints of roots in African-American jazz. The melodic minor third is a primary motive that is highly suggestive of the spirituals which were the inspiration of many of Still's writings:

Example 2, Still, "Ring Play," measures 1-4

The third style, which I have called the neo-romantic, film music style, is best illustrated in "Summerland" from *Three Visions*. The earliest of the major piano works, *Three Visions* was first published when Still was earning his living composing for films. Notes on this work preserved in family files suggest a programmatic interpretation as follows:

> *Summerland* is a vision of that beautiful haven the Spiritualists consider our home after death.

"Summerland," implicates a Black aesthetic while making full use of the harmonic language used simultaneously in jazz and in European impressionism with the drifting qualities of parallel chords and the harp-like arpeggios. Organized in ABA form, it begins with a metrically mixed, falling modal melody which could place it in the context of African-American music or within the neo-romantic traditions of early twentieth century film music. The phrygian melody continues with a sequential statement followed by an outline of the G maj7 chord, the focal harmony in the opening section and in the cadential "arrival" in measure seven:

Example 3. Still, "Summerland," measures 1-8

185

The consistent use by William Grant Still of seventh and ninth chord harmonies, the drifting quality of the melody and harmonic relationships, and the frequent parallelism in chord progressions give "Summerland" the flavor associated with American film music of the 1930's and 40's. Although the harmonic material is clearly based in jazz and blues, the functional use of chords in this piece reflects their association with French impressionism more clearly than with the traditional blues forms. The melodic intervals, however, emphasize the minor thirds of modal, African-American, spiritual melodies, thus subtly combining in "Summerland" impressionistic, European-based harmonies and a clear Afro-American, or as Still called, it, "Negroid," identification.

This significant American composer incorporated elements of jazz, blues, spirituals, and Western art music into a twentieth-century idiom that maintained its appeal to audiences while defining a distinctive American sound through the incorporation of music from his heritage. Still, who received honorary doctorates from Oberlin Conservatory, Howard University, Wilberforce, Bates College, the University of Arkansas, and others for his outstanding accomplishments as a composer, wrote piano works that have broad appeal to performers and audiences alike and that incorporate twentieth-century techniques so important in the establishment of style in this century. Because of their strong base in melodic composition, they consciously maintain their appeal to audiences.

Dr. Still's works are not only important because he was a Southern, African-American composer, but because he was a highly-skilled artist who paved the way for an American national identity. His piano music offers the performer an opportunity to explore modern techniques within harmonic frameworks that are familiar. The beauty of his melodies, the delightful humor in his playful pieces, and the sublime harmonies throughout all the works make these pieces refreshingly intriguing.

Unlike their counterparts in Still's vocal or theatrical music, the piano works offer no texts for readily pointing to an African-American consciousness. There are no Dunbar poems, no Langston Hughes quotations, or Caribbean writers' texts to guide the way. The clues are there, nonetheless, embedded in the music, without even a programmatic title offered as a clue. William Grant Still maintained his deep sense of who he was, his lifelong interest in folk music of all people, and his unique American sound in his piano works. Though small in number, the piano works provide an easily accessible performance medium through which audiences can hear stylistic characteristics the composer used throughout his lifetime. They represent a microcosm of his intellectual and spiritual approach to music in the idioms he chose to use.

In summary, the piano works represent the blending of folk elements and classical compositional techniques into three varying styles that share characteristics based in the composer's lifelong interest in the music of the American Negro. William Grant Still was a well-educated craftsman of his art, which was the composition of music. In his piano pieces, he consciously sought to use modern techniques of composition whether they be polytonality, mixed meters, parallel chords, or programmatic suggestions. He knew the rules of classical music of the nineteenth and twentieth centuries, and he spent his lifetime collecting folk materials from all over the world, with the hope that by blending these traditions, he would create a truly American sound. In the piano works, he has achieved the fusion of styles he intended with their composition.

Carolyn L. Quin

The 1911 graduating class from M.W. Gibbs High School, Little Rock, Arkansas. William Grant Still, third from the left in the top row.

William Grant Still in the Wilberforce University string quartet, seated on the right, with violin. About 1912.

William Grant Still playing the 'cello in New York, early twenties.

W. C. Handy's office in New York, William Grant Still seated
on the left, next to the stenographer. Early twenties.

William Grant Still conducting at the
Black Swan Recording Company. Early twenties.

William Grant Still at the time of the Paris
performance of AFRICA, 1933.

Abstraction of the LENOX AVENUE music,
by Sargent Johnson, San Francisco, 1938.

Carl Van Vechten's photograph of William Grant Still at the time of the
New York production of TROUBLED ISLAND, 1949.

William Grant Still at work in his studio, early fifties.
Photo by LeRoy V. Brant.

Dr. Fabien Sevitzky with William Grant Still at the University of Miami
production of the opera, HIGHWAY I, U.S.A. in 1963.

William Grant Still conducting the Seattle Youth Symphony, 1968.

Dr. William Grant Still, Louis Kaufman - violin,
Annette Kaufman - piano.

William Grant Still at Oberlin College, 1970.

William Grant Still receiving the honorary degree of
Doctor of Laws at the University of Arkansas, 1971

Dr. and Mrs. William Grant Still at the Oberlin College celebration of his 75th birthday (seated). Three of the participants in the celebration were (standing left to right) Doris Mayes (mezzo-soprano), Natalie Hinderas (pianist); and Dr. Eileen Southern (author of the book, *The Music of Black Americans*, 1970).

Joseph D. Portanova's portrait bust of William Grant Still,
made in 1939-40.

VIII

FRIENDS OF THE STILLS ON STILL

PHYLON PROFILE, XXIII:
William Grant Still -- Composer

For a man who has been awarded many honors and achieved international recognition for his work, the distinguished composer, William Grant Still, is singularly modest and retiring. Like a scholar in his ivory tower he devotes himself tirelessly to his work, day after day, begrudging every hour spent away from his composing room. He travels infrequently, as a rule, only when his presence is required in connection with the performance of his work.

His home, a small California cottage, is his studio. There he lives quietly and contentedly with his wife and two children. Long ago he discovered that a great deal of social activity interferes with the orderly progress of his creative work, so he finds relaxation in making children's toys and small gifts for friends in his well-equipped garage workshop.

Though deeply religious, he is not a joiner. He belongs to no particular church but finds some good in all of them. In his relationships with other people, he is simple and unaffected. Expressing admiration only if he actually feels it, he is honest enough to give a true judgment when asked for his opinion--qualities which do not endear him to people who continually expect flattery.

William Grant Still is what is known as an independent thinker. He dares to go against prevailing modes of thought. For many years, ever since his unsatisfactory experiments with ultra-modernism in music, he has been convinced that the present trend toward music-less music and melody-less songs and operas is unhealthy. Not hesitating to state his views in print, he has crusaded for better craftmanship, for more attention to the structure of music and for memorable melodies. More outspoken even than the majority of composers who share his views, he has come to be regarded by a portion of the music public as the spokesman for sanity in music as opposed to the whole ultra-modern school (William G. Still, "The Structure of Music, " *Etude*, March, 1950.)

As a Negro, Mr. Still is responsible for many firsts--the first to have a symphony performed, the first to conduct a major symphony orchestra, the first in the United States to have a full-length grand opera produced by a major company, and the first to conduct a white radio orchestra. Introduced in 1931 by Dr. Howard Hanson and the

189

Rochester Philharmonic Orchestra, his *Afro-American Symphony* was an immediate success. Several years later in 1936, Mr. Still was asked to conduct the Los Angeles Philharmonic Orchestra in a performance of the same work in addition to his symphonic suite, *Africa*, during the Hollywood Bowl summer symphony series. While doing arrangements for the "Deep River Hour," broadcast over CBS and WOR in New York in the early Thirties, Still not only directed the orchestra but also developed a style which was copied later by other radio orchestrators. His opera, *Troubled Island*, based on Haitian history, was produced by a major opera company at the New York City Center of Music and Drama in 1949. Immediately after this production, a citation for "outstanding service to American music" was bestowed upon the composer by the National Association of American Composers and Conductors.

Besides making a valuable contribution to the field of music and the esthetic enjoyment of music lovers, the music of William Grant Still is an important force in the field of race relations. This stems both from the content of his more radical compositions as well as from wide public recognition of a Negro creator of the highest musical forms.

William Grant Still has clearly demonstrated that to be racial in music one does not need to draw literally upon the folk heritage. He seems to have been more successful in this respect than any other composer, regardless of race. Apparently this was recognized by a Princeton University professor of music when he wrote about the borrowers of spirituals in 1932, for he had this to say about Still:

> Yet oddly enough, William Grant Still--himself a Negro--has treated of his race in many authentic pages without literal quotation. (Randall Thompson, "The Contemporary Scene in American Music," *Music Quarterly*, January, 1932.)

It is this special ability that gives his music its typically American quality. His *Afro-American Symphony* and his symphonic requiem, *In Memoriam: The Colored Soldiers Who Died for Democracy*, are two examples of orchestral works that are recognizably racial, yet definitely original with the composer as to thematic material and treatment. The latter was written in 1943 when the League of Composers commissioned sixteen American composers to write on patriotic themes. Their works were given first performances by the New York Philharmonic Orchestra under the direction of Artur Rodzinski, both in concert and over the radio, and later recorded for Government distribution abroad.

The New York Times for October 10, 1943 carried William Grant

Still's statement regarding the inspiration for his composition, which seems to have attracted more attention than any of the others:

When you suggested that I compose something patriotic, there immediately flashed through my mind the press release which announced that the first American soldier to be killed in World War II was a Negro soldier. Then my thoughts turned to the colored soldiers all over the world, fighting under our flag and under the flags of countries allied with us. Our civilization has known no greater patriotism, no greater loyalty than that shown by the colored men who fight and die for democracy. Those who return will, I hope, come back to a better world. I also hope that our tribute to those who die will be to make the democracy for which they fought greater and broader than it has ever been before.

A short time after the radio performance of *In Memoriam* by George Szell and the Boston Symphony Orchestra in January 1945, the composer received the following communication from Syracuse:

I wish I might convey to you the thrilling gratification which I felt in the thought that an American had produced so fine a composition. We have looked into the past so long for the finest and best that it is a startling experience to find that the present has so much to offer.

Even Still's symphonic works classed as abstract music, such as *Poem or Orchestra*, include a racial twist here and there. Certain melodic lines in his opera, *Troubled Island*, also reveal kinship to the Negro folk song, yet this was missed by the majority of American critics, attributable no doubt to their closeness to the native idiom. It was immediately recognizable, however, by the Belgian critic, Nelson H. LeKime, who has long been associated with such masters as Saint-Saens and Rimsky-Korsakof.

The sensitivity of the composer in regard to other musical idioms has made him extremely versatile. His symphonic poem, *Old California*, written to commemorate the one hundred and sixtieth birthday of Los Angeles, September 4, 1941, is a compact blend of Indian, Spanish and American idioms containing only one brief excursion into the folk, and that a very free interpretation of an American Indian theme which appears near the opening. Virtually the same is true of *Costaso*, latest of Mr. Still's operas. It is an authentic picture, in music and drama, of Spanish colonial days in the American Southwest.

Having made an extensive study of the occult, the composer has a passion for translating some of the atmosphere surrounding that study into earthly music. It is to be found in the strange mystic melodies and exotic polyharmonies of two piano suites, *The Three Visions* and *Seven Traceries*, in certain portions of his operas, and in a new choral work, *From A Lost Continent*.

Yet, despite these many facets to his musical personality and despite the variety in the subject matter of his works, everything William Grant Still writes is so permeated with his own individuality that he has succeeded in establishing an idiom of his own, so that anything he writes is recognizable as his. One might say that he has succeeded in obtaining unity through diversity--an achievement of tremendous help in the writing of operas and ballets, in which every mood and every situation must have its appropriate musical counterpart.

A musical career was a natural selection for William Grant Still, for one might almost say he was born with music in his blood. Both his parents were musicians and teachers as well. His father died a few months after he was born in Woodville, Mississippi in 1895. A short time later his mother took him to Little Rock, Arkansas where she taught English in the public schools for thirty-two years. An early graduate of Atlanta University, she was a woman of sterling character and reared her son well, giving him all the advantages of a cultured, middle-class home.

His maternal grandmother, who lived with them in Little Rock, provided his earliest musical memories when she sang spirituals and hymns as she went about her daily tasks. He looks back on that experience with great affection now, but says he did not fully appreciate its value until later in life when he began to see the beauty in racial music and to study it in detail.

A stepfather, acquired when he was eight or nine years old, helped develop Still's interest in fine music by taking him to see operettas and buying a generous supply of operatic records.

Soon after young Still started taking violin lessons and had learned his notes, he began wanting to write them down. He made his own manuscript paper and scribbled notes in his spare moments at home and at school. By the time he finished high school at the age of sixteen, Still was certain he wanted to become a composer. Although secretly in sympathy with this desire, his mother insisted that he plan for a medical career because she saw little future ahead for a Negro composer.

During his four years at Wilberforce University, although studying for a Bachelor of Science degree, William Grant Still became composer, arranger and conductor for the college band and received unusual encouragement and praise from his instructors and fellow students. Leaving college shortly before graduation because of an unfortunate incident, he took various jobs as a professional musician in order to earn a living. This gave him first-hand experience in popular American music, an experience that is seldom given to conservatory students. It had a profound influence on his later development.

He taught himself to orchestrate by observing the possibilities and limitations of each instrument, learning to play several different ones. Without a teacher, he was not hampered by preconceived ideas and developed a unique style in orchestration which he employed for such individuals as W. C. Handy, Sophie Tucker, Don Voorhees, Willard Robison, and Paul Whiteman.

A delayed legacy from his father permitted him to study at the Oberlin Conservatory of Music. Later, he received a scholarship to study with George W. Chadwick, pioneer American composer, at the New England Conservatory of Music. He began experimenting, developing and learning the tools of his trade, but his musical expression was still quite lacking in individuality. It was not until Edgard Varèse, noted French ultra-modernist, offered him a free scholarship that he began to branch out into entirely new fields of musical thought. For a time he adopted an uncompromisingly dissonant style. Soon he discarded it, beginning to work as an individual, to develop his craftsmanship and personal style. Finally he succeeded in making a tasteful blend of all the elements that had gone into his education.

It is one thing to have a gift for making beautiful music and quite another to gain a public hearing for it. Even though he had been engaged in commercial work in New York in the early Twenties, Still was puzzled about the best way to make himself known as a creative musician. His teacher, Edgard Varèse, well known in the world of serious music and acquainted with some of the leading artists of the day, helped his pupil to get hearings for his work.

To some of the concerts featuring Mr. Still's early works came musicians like Eugene Goossens, Arturo Toscanini and the late George Gershwin. The latter was known to be a devotee of Negro music in all its forms (*Opera And Concert*, April 1948). He went everywhere to hear it, from small Negro churches to Harlem cafes, thence to Negro shows and finally to concert halls. The inspiration he received formed a definite background for his own compositions. As a matter of fact, Eubie Blake, conductor of the "Shuffle Along" orchestra in which Still played oboe, reminded him of a little tune of his that sounded very much like Gershwin's "I Got Rhythm." Mr. Still did not remember the tune, but Mr. Blake insisted that it was one of those that Still had improvised during his nightly performance of the "Shuffle Along" score. Many notables came to see "Shuffle Along" and returned to see it again and again. George Gershwin certainly saw it. Who knows whether he happened in on one of the nights that tune was played?

One of the most memorable of those early concerts was held at Aeolian Hall in New York City with Eugene Goossens conducting and Florence Mills singing William Grant Still's *Levee Land*. Musically, it was epoch-making since it was one of the very earliest attempts to lift jazz to the symphonic level. Moreover, it was a distinct triumph for Florence Mills and widely publicized on both sides of the Atlantic.

Just before the first performance of his ballet, *Sahdji*, by the Eastman School of Music in 1931, Dr. Howard Hanson wrote Still:

> You will be interested to know that after my first rehearsal with the orchestra, the orchestra members put down their instruments and applauded the work. As you know, this is most unusual for a professional group and it only shows how deeply impressed they were with your music. I think myself that it is a stunning piece of work and should make a deep impression.

Today Mr. Still's work is being played regularly by top-ranking conductors and musical organizations throughout the world. Performances here and abroad have been increasing every year to such an extent that it is difficult to keep track of them, especially since the music is being handled largely through publishers.

Notable performances of his work have been given by symphony orchestras in all the leading cities of America and over various radio networks by Leopold Stokowski, Hans Lange, Artur Rodzinski, Werner Janssen, Rudolph Ringwall, Pierre Monteux, and many others. *Plain-Chant For America*, scored for baritone solo and orchestra with the text by Katherine Garrison Chapin (Mrs. Francis Biddle), was commissioned by John Barbirolli and dedicated to the late President and Mrs. Roosevelt in October 1941, for the celebration of the one hundredth anniversary of the New York Philharmonic-Symphony Orchestra. *Festive Overture* won the Jubilee Season Prize for Still in January 1945, when it was given a first performance by the Cincinnati Symphony Orchestra under the direction of Eugene Goossens. A first performance of Still's new *Fourth Symphony* was just given this spring by Victor Alessandro and the Oklahoma Symphony Orchestra over the Mutual network.

Millions heard the music of William Grant Still at the New York World's Fair in 1939 and 1940, for it was played continuously in the Perisphere for the Theme Exhibit during the entire run of the Fair. The commission to write this music was awarded to Still after a group of judges had listened to non-commercial recordings of all the leading

American composers at a large New York broadcasting studio. They finally narrowed their selection to two works, *Lenox Avenue* and *A Deserted Plantation*. When the judges agreed that the composer of either piece would be acceptable they were agreeably surprised to learn that both pieces were the work of one man--William Grant Still!

The Afro-American Symphony has been played abroad by Rudolph Dunbar in France, Germany and England; by Franz André in Belgium; by Sir Hamilton Harty and the British Broadcasting Company Orchestra in England; by the Australian Broadcasting Company Orchestra in Sydney, Australia, under the direction of Leith Stevens; and by Marti Simila and the Helsinki Municipal Orchestra in Finland with top officials of the Finnish Government and members of the diplomatic corps in attendance.

John Barbirolli played *Plain-Chant For America* at Albert Hall, London, in November 1944, as a Thanksgiving Day tribute to America, with speeches for the occasion being made by Winston Churchill and the American ambassador to England. Still's *Dismal Swamp* was performed in Mexico by Samuel Marti and the Orquesta Sinfonica de Yucatan, and in Rio de Janeiro, Brazil, by the Symphony Orchestra of O. Lorenz Fernandez more than ten years ago. Several complete programs of William Grant Still's music have been presented during the years over the Belgian National Radio (INR) from recordings made by the U. S. State Department which are not available in this country commercially.

Besides many special prizes and commissions, some of which have already been mentioned, William Grant Still has received extended Guggenheim and Rosenwald Fellowships, a Harmon Award (1927), a trophy of honor from the Musicians Union, A. F. of M., and three honorary degrees--a Master of Music from Wilberforce University (1936), Doctor of Music from Howard University (1941) and from Oberlin College (1947). He is mentioned at length in almost a score of books including *Who's Who In America: A Guide To Great Orchestral Music*, by Sigmund Spaeth; *Composers of Today*, by David Ewen; *Composers In America*, by Claire Reis; *Thirteen Against The Odds*, by Edwin R. Embree; *The Story Of One Hundred Great Composers*, by Helen L. Kaufmann; and *Our Contemporary Composers*, by John Tasker Howard.

Glowing tributes have been published in various foreign publications such as *Ritmo* (Spain); *Micro* (Belgium), *Melody Maker* (England), *Neue Zeit* (Germany), *Uusi Suomi* (Finland), and the *Courrier Musical* (France). They have called William Grant Still "the greatest American composer of this epoch" and "the most remarkable man in American music today." His music has been described as "characteristically

American" and "a spiritual bridge between two continents."

Despite widespread recognition of his work, William Grant Still does not feel he can rest on his laurels. He works just as hard now as he did at the inception of his career and judges his own work more severely than any critic. Still wrote and destroyed a great many operas before he composed some he considered good enough to keep. Even *Blue Steel*, which he wrote on his Guggenheim Fellowship soon after coming to California in the early Thirties, he now considers faulty, particularly in plot, and is no longer offering it for production even though it contains some very effective music.

Success has not come easily to Still, nor has it brought him extremely large financial returns. He looks forward to the day when all his major works will be made available for wide distribution through commercial recordings. Although his income is modest, he never sacrifices principle for material gain, nor does he hesitate to help individuals in whom he believes, especially young musicians with talent. At one time he resigned from a lucrative post as a musical supervisor with a Hollywood movie studio rather than lower his musical standards.

These traits are shared by his wife, the former Verna Arvey, well known as a pianist and writer, who is the perfect helpmate for Still. Besides giving him the proper wifely encouragement, she has played his works in concert and written librettos for his ballets and operas. A frequent contributor to leading musical publications, she is also author of *Choreographic Music*, a history of dance music, a brochure on William Grant Still, and a full-length biography of her noted husband, the latter as yet unpublished.

Because he believes so thoroughly in and depends entirely on the inspiration he receives, Still has said, "No man is a creator. Only God is the Creator and man the instrument through which he speaks." At the end of everything he writes, he adds these words:

With humble thanks to God,
The source of inspiration.

Miriam Matthews

196

WILLIAM GRANT STILL

Eighty years ago, on May 11, 1895, in the little town of Woodville, Mississippi, William Grant Still first saw the light of day.

This year, on Saturday, May 24, the Friends of Music of the University of Southern California honor Dr. Still and his contributions, as a distinguished American musician and composer, with a dinner and program of his works. The "Tribute to William Grant Still" inaugurates a new and exciting program to honor each year an internationally known musician. The Tribute will establish a permanent music scholarship in Dr. Still's name at USC, serving as a fitting commemoration of the eminent composer's eightieth birthday.

Through his own perspicacity and the cooperation of his mother and father he chose as his birth-time the prestigious class of the 1890's, a decade in which, apparently, the planets which favored composers were in the ascendancy.

The decade of the 1850's had brought to the American scene that most American of all early American composers, the great George Whitefield Chadwick--with whom William Grant Still studied--Arthur Foote, Edgar Stillman-Kelley, and Victor Herbert.

The 1860's brought Edward MacDowell--the first American composer to win an international audience--Horatio Parker, that distinguished transplanted American from Alsace, Charles Martin Loeffler, Henry Gilbert, Charles Skilton, of Indian fame, and America's most famous woman composer, Mrs. H. H. A. Beach.

The '70's introduced John Alden Carpenter, whose centennial we shall celebrate in '76, together with our nation's birthday, Henry Eichheim, Blair Fairchild, Rubin Goldmark, Henry Hadley, Edward Burlingame Hill, Charles Ives--whose centennial we observed last year--Daniel Gregory Mason, my old teacher, Arne Oldberg, that great iconoclast, Carl Ruggles--whose centennial we should also observe next year--Ernest Schelling and David Stanley Smith.

The class of the 1880's produced Ernest Bloch, Charles Wakefield Cadman, America's great impressionist, Charles Tomlinson Griffes, Louis Gruenberg of "Emperor Jones" fame at the Met, John Powell, Wallingford Riegger, another composer born before his time, Lazare Saminsky, Arthur Shepherd, Deems Taylor, and Emerson Whithorne.

Which brings us, at last, to the famous class of the 1890's. The class roll begins with the distinguished Philip James, now in his 85th year;

Frederick Jacobi, Timothy Mather Spelman, and Samuel Gardner, born in 1891; Douglas Moore and Bernard Rogers, 1893; Albert Stoessel and Bernard Wagenaar, 1894; Carl McKinley, Leo Sowerby, and--so important in the history of American music--William Grant Still, 1895.

This would unfortunately, in my opinion, leave some of us yet unborn, for I followed, respectfully, a year later, in 1896, together with my distinguished colleagues, Roger Sessions and Virgil Thomson; Henry Cowell and Quincy Porter in '97; Herbert Elwell, Roy Harris and George Gershwin in '98; Werner Janssen and Randall Thompson in '99, and George Antheil and Aaron Copland at the turn of the century.

The historic background is important, for William Grant Still came on the American scene at a time when the new music of America was being born. Into this melting pot of the new America, the America of the up-coming 20th century, came this new composer bringing with him the rich heritage of a race which in the past had had only slight opportunity to make its contribution to the music of America.

William Grant Still brought to music a new voice, a voice filled with lovely melodies, gorgeous harmonies, insidious rhythms and dazzling colors. But it was new music deeply rooted in the great traditions of the past.

He has, from his earliest days, been a master of orchestration. A Still score may not be quiet but it always sounds the way the composer intended. Some of our most cerebral of composers might well profit by a study of the William Grant Still scores. They might learn something.

And yet, with all his expertise, his music speaks to the common man. Boys and girls listening to his music need no analytical tables, seismographic charts nor digital computers. It is necessary only to bring a sensitive ear, a mind and a heart.

My first acquaintance with Bill goes back almost a half century when we performed his "Darker America" in the season of 1927-28. At that time it won one of the earliest of the publication awards which had been established by the Eastman School. The chairman of the award committee, as I recall, was the late Olin Downes, at that time music critic of the *New York Times*. Downes was enormously impressed with the freshness of the work by this young and comparatively unknown American composer. We apparently liked it too, for we repeated it the next season and it remained in our repertory into the 70's.

The following year we gave the first performance of a fascinating suite "From the Journal of a Wanderer." There followed in 1930-31 the ballet, "Sahdji" and the suite, "Africa," and the following year, 1931-32 the famous first symphony, the "Afro-American."

198

"Sahdji" was a block-buster, a powerful, dramatic story with music which was made to be danced. All of us in the Eastman Theatre, dancers, choristers and orchestra were quite enthralled with it. And so was the public. Even the critics applauded, although some thought that the music was very "rough," even rude. But I suppose this proves only that, at some time, all of us were modernists!

The "Afro-American Symphony" was, again, something else. Here was a symphony in the conventional four movements, beautifully constructed, architecturally secure, but yet with a new ingredient never before seen in an American symphony. For it was a symphony, an American symphony, but it was an Afro-American symphony with all of the ethnic background that the name implies.

In 1933-34, when I was invited by the Weimar Republic to give a series of programs of American music in Germany, the "Afro-American Symphony" seemed highly appropriate. I had been warned that German audiences might not approve of this symphony, far removed as it was from Beethoven and Brahms. When we played the scherzo movement, a movement which can only be described as infectiously jazzy, the Berlin audience was completely carried away and demanded two repetitions. I doubt if that has ever happened in Berlin before or since. This symphony must be one of the permanent symphonies of the American repertory.

In later years we performed the ballet, "La Guiablesse," the suite, "From the Black Belt," "Kaintuck'," "Dismal Swamp," "Summerland," and, finally, the "Second Symphony in G Minor" in 1938.

And just before we concluded our American Festivals at one of our last concerts, we performed one of Bill's most charming, most appealing compositions, a work entitled "The Little Song That Wanted To Be a Symphony," for voices and orchestra. It is an appeal in the gentlest of voices for human understanding, a veritable sermon in sound.

I think it is appropriate that, as the first composition of William Grant Still in Rochester, "Darker America" won the publication award; so did also the "Little Song" win the final publication award of our fifty year series. It is now published and it is our hope that it will soon be recorded to bring its message of peace, goodwill, and human understanding to all people.

For William Grant Still is not only a great American composer, he is a great man. And, above all, he is a gentle man. We salute him on his eightieth birthday, together with his wife, who has been his constant source of courage and strength.

The University of Southern California Friends of Music "Tribute to William Grant Still" is a fitting reminder of Dr. Still's lifetime devotion to his art. We wish him many more years, and we thank him for the rare gift of his music.

Howard Hanson

OF ONE BLOOD, THOU & I

William Grant Still and I sprang from the same rich and common soil of Southwest Mississippi. Although his mother took him as an infant after his father's death from Woodville to Arkansas, I categorized his accomplishments as those of a native Mississippian.

His music came to my attention when I was editor of my hometown weekly newspaper. On March 25, 1937, I wrote in *The Summit Sentinel* that although Mississippi had contributed richly to literature, there was a dearth of musical talent, with the exception of William Grant Still.

"He is probably the best of modern composers who specialize in definitely 'American' music. At the present time Still is in Hollywood writing and arranging music of the heavier type for the movies. He is a young man," the editorial stated, "and certain to make a name for himself in the world of music for all time."

When I sent him a copy of the editorial, he responded, beginning a friendship that covered some forty years. Unfortunately we never met, but through his letters I received a sense of the depth and lasting significance of the man and the composer. We congratulated each other on the birth of our children, compared views on music, agonized over the tragedy of racial tension in America, and came to know each other as persons.

We shared admiration for Debussy, Delius, and Puccini. I saw their mark on his work and was bemused when someone callously suggested influences from Gershwin's "I Got Rhythm" on the scherzo of *The Afro-American Symphony*. We were early discoverers of the author Lillian Smith.

I was pleased when he withdrew from the dubious influence of the Hollywood music scene and devoted his full energies to serious music. He constantly encouraged me in creative writing, through my years in radio writing and programming in Birmingham, Alabama, and my eventual studies for the Unitarian ministry at Tufts University in Boston, and ministries in Upton, Massachusetts; Jacksonville, Florida; and Chattanooga, Tennessee.

Shamefully, despite that music is a major influence on my life, I have never learned to read music. Thus I was both flattered and amused when he twice suggested that I belonged on the staff of a major newspaper as music critic.

"You ask what I am working on now," he wrote on October 12, 1945, "and no doubt you'll be surprised to know that I have a new method of relaxation. I have taken to building furniture. You see, I've worked for so many years so steadily at music, that this year, after I'd finished a large work, I became very tired, and didn't want to write music any more for a while. So far, I have made a desk, a chair, a magazine rack, a humidor, and two bookcases. I'm now working on a tea table which my wife requested, and sandwiching in work on a little piano piece that a local publisher wants for an album . . .. " Products of this activity were two skillfully crafted pairs of bookends, one for my older son, mine displayed on a shelf in my study.

Some interesting lines converged. The first symphony concert I ever attended was in New Orleans when the Philadelphia Symphony was on tour, conducted by Leopold Stokowski. My admiration for Stokowski across the years became near-idolatry for the extra-dimension he added to whatever he conducted; for the Bach transcription; and for his sponsorship of new compositions, especially those of William Grant Still.

So I had a sense of proximity to Valhalla when my friend mentioned in a letter that during a visit to his home by Stokowski, he had read to him a letter I had written to Goddard Leiberson of Columbia records. Later he sent to Stokowski a radio script I had written.

During those troublesome years of World War II, I remember being quite fond of the Artie Shaw recording of *Frenesi*, hearing it on the radio, in jukeboxes, and in the spots along Bourbon Street in New Orleans. Then I learned that not only had William Grant Still made the arrangement, but that he and Artie Shaw were friends.

Once, after having read Richard Wright's *Native Son*, a novel which I consider a major work, I suggested to my friend the possibility of his writing some incidental music, perhaps an opera, based on this writing of a fellow Mississippian. He replied that Artie Shaw had given him the book to read, but that he gave it up after the first few chapters because the central character "was so repellent to me." He then stated that his wife, whose judgment he deeply respected, had said that it was a significant book and that if he had gotten past the opening chapters, he would have found it valuable.

Later I concluded that an element of bias entered into his judgment of *Native Son* because of Wright's affinity for communism and his voluntary abandonment of America for France. Still was deeply sensitive to the ramifications of Marxist influence on Blacks. Fearful of the connotations of the move of the American communist party to Harlem, he wrote on October 3, 1951, "I hope that the public in general doesn't get the idea that colored people are prominent in the movement, because only a few have been duped. I am doing my best to try to right this impression, even though my efforts are small."

202

Convinced that his anti-Communist views had a negative influence on performance of his works, he wrote on January 4, 1951, that he had had the disheartening experience of having several performances of his music stopped by "a peculiar sort of intrigue, which differs in each instance--and which I definitely suspect to be the work of communist sympathizers, who have been against me for years."

He mentioned a cliquishness of the more politically radical composers which made performances of those outside their circle difficult. His disdain of those "leftist" contemporaries by no means drove him to a leaning toward the opposite political spectrum. When Rudolph Dunbar conducted *The Afro-American Symphony* in a BBC broadcast in July 1942, he informed me that the Nazis had publicized the event "in their own way. I can just imagine what they said, can't you? When they have persecuted so many Jewish composers on account of their racial origin, they surely must have said that my music was degenerate, etc.. However, in my view, any Nazi knock nowadays is a boost."

We were of differing opinions about the Russian composers. Whereas he thought that they were increasingly played in America for political reasons, I was convinced that they were writing the most enduring serious music of the time.

Still's usual fairness exerted itself in an article in *Opera and Concert* in May 1948. "Whatever the political and philosophical intrigue," he wrote, "whatever the racial or musical prejudice, I am convinced that the final decision will be made on the musical merit and on the value of the composer to the world, rather than on propaganda, political ability, literary efforts, aggressiveness, selfishness, or the number of performances the composer's work has during his lifetime."

An optimist in the midst of the impending struggle for racial justice, he felt that things would work themselves out. "What the prejudiced person fails to realize is that his prejudice not only hurts the man he hates," he wrote me on February 29, 1948, "but hurts the nation as a whole in the eyes of other nations and eventually hurts himself."

My militance in these matters exceeded his. This may have been because of my proximity to the bitter action in the South. In a letter on January 1, 1963, as the racial tension began to reach its apex, he still considered it "a condition that will gradually yield to the times. I still feel that the ultimate solution over the entire South will come through the emergence of the White Southerners who are basically men and women of good will and good sense. As you know it has been our good fortune to count many of these among our friends, and we would like to see the day arrive when their opinions and their wishes will be deferred to rather than the ignorant and the bigoted. This is not an impossibility, and we

203

welcome the day when it will become a fact."

As I participated in such events as the Selma March, he expressed pleasure. But he continued to criticize the extremists who occasionally expressed hostile views when he spoke on college campuses. When the Black radicals turned to violence, a reaction which I am certain history will place into perspective, the tone of our mutual correspondence was against separatism and against the scorn of White liberals.

"As you must have gathered during the years we have known each other," he wrote on September 13, 1959, "we are strongly on the side of love (not hatred) and strongly for integration, for all of us being *Americans* together (not separatism as it is being ballyhooed today)."

He was convinced that the objective in all relationships is to "build friends." This he did, particularly with his music, but with equal effectiveness through his wisdom and gentility.

Charles W. McGehee

RECALLING STILL

William Grant Still was a virtually legendary figure in the 1950's in Southern California when, along with Still's academically gifted daughter, I entered the seventh grade at James A. Foshay Junior High School in Los Angeles. Since both of us, Judith Anne Still as well as myself, were assigned to the same college preparatory programs, we would get to know one another very well by the time we graduated from Manual Arts High a distant six years later. As it turned out, her brother Duncan (two years her elder) also became a good friend through our mutual fascination, his and mine, with railroad locomotives and model trains; not to mention such heady stuff as chemistry and physics. This was my passport into the Still household--a teenage enthrallment with diesel locomotives and atomic nuclei. But I would become a frequent visitor, for there was much more to the Still family than the opportunity to indulge one's teenage fantasies of model railroading and nuclear science.

The Still home, at that time a modest stucco dwelling on Cimarron Street, was in all ways as culturally absorbing as my own, except more so. For my family, music and art were vital tools of mental enrichment and social refinement, as well as sources of pleasure. As a teenage guest in the house of William Grant Still, I was amazed--no, thunderstruck--with the thrill which only a teenager could know of being inside a home where music was the *key centrality* around which everything else revolved. Music was no mere tool here. For this was a sanctuary for its conception, gestation, and birth. The lives of the human adults who lived in this place were as intimately bound up with the creation and business of music, as the lives of the rest of humanity seemed bound up with work-a-day employment which too often revealed only scant connection to the "inner person." But William Grant Still's profession was his job; and his profession was music--the "genuine article"--the kind one heard at the stately Philharmonic Auditorium and on radio stations that played the works of the great masters.

It was Still's calling, the same sort, no doubt, that quickened the likes of the Bachs and Schuberts long before his time. In this, he was one of the favored fortunates of the modern age whose "calling" became his career. Indeed, Still would come to be known--at least, in the music education community in Southern California and beyond--as the "Schubert" of his day. I think it more likely the other way around, that Franz Schubert was the "William Grant Still" of his day. Although separated by great lapses of real time, both Schubert and Still exhibited a shared skill--less well-appreciated in today's world of fads, glitter, and transient values--of translating the artistic output of their imaginations into "finely crafted" scores. And while this did not create for Still anything close to financial riches, there was in the house of Still an undeniable peace, spiritual richness, and creative intensity that was unmatched in most places I had ever been. The great luminous presence that was William Grant Still bathed his surroundings in a gentle, artistic energy.

The Venerable and Still families discovered in one another a steadfast and mutual admiration. My personal friendship with the elder Stills, the composer and his wife, Verna Arvey Still, would continue through the culmination of their lifetimes. For theirs was a unique personal style--down-to-earth and homey, yet culturally sophisticated, intellectually penetrating, and socially aware. I shall not forget being at their home one Saturday evening, and asking if we might watch my favorite, "Old West" adventure series (one of the top-rated programs on television in the 1950's and 60's). By no means avid television viewers (at least in today's inflated sense of the term), the Stills were unacquainted with this particular program. Furthermore, it was one of the few programs that my father had "certified" for Venerable family viewing--and that helped to decide the issue. Although the Stills seemed to enjoy this true-to-life drama set in Dodge City of a bygone era, opportunity for a discussion of the program's merits somehow never presented itself. That is, not until some years later when, during one of my visits home to Los Angeles (from the University of Chicago where I completed my doctorate in chemistry), I happened to drop in on the Stills--only to find them in the middle of a suspense-filled episode of "Gunsmoke." After being warmly welcomed and then receiving (for my interruption) one of the friendliest "scoldings" that I have ever had, the Stills reminded me that I was the instigator who started them years before in what had become a time-honored, weekly family ritual.

Early on, I felt a special kinship with the man, William Grant Still. It was a bond of which I was not consciously aware as a teenager, but surely felt. It would become the compelling basis for my visits to the Still's home, first on Cimarron Street and later on Victoria Avenue. Perhaps it was because I felt as welcome there as I imagined friends felt when they visited the Venerable household on Budlong Avenue. But perhaps there were other, more compelling considerations, such as the shared commonalities between our two families. These were commonalities that would indelibly impress the mind of the artistic, scientifically inclined adolescent that I was when I first met up with

206

William Grant Still in 1954.

Aside from the obvious fact that both Still and my father shared the name "Grant," which each inherited from his father, both shared a similarly diverse racial and cultural ancestry and a heritage of early musical and intellectual experience; and both had roots in the Arkansas-Missouri region--all of which shaped their unique perceptions of life. Both produced offspring who were born on the same day (of the same year) and in the same place (Los Angeles). Both shared a beloved mutual friend, Bessie Lawson Blackman, a nurse in Los Angeles; a widely-respected woman of color who was a direct descendant of Martha Washington (wife of the first president) and her first husband Daniel Custis. But most of all, Mississippi-born William Grant Still and Missouri-born Grant Venerable shared a more universal accomplishment. Both were pioneers, the first of their race to excel in their respective fields which, by tradition and practice, had been previously uninhabited by or closed to people of color.

They were trailblazers--"Billy" Still in the musical world of symphonic composition and conducting--and Grant Venerable in the technical world of civil engineering. Both wore their laurels with a quiet dignity. Both suffered rebukes and obstacles thrown in their path because of the pigmentation of their skin. Yet they wore their racial identity unselfconsciously, as though a wonderfully fitting garment. Both transcended social obstacles and periods of financial scarcity. Both were formed from the elements of a uniquely principled integrity. And both demonstrated a profound reverence for the life-force and the higher power that informed it.

Such important commonalities would not only influence the quality of my relationship with composer Still, but they would also provide a kind of "chemical oxidant" for my own development; not just as a scientist and musician, but as a whole person.

Thus, in reflecting on the essence of William Grant Still, I am put in touch with intensely personal forces which are key to everything that I am as an individual and a spiritual entity. They are dynamic yet poetic forces which carry me out of the immediate moment into a universal dimension where there is no time. I am transported to a place where the essence of Still fuses with all that is universal. I am transported also to childhood when, long before meeting Still, I sat often transfixed with fellow elementary school classmates in the Shrine Auditorium in Los Angeles, where I first heard performed the music of William Grant Still.

His rhythmic creation, the *Afro-American Symphony*, with its splendid colorings and lilting tempos, moved me in the depths of my being. But

207

so did Still's spirituals with their lively syncopations. How amazing it was, being so unable to sit still when the Foshay Glee Club sang, "Is there anybody here who loves my Jesus?" But one could not help, could not avoid, would not wish to avoid, being all stirred up inside with the joy that one felt. And irrespective of religious persuasion, it was impossible not to love the "Jesus" in question. During my undergraduate years at the University of California at Los Angeles, it was Still's ballet, *Sahdji*, that seemed to reaffirm the roots of my being, not simply as a young American with roots in Africa--but as a unique member of the human group itself which, we have since learned, originated in the heart of the African continent.

Who was William Grant Still, aside from the fact that he was a most remarkable man in his own time? He was, paradoxically, eminently knowable--a familiar and folksy quality--and yet unknowable, private, without being distant or remote. He was *in* the world of everyday experience, but not really *of* it. The primacy of the human experience, he believed, was the substance and basis--must always be the substance and basis--of music. This he impressed upon me during one of many sessions I enjoyed on Still's old and resonant baby grand piano. It was a session in which I performed free improvisations on a well-known romantic composition, in which I imagined the various interlinking themes as metaphorical of the behaviors of electrons in atoms. (This was a time, it should be remembered, when I was fully immersed in graduate studies in quantum chemistry and molecular structure.) His "lesson" was not lost on my personal development. It was a lesson that was to influence the direction of my journey which led to my becoming a scientist--a professor of chemistry and ethnic studies in California's public university system--who would be guided by a greater measure of humanity than otherwise.

As a musician who would more sensitively "feel" his subject matter, I became accomplished on the organ. In all of our conversations about music and his student days at Oberlin (when he occasionally sneaked into the organ practice rooms to play), the composer never spoke of his own compositions for organ, which are not as well-known as his instrumental and choral music. In kind consideration of my life-long interest in the organ, Judith Anne Still presented to me in 1984 a much-welcomed gift of her father's organ scores. My favorite, entitled "Reverie," was composed by Dr. Still in 1962. A quiet, meditative litany, expressing the timeless perfection of a Bach chorale and suffused with the soul uplifting qualities of the Negro spirituals, it evokes the essence and spirit of William Grant Still.

When I play "Reverie" on the organ and yield myself to its subtle, nearly understated beauty, the music itself seems to take life in the well-spring of my own human experience; not merely in my experience of Still, the figure of legendary proportions whom I met when I entered the seventh grade, but in my experience of Still, the devoted family man and father of my childhood friends, Judith and Duncan. It takes life in my experience of Still, the dedicated apostle of twentieth century music and chronicler of the African-American heritage. But most of all, the ethereal "Reverie" takes life in my experience of William Grant Still, the gentle artist who lived in a modest stucco dwelling on Cimarron Street and created music that could move an entire universe.

Grant D. Venerable II

IX

CLOSING

OUT OF THE WILDERNESS,
OR "THE LAST BEST HOPE OF EARTH"

They wandered in the wilderness in a solitary way (Psalms 107:4).
He turneth the wilderness into a standing water . . . that they may
prepare a city for habitation (Psalms 107:35-36).
The stone which the builders refused is become the head stone of the
corner (Psalms 118:22).

In the early seventies, Dr. Robert Bartlett Haas planned the book, *William Grant Still and the Fusion of Cultures in American Music*, with the intention of introducing a totally unknown composer to the artistic community. The response to his plans at the university where he taught was negative, and he was forced to solicit private funds to publish the volume. Members of the Fine Arts Committee in his institution even turned down his request for monies to present a William Grant Still Festival for the composer's seventy-fifth birthday. Haas was so disappointed over the lack of interest in his project, that he committed himself to selling every copy of the book himself, if that became necessary.

It did not become necessary. Two printings of the book were sold in due course, and requests flowed in for a second edition. Twenty years later there are several books about William Grant Still either printed or planned, and there have been over a dozen festivals for the composer across the country. Whereas the material in the original *Fusion* was completely new to the public, today there are other books in print, or soon-to-be in print, which contain some of the same material. So much has happened for Still since the first edition saw the light of day that the book has almost outlived the need for a new edition. However, my feeling is that a second edition is important, not because it rescues a great man from obscurity, but because it continues to make clear the nature of his achievement where artistic change and social reform are concerned. The title itself is sufficient to carry the message that he wished to convey to the world.

This is not to say that I have always been aware of the importance of the book and its title. I haven't. Its significance only came home to me last month, when I was not involved with my father's work at all, but was, rather, taking an off-road excursion into a study of the career of the Great Emancipator, Abraham Lincoln.

My father had always been fascinated by the life of Abraham Lincoln, less because Lincoln had freed his grandmother from slavery, than because the sixteenth President was an intensely spiritual person who experienced dreams and visions not unlike his own. In fact, Lincoln was so much-admired in our household that I never knew, until my college years, that he had been one of the most beleaguered and severely criticized political leaders in history.

When I began to travel across the country to talk about my parents and their work, I frequently found myself in places where Lincoln had been, especially in Illinois, in Pennsylvania, and in Washington, D. C.. In each of those states, when I stood on certain spots in front of particular buildings, I was told that I was standing on the very spot where the President had stood to address the crowd. At once I felt a sense of immediacy and pride, probably like that visited upon any impressionable tourist in the East, in discovering that I was following in the tracks of a sainted and saintly person.

It was natural, therefore, that on February 12th of this year, when I had the opportunity to see the Lincoln Exhibit at the Huntington Library in California--a display of letters, photographs and personal effects belonging to Honest Abe--I dropped everything and went to the Huntington. Actually, I was a little annoyed with myself for taking time away from my labors at the William Grant Still Music company to indulge in another sort of hero-worship. Why search into the life of a person whose fame did not really require additional study or admiration? My time was needed elsewhere to educate the world about William Grant Still and Verna Arvey, and about what they had given to the growth of civilization. And, there were manuscripts to correct in order to get the *Fusion of Cultures*, Second Edition, ready for the printer. What did Lincoln have to do with *Fusion of Cultures*?

I spent a good two hours in the exhibit, reading every line of every letter, trailing after the thought-forms of a giant mind toward some philosophical whole. I saw at once that Lincoln had always had the best interests of the colored races at heart, despite modern allegations that he had freed the slaves out of expediency. His statement that Negroes were not equal to Whites in the Lincoln-Douglas debates was his ploy to gain election: he was painfully aware that he would not have been elected had he spoken otherwise. Moreover, any graphologist could see the secret side of his nature in his handwriting; the gap under his small "s" revealing his ability to withhold the truth toward some higher benefit. He had a job to do for humankind, and he knew it; he would get it done, ignoring any circumstances to the contrary.

Ultimately he did the job better than anyone else might have done, validating and completing the American Revolution, spending over 18,000 sleepless hours in clerical and hands-on diplomacy, displaying wit and humility, spiritual resolve, a huge intellect, and a knack for reflecting and touching the poetry and feelings of civilized humanity. He sacrificed health, personal luxuries, and the approval of many individuals of reputed stature in order to do that work. While he labored, he was so widely misunderstood and, indeed, looked down upon, that the Public Broadcasting System has correctly dubbed him the "most reviled American President." Even his Gettysburg Address was assessed by a reporter of the day as "silly, flat" and "dishwatery."

As I discovered for myself what Lincoln had accomplished, and against what odds, I was struck by the humanness of the man. There, amid his jocular, biting, profoundly literary writings, alongside his gloves, spectacles, wallet, handkerchief and beaver hat, the mythological figure took form. What was familiar about him? I suddenly realized that he reminded me of my father. My father smiling, joking, sometimes childlike, sometimes firm, and, at the end of his life, tired, ill, somewhat sad over the cruelties of a number of people. The difference was that William Grant Still's letters and personal effects were not on exhibit at the Huntington; his spectacles, his wallet, his handkerchiefs and his hat were packed away in our storeroom at home awaiting a place in the halls of history.

Once home from the exhibit, I could not get Lincoln out of my mind. His life nagged me, as when a student of American literature, I had been haunted by the coffins of *Moby Dick*: what was the meaning? That night I had a crazy dream, born more of fatigue than of any depth of thought. In the dream I was at the exhibit again, wandering among the display cases over and over, until a barrier rolled away from the cavern of time, and there the persona of the President rose and stood among the onlookers, seeming to mingle with the crowd to muse over his own belongings. When he looked into the glass of the cases, he saw his own face reflected twice, first ruddy and then pale, in the here and hereafter, part of the past, the present and the future simultaneously. When he came to the tableaux from Ford's Theatre, he walked by it and went to shake hands with my father who had come to meet him. Lincoln grinned at the composer and said, "We foxes and hounds surely did turn the Lords out of the manor." Then the two of them walked off side-by-side across the lawns of San Marino toward the sun.

Clearly my subconscious mind had found its own meaning in Lincoln, just as it had once made peace with Melville's coffins. Foxes and hounds? An interesting way to describe a politician and a musician, but, then one never approaches ideas in dreams as one does in the daytime. Certainly what could be said was that most of the things that were true of Lincoln were also true of William Grant Still. Both had a capacity for love and

213

empathy, as well as a knowledge of the truth beyond what their contemporaries professed to be the truth. Both displayed the strength to define their sense of the absolute in the face of great psychological abuse. Lincoln unshackled the slaves, Still worked to sever the chains of preconception and prejudice that pursued the dark-skinned peoples long after slavery. The composer not only wrote music that demonstrated the powerful desserts of the minority races, but he also penned hundreds of articles, letters and speeches throughout his life which spoke out against racial hatred and artistic mediocrity. His work manifested wit and humility, spiritual commitment, a massive intelligence, and an ability to reflect and to touch the poetry and feelings of civilized creatures. He sacrificed health, money, and the approbation of the leaders in the arts, and his work was so undervalued while he lived that critics called it everything from trite to passé.

Perhaps the most poignant similarity in the two men was their propensity for finding a refuge from criticism in humor. The Statesman who told McClellan that, if he wasn't using the Union army, he would like to borrow it for awhile, was followed one-hundred years later by the composer who wrote little friendly messages to the instrumentalists at the end of each of his orchestra parts, such as, "I wouldn't play anymore if I were *You*; and, "Cease bowing--it's time to pack up." Both men could laugh until they swayed in their chairs, both men could see the fun in the worst situations, both could joke in public, strive mightily in private, and fill the intervening moments with profound and concerted labor.

Moreover, it is in the lives of both men that I have found the importance of *The Fusion of Cultures*. Lincoln and Still were two of the figures in the West (like Gandhi in the East) who were responsible for inviting the coming age of universal understanding and of the fusion of races, cultures and nations. Lincoln struck down the barriers that stood in the way of brotherhood, Still demonstrated the need for, and urged society toward, brotherhood and sisterhood. Both espoused the message of union and concord among all peoples. Both were part of a movement toward social and artistic reform that will be realized in the twenty-first century. Our memories of their accomplishments will serve as a map for the future, for, in metaphysics, a noble memory is a divine directive.

This book is, therefore, an attempt to keep the idea of cultural concord available until society is ready to embrace it. However, before this volume can be appreciated, the question must be asked and answered, "Why is the fusion of races and cultures important?" Some elements in our current social order seem to suggest that it is more desirable for races to remain separate and significant and unique, each in its own way. William Grant Still would have been the first to deny the validity of separatism, even as he insisted upon the importance of fusion. Why?

According to my father, fusion is the essence of creation itself. Because life in the cosmos can develop only through harmonious interaction, separatism leads only to destruction, decay, discord and world war. Interaction enriches, brings growth, compassion and expansion of possibilities. In nature, all creatures and natural substances maintain their uniqueness and singularity, and yet they are fused into a whole through a system of interrelatedness that is both beautiful and functional. Without balance and symbiosis in nature, a fertile plain can become a desert. And, of all the wastelands caused by imbalance, the most terrible are those found in the human sphere. Humankind is the only species which seeks division, and assumes a superiority apart from the concerns of survival. Only human beings have a sense of self-importance that prevents them from realizing that they are not only not superior to other humans, but also that they are not more significant in the cosmic complex than other aspects of creation.

At no other time in history has this sense of self-importance been more pronounced than in the last half of the 19th century and in the whole of the 20th. Past centuries have been characterized by labels such as "The Middle Ages," "The Age of Enlightenment," "The Age of Reason," and so on, while the personality of our period in the course of civilization has been variously designated as "The Age of Technology, "The Atomic Age," or "The Age of Humanism." In my estimation, however, this century might well be christened "The Age of Alienation," or, "The Age of Egotism." Indeed, the most visible landmark of our time has been its lack of nobility and its absence of substantive greatness.

Consider the credentials of this century and the last. We have sought scientific advances without regard for the integrity of the natural system which surrounds us, and without belief in the equal importance of advances in the liberal arts. We have seen attempts to validate racial injustice at the expense of millions of lives. The frequent assertion that the Civil War was not about race at all is itself an injustice--when bigotry and propaganda masquerade as historical fact we all become party to the perpetuation of racism. The truth is that the Civil War was not fought over states' rights, it was fought over slavery, for it is clear that the conflict would never have occurred if slavery had been permitted to enter the territories of the expanding nation. The Civil War was, in actuality, a monumental effort exerted by people with certain physical characteristics to place their concerns over and above the comforts and concerns of people with differing physical characteristics. The racial injustice inherent in the War for the Confederacy was the same racial injustice which impelled the Ku Klux Klan and the Nazis, and it was the same injustice which led to the second greatest war of our century, a war predicated on delusions of superiority based upon artificial and superficial considerations.

During World War II, Hitler and Stalin were the personifications of ego asserting its power over society in the most destructive way possible: through genocide, or the establishment of tyranny through annihilation. Marxism pretended to support the rights of the individual, but maintained its control via the suppression of individual rights. Marxism, Nazism and the World Wars are to be blamed for the rise, after 1914, of a popular sense of alienation from the cosmos, and the popularity of philosophies of repudiation and self-service.

Following the two great wars, the intelligentsia flocked to the doctrines of Hedonism, Existentialism, Nihilism, Relativism, and Deconstructionism, as well as to artistic Realism, Absurdism and Abstractionism, and to any other "isms" which rejected a higher law and a belief in universal absolutes. Freud taught the importance of sexual desire, so that physical satisfaction took precedence over love and idealism. Psychologists inspired malcontents with talk of the supremacy of the self, and of "identity," and seemed to suggest that personal happiness was more to be valued than serving the needs of others. The social order began to disintegrate, and high crime and drug abuse moved in to fill the vacuum left by the flight of community solidarity.

The worst casualties of the Age were the arts. Through the rejection of idealism and the belief in personal, not universal, standards of taste, civilization entered into a period of artistic chaos unlike any before it. Under the aegis of institutions of higher learning, the most mediocre work could pass for products of genius. In fact, the height of egotism in the present century arrived when it was no longer possible to tell the difference between a work of art, and the playful smears of a pet chimpanzee.

The result of the idolatry of non-accessibility in art and music was that the general public, the "common" people, unimpressed by the lofty language of the academics--who insisted that the Emperor *was* fully clothed--turned away from the high arts in droves. From a time when music, art and dance were an integral part of the landscape, when children and adults learned notes and instruments as avidly as they conquered geography and ciphering, the nation fell into a vast creative landfill in which it was believed that inspired harmonies, organized rhythms and communication through non-verbal means were no longer necessary to social life and development. From that moment on, city fathers could always find support for sports programs, and student computers, but never for the luxuries of music and dance in the schools.

216

Now, as the century comes to a close, the time approaches for a revolt against the worship of false gods. Civilization has stumbled about aimlessly for too long a time, trying to cling to a sense of purpose, searching for heroes, craving beauty and joy, wondering how it got into this desolate expanse in the first place. Those who have known the way out have been largely ignored, particularly those who have spoken up for a return to artistic truth and cultural harmony.

Just as William Grant Still had campaigned for racial justice and brotherhood throughout the century, so also had he spoken out bravely against the atonal-serialistic-twelve-tone-avant-garde-nonrepresentational-art-and-music-mania of the time. His genius was proof against the assertion that anyone who denied the validity of "Modern" or "New" music did so out of incompetence and lack of elevated tutelage. Possibly one of the causes of his neglect, aside from his color, was his continual advocacy of melody, form and spiritual attunement as the source of all creative fecundity.

Real music, Still believed, was the sound of the life-force at work, the creative process revealed; therefore, compositions which had charm, romanticism and timeless loveliness were more difficult to write than solidly discordant pieces. Few composers could capture the God-Sound, effecting a linkage with cosmic forces, but, once they captured it, the works that they produced could act upon their hearers to improve the complexities of the brain, to heighten self-discipline, to foster the mastery of disciplines outside the arts, and to increase the capacity of the hearers for moral and spiritual activity. Good music could reduce crime and increase productivity in the workplace. Accessible melodies that spoke to the emotions were as powerful as medicine for bodily health, mental capacity, and maturity. There could be no fusion of cultures if the non-verbal expressions were not clearly apprehended and translatable. So thought Still, and yet his repeated efforts to bring value to music and art, and an integration of the arts across racial and national barriers, were unrecognized. Lincoln had been given the power of state to sway the populace, Still had not. He died forgotten in 1978.

After the composer's death, five years passed before anything was done to try to popularize his music and his writings. His wife, my mother, Verna Arvey, was very ill with diabetes and congestive heart problems, and I did not at first want to have anything to do with the world of music and social reform.

When I was a young girl, I recall that it was always accepted in our metaphysically-oriented family that my father and my mother had been chosen before birth to do an important spiritual and historical work in life. Psychics had told them that the music that would come out of their years together was destined to be heralded as some of the finest that the world would have to offer, not for its own sake, but because its unique qualities would call attention to the need for change in social attitudes in the coming Aquarian Age. Other persons of color had been gifted in the arts, other couples had been intermarried, others had fought for civil rights, but none before Still and Arvey had been so persistent and so exemplary in affirming the cause of cultural interaction.

I was quite proud that my parents had been brought to this exalted calling, but I did not expect to share in their achievements, even as I was aware I had not been blessed with their enormous talents and gentle natures. My father's own dreams and visions had made it manifest that his would be a life of hardship which would go on "to the bitter end." I admired him for bearing up in the wilderness for forty years, for bringing the tablets down to the unbelievers, but surely I could do very little to assist, being so ill-prepared in the arts and in public relations. Moreover, I was not schooled in the techniques of self-sacrifice.

My father did not encourage me to join him on the "Cross," but he did tell me of a dream which I have recounted in detail in my book, *A Voice High-Sounding*. The upshot of the dream was that someday I would have to take care of the music, and that his catalog of compositions was to become a very valuable asset indeed. When he had finished describing the dream, I observed that there was no chance of my taking care of the music, because I expected my mother, who was fifteen years his junior and an astute businesswoman, to continue to run William Grant Still Music until the company came into its own. My father replied, "You never know what God has in store."

When my father had been dead two years, and my mother was bedridden, I wanted to resist the nagging sense that something had to be done with the music. But the thousands of pages of handwritten manuscript, some brown with age, some eaten by silverfish and stained by water from the leaky roof, all packed in neat butcher paper and manila packages, stood in stacks all over my mother's house, like thread-bare wayfarers begging for sustenance. When I thought of how my father had carefully penned the last works of his career, in spite of his eye trouble and stomach upsets--when I remembered how he had meticulously wrapped the onion skin master sheets and tied them neatly with strings, as if they were to be sent to a prestigious orchestra for performance--when I realized that so many of them had never been touched since, and that, regardless of all his attempts to interest conductors in them, they remained just as he had left them, my sorrow flowed in streams and torrents. Something had to be done, even though I was hardly the person qualified for the task.

At first I believed the job could be done in short order. It was good music, and my father's worst enemies might be expected to lose credibility after their victim had been dead for some time. I was told that once I had contacted a great conductor or two who would champion Still, and one or two interested New York publishers, the rest would be no problem. It did not occur to me that my father had, in the 20's, 30's and 40's, the greatest of conductors as his champions, and the finest publishers, and that even they had not been able to bring Still to the public. But, I was inexperienced, and from 1980 to 1983 I spent time and money seeking performances and publications, until it became clear that an increase in visibility of the name on concert programs did nothing to enhance its status.

I realized, after hearing again and again, "Where can I get recordings of your father's music?" that the vast audiences were no longer in the concert halls. They were in their cars and in their kitchens and in their bedrooms, playing cassettes and discs, making private decisions about what to play from a sense of taste and pleasure that had no connection with stereotypes or pseudo-sophistication. I went to the record companies.

Most big recording companies in 1983 were not ready to lay out a welcome-mat for me. They greeted me with legions of stereotypical notions and mindless rejections, in varying degrees of politeness. "American music is out of favor these days." "Black music doesn't sell." "We do not feel that your father's work has commercial value." "We don't plan to do a collection of Black works unless you can bring us a substantial grant." "We are not familiar with your father's work." "We have just done an album of Gershwin [or Joplin or Ellington], and we feel that we have made a significant contribution to the recognition of your father's heritage." And all this without ever having seen a score, or heard a note, of the music that I was proposing for the recording.

I was not perturbed, I was enraged. Who said that Civil rights were being given their due? Who said that the American people were blessed by artistic freedom and the freedom to know? I saw that I would have to make the first recordings myself, using all the resources that two widows and four children could bring to bear. We cinched up and began the rocky ascent. We borrowed money, moved to cheaper quarters, and, in the next five years, we made and/or distributed nine LPs and cassette tapes of the music of William Grant Still. We were assisted greatly by the University of Arkansas, Fayetteville, which produced the recording of the *Third Symphony*, and by the Arkansas Arts Council, which gave copies of that LP to universities all across the country.

When the LPs and tapes were successful, achieving critical acclaim, and when the Library of Congress decided to put the *Afro-American*

Symphony on compact disc, it became easier to convince other companies to make all-Still CDs. We began to get money back. We used that money to expand our efforts, to send letters to music professors across the country, and to offer promotional CDs to radio stations. We also planned the publication of several books, among them the second edition of *Fusion*, but we decided to wait on those until there were at least two-dozen Still recordings on sale to the public. *Fusion* made no sense to anyone unless the music could be heard. Always we spent more than we had, always we robbed Peter to pay Paul, but always we made progress.

The music on the recordings was scattered like seeds in the hearts of the people, where it now germinates and brings forth a growing awareness of what the composer and his wife tried to accomplish. We return now to the job of reprinting *Fusion of Cultures* for the Centennial, with full confidence that, in the next century, William Grant Still will be recognized as a prophet of a new age--the Age of Cosmic Consciousness. In this new age, which the composer heralded and advocated, there will be freedom to be part of the multiplicity of life as unique individuals, as well as the enlightened desire to understand and to participate in the differences of others. In culture and in society, when human intercourse becomes as harmonious and strikingly various as the natural world, then will civilization advance to the level of its technological competence.

It is unfortunate, of course, that our spirituality has lagged so far behind our technology for these one-hundred years, and that the road to an advanced level of civilized life has not been a straight one. In the Civil War, in the race riots, in the pogroms in Europe, in the World Wars, in the years of discrimination of every sort, and in the years of degradation in the arts, mankind has veered from the uphill route, and, self-serving ever, has taken the path of least resistance and most injustice. Thereupon, a higher source sent down a few kindly spirits, such as a Lincoln, a Gandhi and a Still, to step to the helm, to redefine good and evil, to affirm that there is a best way toward beauty and virtue, and to prove that the roughest, longest road is a small price to pay for progress.

In his journey on that long road, Lincoln created the conditions necessary to bring about interaction among the races: a unified nation and the freedom of all persons in that nation. Still demonstrated the value of that interaction, and the means to achieve it. Lincoln said, "I believe I have made some mark which will tell for civil liberty after I have gone." "In giving freedom to the slave, we assure . . . the last best hope of earth." "If my name goes down in history, it will be for this act." William Grant Still said, "If I have a wish to express, it would be that my music may serve a purpose larger than mere music. If it will help in some way to bring about better interracial understanding in America and in other

220

countries, then I will feel that the work is justified." These two men pushed humankind along in the same direction. Lincoln's ultimate vindication, and the enormous fascination of people with his life and work, gives us assurance of the coming vindication for William Grant Still.

This book marks a part of the path toward that vindication. The book began the process of recognition in 1972 when it was first printed, and the fact that it retains its importance and interest value twenty-two years later, reveals how far we have come here at William Grant Still Music, and why we have made the journey. Like an oaken gate outside a capacious, century-old inn, its historical varnish shines and beckons, welcoming us to the new century, and to the hospitality of the kindly Host and noble ghosts who ushered in that century. The arch over the entry bears the inscription: Memorial to *William Grant Still and His Fusion of Cultures in American Music.* All travelers welcome.

Judith Anne Still

THEMATIC CATALOG OF WORKS
(1921 - 1972)

Celeste Anne Headlee, Editor

The editor would like to
acknowledge the contribution of
Verna Arvey
for the initial compilation of material
and the contribution of
Dr. Jean Matthew
who assisted in the compilation of the
thematic catalog and deduced the themes for
Three Negro Songs and *Black Bottom*.

WILLIAM GRANT STILL
Thematic Catalog Of Works

|
|

*All works published by William Grant Still Music
unless otherwise noted.*

WILLIAM GRANT STILL MUSIC
4 So. San Francisco, Suite #422
Flagstaff, AZ 86001-5737
(520) 526-9355

WORKS FOR STAGE

LA GUIABLESSE   *1927*   *30 min.*

A ballet for symphony orchestra and corps de ballet, with a scenario by Ruth Page after a Lafcadio Hearn story and based on a legend of the West Indian island of Martinique. It was first performed at the Third Annual Festival of American Music in Rochester, New York on May 5, 1933, with Dr. Howard Hanson conducting and Thelma Biracree as solo dancer. The Rochester *Democrat and Chronicle* commented that the music "is charming, picturesque and dramatically suggestive, never padded, never divorced from the action, yet with individual appeal of its own." This work requires 1 stage set, corps de ballet, 4 solo dancers, and full orchestra. Three of the dances ("Dance of the Children," "Dance of Yzore and Adou," and "Entrance of Les Porteuses") comprise an orchestral suite which has often been played separately. The latter dance has also been arranged for solo piano. Dedicated to Adrian Michaelis.

SAHDJI   *1929-30*   *30 min.*

A. Introduction

B. Opening Dance

A ballet for orchestra, mixed chorus, bass soloist and corps de ballet, with a scenario by Richard Bruce Forsythe and Alain Locke on an African tribal subject. It was first performed at the Eastman Theatre in Rochester, New York on May 22, 1931 with Dr. Howard Hanson conducting and

Thelma Biracree as solo dancer. The Rochester *Democrat and Chronicle* said that the ballet "is a vividly impressive work . . . Mr. Still gives evidence of an excellent sense of dramatic appeal in stage music." This work requires 1 stage set, corps de ballet, chorus, bass soloist, 3 solo dancers, and full orchestra. Dedicated to Howard Hanson. Available through CFI-ESM.

A. Introduction

B. Opening Dance

THE SORCERER   1933   Undetermined

A discarded ballet for which only the piano score remains.

BLUE STEEL   1934   120 min.

An opera in three acts which was eventually discarded by the composer. The libretto is by Bruce Forsythe and based on a story by Carlton Moss. It is unperformed in its entirety, however, an excerpt ("Entrance of the Priests and Dance of the Priestesses") was played by the Eastman School Little Symphony under the direction of Karl Van Hoesen on April 3, 1935. Written for full orchestra, vocal soloists, chorus, and three stage settings. The composer later incorporated this opera's musical material in other works.

LENOX AVENUE   *1937*   *23 min.*

A full-length ballet for orchestra, chorus, and narrator. The scenario, by Verna Arvey, is descriptive of New York's Harlem street scenes. It was first performed on CBS Radio on May 23, 1937 with Howard Barlow conducting (no reviews). Later, on January 19, 1938, the composer conducted the Los Angeles Federal Symphony in a concert performance. The Hollywood *Citizen-News* wrote of this performance that Still's piece "possesses the power to hold one in its spell and to create a vivid, lasting impression. It seems destined to endure." Richard Sheridan Ames described it as "original in outline, imaginative, simply poetic, genuinely powerful in several passages. Mr. Still acknowledged an ovation by repeating the final episodes." The "Blues" and spiritual for chorus from this ballet are published separately. (A recording of this performance entitled "William Grant Still Conducts William Grant Still" is available through WGSM.) The work was commissioned by the Columbia Broadcasting System and later converted into a ballet which was first performed by the Norma Gould Dance Theatre Group in Los Angeles. It was scored for reduced orchestra, narrator, chorus, and piano soloist. The ballet version does not require a narrator, but does require two solo dancers and a corps de ballet.

TROUBLED ISLAND   *1938*   *160 min.*

An opera in three acts with libretto by Langston Hughes and additional text by Verna Arvey. Based on the life of Haiti's first Emperor, Jean Jacques Dessalines. It became the first American premiere ever performed at the New York City Center on March 31, 1949 under the direction of Laszlo Halasz. The New York *Times* wrote that "there is evident in it an operatic talent, a structure of considerable breadth and melodic curve which commended it to the audience." Requires full orchestra, eight vocal soloists, chorus, ballet, and four stage sets. It is dedicated to Leopold Stokowski.

MISS SALLY'S PARTY   *1940*   *30 min.*

This ballet is written for full orchestra, corps de ballet, seven solo dancers and requires one stage set. Based on the composer's knowledge of Negro parties and traditions in the Old South, the scenario is by Verna Arvey. It was premiered at the 11th Annual Festival Of American Music in Rochester, New York, on May 2, 1941 with Dr. Howard Hanson conducting and Thelma Biracree as principal dancer. The *Democrat and Chronicle* wrote: "Here was tuneful music, animated, clean-cut, and the choreography was delightfully fashioned." The cakewalk in the ballet is a highlight of the piece. Dedicated to Thelma Biracree.

I'M PICKING MY LAST ROW OF COTTON *1941*   *Undetermined*
A short piece for chorus and pantomine which was discarded by the composer. It later became the song, *Bayou Home*.

A BAYOU LEGEND   *1941*   *75 min.*

An opera in three acts for nine vocal soloists, chorus, full orchestra, and three stage sets. The libretto, by Verna Arvey, is based on a legend from Biloxi, Mississippi about a romance between a man and a spirit in the early 19th century. This was the first opera on which William Grant Still and Verna Arvey collaborated fully. It was premiered on November 15, 1974 by Opera/South of Jackson State University with Donald Dorr directing and Leonard de Paur conducting. Opera/South also filmed this opera for television and, in November 1981, it became the first opera written by a Negro to be televised over a national network. Dedicated to Sir John Barbirolli.

A SOUTHERN INTERLUDE _1942_ _60 min._

This opera was actually an early version of _Highway I U.S.A._ with libretto
by Verna Arvey. It was in two acts and required 1 stage set, reduced
orchestra, small chorus, and four vocal soloists. It was never performed
and was later discarded by the composer.

COSTASO _1949_ _120 min._

An opera in three acts, requiring ten vocal soloists, chorus, ballet, full
orchestra, and four stage sets, with a libretto by Verna Arvey. It is based
on a legend of the Spanish-Colonial period in the American Southwest.
An amateur presentation of the opera was done by the young adults of the
National Association of Negro Musicians in Pasadena, California on May
16, 1992 in Rufus Mead Auditorium. Vittes of the _Los Angeles Times_
said that production "was mostly amateur but the work was not." He
commented on "the work's power and vision" and "the imagination and
turbulence of Still's vivid scoring." This opera has never been performed
professionally. Dedicated to the composer's friend, Don Voorhees, "in
appreciation of his service to American music."

MOTA _1951_ _120 min._

An opera in three acts requiring eight vocal soloists, chorus, full orchestra,
and two stage sets. The libretto by Verna Arvey concerns political
intrigue in an ancient African village. This opera will receive its world
premiere at North Carolina A&T State University in 1996, under the
auspices of William Grant Still's friend and fraternity brother, Dr. Clifford
Watkins. This will be the first important world premiere of an opera ever
presented by a historically Afro-American college or university.

THE PILLAR   *1955*   *120 min.*

An opera in three acts with a libretto by Verna Arvey, based on the story of an American Indian tribe. Mani becomes the chief of the tribe over his brother, Yona, and a divine Spirit promises plenty to their people if Mani will keep the tribe out of war. Yona, however, despite the prosperity that the people enjoy, incites the people to battle and kills Mani. Desolation returns to the tribe. Dedicated to Mrs. Leiland Atherton Irish "in appreciation of her service to American music and in gratitude for her friendship." The opera has never been performed.

MINETTE FONTAINE   *1958*   *120 min.*

An opera in three acts requiring ten vocal soloists, chorus, full orchestra, and five stage sets. The opera is based on voodoo rituals in Louisiana and the tragedy that befalls a 19th century operatic diva when her jealousy and selfishness drives her to use the occult in order to gain the love of another woman's man. The libretto is by Verna Arvey. Premiered by the Baton Rouge Opera Company at the Centroplex Theatre in Baton Rouge, Louisiana on October 22, 1984. The production was directed by Donald Dorr and was more financially successful than any previous opera performed by the Baton Rouge Opera. Dedicated to Joan Palevsky.

HIGHWAY 1, USA   *1962*   *60 min.*

A one-act opera requiring four vocal soloists, chorus, full or reduced orchestra, and one stage set, with a libretto by Verna Arvey. The opera tells the story of two brothers and their conflict, and is set in a gas station on Highway 1. It was premiered on May 11, 1963 in honor of the composer's birthday at the fourth annual Festival of Contemporary

International Music, University of Miami, with Fabien Sevitzky directing and conducting. Dedicated to Judith Anne Still and Larry, Daniel, and Lisa Headlee.

INCIDENTAL MUSIC from THE PRINCE AND THE MERMAID
1965   *20 min.*

Music for a children's play by Carol Stone based on a fairy tale. The musical segments are entitled "Song of the Sea," "Waltz," "Minuet," and "Scherzo". The play, which requires seven characters, soprano soloists, chorus, and chamber group, was premiered at the San Fernando Valley (California) State College on March 4, 1966. It was directed by Carol Stone.

WORKS FOR ORCHESTRA

FLORIDA BLUES   *Early 1920's   Undetermined*
A composition by William Philips which was arranged for small orchestra by Still. Published by WGSM-Handy Bros.

TEXAS MOANER BLUES   *Early 1920's   Undetermined*
Arranged by Still for Clarence Williams. Published by MCA.

WHAT MAKES ME BELIEVE YOU?   *Early 1920's   Undetermined*
An early work by Charles Lawrence which Still orchestrated.

YAMEKRAW   *Early 1920's   Undetermined*
A composition by James P. Johnson which Still orchestrated.

THREE NEGRO SONGS   *1921   10 min.*

These songs, written in New York and scored for reduced orchestra, were never performed. Discarded by the composer, only the conductor's score is available. The titles of the songs were: "Negro Love Song," "Death Song," and "A Song of the Backwoods."

BLACK BOTTOM   *1922   10 min.*

This short piece for chamber orchestra has never been performed. Only a portion of the piano score remains, as it was discarded by the composer.

FROM THE LAND OF DREAMS   *1924   8 min.*
This piece, written in New York City while Still was under the tutelage of Edgar Varèse, uses three voices instrumentally rather than soloistically. It

was first performed at an International Composers' Guild concert in New York City on February 8, 1925 with Vladimir Shavitz conducting. Paul Rosenfeld, in *The Dial*, praised the work, saying that Still's use of jazz motives was "more genuinely musical than any to which they have been put, by Milhaud, Gershwin, or anyone else." Another critic, however, attacked the piece saying that Edgar Varèse had driven out of Mr. Still all of the rollicking, entertaining and original music attributed to Negroes. Still agreed and scrapped the work. Scored for woodwinds, strings, percussion, and three female voices.

DARKER AMERICA   *1924-25   17 min.*

A.

B.

This symphonic poem for chamber orchestra and reduced orchestra was first performed at an International Composers' Guild concert at Aeolian Hall in New York City, with Eugene Goossens conducting, on November 28, 1926. The *Musical Courier*, though recognizing that Still was still influenced by Varèse, said that, "There is no doubting the man's power and his music on this particular occasion was like a bright spot amid a lot of muddy grime," also adding that someday, Still "will blossom forth as one of America's really great composers." This symphonic poem won a publication prize at the Eastman School of Music and is published by CFI-ESM.

FROM THE JOURNAL OF A WANDERER   *1925   20 min.*

A. *Phantom's Trail*

B. *Magic Bells*

C. *Valley of Echoes*

D. *Mystic Moon*

E. *Devil's Hollow*

Divided into five separate movements, this orchestral work was first performed at the North Shore Festival by Frederick Stock and the Chicago Symphony Orchestra in 1926. The titles of the movements are: "Phantom Trail," "Magic Bells," "Valley of Echoes," "Mystic Moon," and "Devil's Hollow." It was eventually discarded by the composer, but the conductor's score is still available.

FROM THE BLACK BELT   *1926*   *20 min.*

A. *Li'l Scamp*

B. *Honeysuckle*

233

C. *Dance*

D. *Mah Bones Is Creakin'*

E. *Blue*

F. *Brown Girl*

G. *Clap Yo' Han's*

Composed for small orchestra and later revised for full orchestra, this suite has seven sections: "Li'l Scamp," "Honeysuckle," "Dance," "Mah Bones Is Creakin'," "Blue," "Brown Girl," "Clap Yo' Han's." It was premiered by Georges Barrère's Little Symphony at the Henry Miller Theatre in New York City on March 20, 1927, with Barrère conducting. The New York *Herald-Tribune* said that this piece, "after starting with a suggestion of jazz, seemed unlikely to shock conservative ears." Another critic commented that, "as there was nothing hyperprismic about the music, these short pieces must have been written while his mentor, Edgar Varèse, was occupied in listening to a League, a Guild, or peradventrue, a Philadelphia Orchestra concert and, consequently, had his back turned." It is published by Carl Fischer, Inc.

FROM THE HEART OF A BELIEVER   *1927*   *10 min.*

This orchestral poem is a musical affirmation of Still's devotion to God. It was never performed and was later scrapped by the composer. The conductor's score, however, is still available.

LOG CABIN BALLADS   *1927*   *10 min.*

This suite was scored for three violins, viola, 'cello, bass, woodwinds, and percussion, and had three sections: "Long To'ds Night," "Beneaf de Willers," and "Miss Malindy." With Georges Barrere conducting, it was premiered at the Booth Theatre in New York City by the Barrere Little Symphony on March 25, 1928. F. D. Perkins in the New York *Herald-Tribune* described the suite as "conservative, distinctly tuneful, and expressively effective, and well orchestrated." The composer, however, was dissatisfied with the piece and scrapped it.

AFRICA   *1928*   *30 min.*

Written for full orchestra, this suite was Still's concept of the land of his ancestors. It has three sections, "Land of Peace," "Land of Romance," and "Land of Superstition." Premiered in 1930 in a reduced version by the Barrere Little Symphony, it was later scored for full orchestra and performed at an American Composers' concert in Rochester, New York in 1930. The Rochester *Evening Journal* said "the music of this suite is impressionistic, strongly marked in rhythm, with passages that are richly harmonic." Other critics noted that it was charming and lyric, and an advance creatively for the 35-year-old composer. It was dedicated to George Barrere, but was later discarded by the composer. The score and parts, however, are still available.

DANSE BARBARE   *1928*   *Undetermined*

A composition by Will Donaldson which was orchestrated by Still. Only the piano score remains. Published by CFI.

DARK MADONNA   *1928*   *Undetermined*

A composition by Will Donaldson which Still orchestrated. Published by CFI.

A.

Moderato assai

B.

Adagio

C.

Animato

D.

Lento, con risolutione

Still's most popular and well-known work, it was written for full symphony orchestra. It was premiered at an American Composers' Concert at the Eastman School of Music on October 29, 1931 under the baton of Dr. Howard Hanson. Amy H. Croughton, in the Rochester *Evening Journal,* wrote: "To give one such composer as Mr. Still an opportunity to have his compositions heard and to hear them himself would justify the entire American Composers' movement." David Kessler, in the Rochester *Evening Journal and Post Express* wrote that, "the Symphony has life and sparkle when needed and a deep, haunting beauty . . . and it always sings." It is based on an original blues theme and has four movements: a) Moderato assai--Longing, b) Adagio--Sorrow, c) Animato--Humor, and d) Lento, con risoluzione--Aspiration. Each of the movements is preceded by a favorite verse from one of Paul Laurence Dunbar's poems. The third movement (animato) is the "Scherzo," so often played separately. It is dedicated to Irving Schwerke and, though originally published by J. Fischer & Bro., it is now available from G. Schirmer.

A. *Spiritual*

Moderately fast

B. *Young Missy*

Andantino

C. *Dance*

Animated

Although only the piano score remains, this piece was originally written for reduced orchestra and has three parts: a) "Spiritual," "Young Missy," and "Dance." Introduced by Paul Whiteman at the Metropolitan Opera House in New York City on December 15, 1933, it was accompanied by excerpts from the poem "The Deserted Plantation," by Paul Laurence Dunbar . Francis D. Perkins in the New York *Herald-Tribune* wrote that it was "skillfully constructed of music, in which the various possibilities in color and sonority obtainable from this type of orchestra are ably and effectively realized." The piano score is available from Robbins Music Corporation (now Columbia Pictures Publications).

EBON CHRONICLE   *1933*   *9 min.*

① *Allegro*   ②

Scored for full orchestra, this orchestral poem was premiered by the Fort Worth Symphony Orchestra in Texas under the direction of Paul Whiteman on November 3, 1936. The composer later discarded it and only the conductor's score remains.

237

THE BLACK MAN DANCES   1935   10 min.

Eventually scrapped by the composer, this suite of three movements for orchestra was never performed. The conductor's score, however, is still available.

DISMAL SWAMP   1936   15 min.

A. Principle Theme

B. Second Subject

C. Final Form of Principle Theme

This tone poem for orchestra is musically descriptive of Virginia's and North Carolina's great Dismal Swamp, forbidding at first glance, but possessing hidden beauty for those who penetrate its depths. This piece was first introduced at the Eastman Theatre in Rochester at an American Composers' Concert on October 30, 1936, under the direction of Dr. Howard Hanson. The Rochester *Evening Journal and Post-Express* described the piece as "an atmospheric, ingenious development of a constantly repeated phrase culminating in an impressive finale," also commenting that it was "the best score on the program."

238

BEYOND TOMORROW   *1936*   *9 min.*

An early version of *A Song At Dusk* for orchestra. It has never been performed and is dedicated to the composer's daughter, Judith, and her husband, Larry Headlee.

SYMPHONY IN G MINOR (Symphony No. 2) *1937*   *25 min.*

Subtitled "Song of a New Race," the second symphony has four movements and is a continuation of the *Afro-American Symphony*. Whereas the first symphony described the Negro in his early days, not far removed from slavery, this symphony described the Negro modern times: "A New Race," which is the fusion of all racial elements. It was premiered by Leopold Stokowski and the Philadelphia Orchestra in Philadelphia on December 10, 1937, it was described by the Philadelphia *Inquirer* as "of absorbing interest, unmistakably racial in thematic material and rhythms, and triumphantly articulate in expressions of moods, ranging from the exuberance of jazz to brooding wistfulness." In contrast, the *Philadelphia Evening Bulletin* for the same date found the third (Scherzo) movement lively and effective, but heard little suggestion of the rich and inventive idiom of the Negro race in it. Scored for full

239

orchestra and dedicated to Isabel Morse Jones. Published by Carl Fischer, Inc.

CAN'TCHA LINE 'EM   *1940*   *5 min.*

Commissioned by CBS and first performed on February 17, 1940 by the CBS Radio Orchestra on the network program, "American School of the Air." It is based on a folk theme and is scored for small orchestra.

OLD CALIFORNIA   *1941*   *10 min.*

A. Indian

B. Spanish

C. American

This is a musical history of the State of California: the Indian tribal dances, the Spanish occupation with its fiestas and its religious devotion, the conflict caused by the coming of the Americans, and the conclusion which speaks of final peace and abundance. Composed at the request of Werner Janssen to honor the 160th birthday of the City of Los Angeles, the first performance was given by Werner Janssen and the Janssen Symphony Orchestra at the Wilshire-Ebell Theatre in Los Angeles on October 30, 1941. It was enthusiastically received, and played frequently since then. The Hollywood *Citizen-News* described it as "a work of strong melodic appeal, magnificently orchestrated, it is worth a permanent place in the orchestral repertoire." It is scored for full orchestra. Dedicated to the memory of his dear friend and publisher, George Fischer, "who worked tirelessly on behalf of American composers and their music."

FANFARE FOR AMERICAN WAR HEROES *1943* *1 min.*

First performed by the Columbus, Indiana Pro-Musica under the direction of David Bowden on February 9, 1991. Scored for full orchestra.

IN MEMORIAM: THE COLORED SOLDIERS WHO
DIED FOR DEMOCRACY *1943* *6 min.*

A. Fanfare

B. Principle Theme

C. Second Subject

This orchestral requiem, commissioned by the League of Composers, was the most successful of seventeen pieces written for the League to commemorate World War II. It was inspired by the report that the first American soldier to be killed in the War was a colored man. Said the composer, "I also hope that our tribute to those who died will . . . make the democracy for which they fought greater and broader than it has ever been before." It was first performed by Arthur Rodzinski and the Philharmonic-Symphony Society of New York on January 5th and 7th, 1944. Olin Downes in the New York *Times* said the work accomplished its purpose "with simplicity and feeling, without affectation or attitudinizing." Henry Simon in *PM* said, "It says what it has to say directly and tellingly, and remains within the five-minute limit without strain as the other works in the series have not done." It has been played many times since with favorable results. It is scored for full orchestra and is available through MCA.

PAGES FROM NEGRO HISTORY   *1943*   *10 min.*

A. *Africa*

B. *Slavery*

C. *Emancipation*

This piece was composed for reduced student orchestras and has three sections depicting the history of the Negro in the United States which are based on narration by Verna Arvey: "Africa," "Slavery," and "Emancipation." It was first performed by the Western Maryland College Orchestra in Westminster, Maryland on March 17, 1944. It is dedicated to the composer's son, Duncan. Published by Carl Fischer, Inc. in the collection "Music of Our Time."

POEM FOR ORCHESTRA   *1944*   *15 min.*

A.

B.

C.

Commissioned by the Fynette H. Kulas American Composers' Fund for the Cleveland Symphony Orchestra, this work was inspired by the composer's belief in the need for a spiritual reawakening in the world. It describes this religious resurgence as coming after a period of darkness and despair. It is accompanied by an explanatory poem for the program notes, written by Verna Arvey. It was first performed by Rudolph Ringwall and the Cleveland Symphony on December 7th, 1944. The Cleveland *Plain-Dealer* described it as "deeply moving and reminiscent of the Negro spiritual . . . The sad, sorrowing beginning in dissonances of brass builds to a musical climax of hope and coming to spiritual consciousness in a singing melody of strings." *Musical America* noted that it had "lovely, lyrical passages and stirring, forthright vitality." Dedicated to Arthur Judson and scored for full orchestra. It is available from Theodore Presser.

FESTIVE OVERTURE   *1944*   *10 min.*

A.

B.

C.

This work was chosen unanimously by three distinguished judges (Pierre Monteux, Deems Taylor, and Eugene Goossens) as the winner of the Cincinnati Symphony Orchestra's Jubilee Season competition from among thirty-nine anonymously submitted scores. Premiered by Eugene Goossens and the Cincinnati Symphony Orchestra on January 19th and 20th, 1945. The Cincinnati *Post* said, "Mr. Still turned in an overture that surges dramatically . . . It is colorful writing, sometimes brilliant and grand." Both the Cincinnati *Post* and the *Cincinnati Enquirer* approved of the music's "American flavor" and "irrepressible march rhythm." It is dedicated to the memory of Eugene Goossens and scored for full orchestra. Published by Carl Fischer, Inc.

ARCHAIC RITUAL   *1946*   *20 min.*

A. *Chant*

B. *Dance Before the Altar*

C. *Possession*

Thematically unified, as was the earlier *Afro-American Symphony*, the *Archaic Ritual* emphasizes the transformation and interweaving of motifs, so that each movement of the Suite ("Chant," Dance Before The Altar," and "Possession" is irrevocably tied to the others. Moveover, each movement builds, so that the opening Chant gives way to a spirited dance rhythm which, in turn, proceeds to a more frenzied section in which the worshippers are possessed by spirits. It was first performed by the Los Angeles Philharmonic Orchestra in the Hollywood Bowl, under Izler Solomon's direction, on August 25, 1949. It was also included as a dance sequence in the Baton Rouge Opera Company's production of *Minette Fontaine* in October 1984. Scored for full orchestra.

SYMPHONY NO. 4   *1947*   *33 min.*

Subtitled "The Autochthonous Symphony," this work was the composer's tribute to the fusion of cultures in the United States and to the spirit of the American people. As the title indicates, this is a work with its "roots in our own soil." It has four movements: a) Moderately--the spirit of optimism and energy, b) Slowly--pensive, then animated in a folky way, c) Moderately fast--humorously, the American idiom, d) Slowly and reverently--the spiritual love of mankind. First performed by Victor Alessandro and the Oklahoma City Symphony Orchestra on March 18, 1951. The concert was broadcast over the Mutual Network. Dedicated to one of the composer's early teachers at Oberlin Conservatory, Maurice Kessler.

A. *Singing River*

B. *Autumn Night*

C. *Moon Dusk*

D. *Whippoorwill's Shoes*

This orchestral suite was inspired by the poems of the Southern poet, J. Mitchell Pilcher, and has five parts: "Singing River," "Autumn Night," "Moon Dusk," "Whipporwill's Shoes," and "Theophany." First performed by Arthur Rodzinski and the Chicago Symphony Orchestra on April 22, 1948. The *Chicago Daily News* described it as "pleasant music, with an occasional flash of personality." Dedicated to one of the composer's early teachers at Oberlin Conservatory, F. J. Lehmann. It is scored for either full or reduced orchestra, but the publication of Peer-Music is for small orchestra only and the fifth movement is left out.

DANZAS DE PANAMA _1948_ _15 min._

A. *Tamborito*

B. *Mejorana y Socavon*

C. *Punto*

D. *Cumbia y Congo*

Scored for string orchestra or string quartet, this work was inspired by Elisabeth Waldo's folk tunes and consists of four parts: "Tamborito" (Negro-Panamanian in origin), "Mejorana y Socavon" (Spanish-Indian in origin), "Punto" (Spanish-Indian in origin), and "Cumbia y Congo" (Negro-Panamanian in origin). This suite simulates the sound of native drums by having the players knock rhythmically on their instruments, and its percussive effects make the work unique in the literature for string quartet. It was premiered by the Waldo Latin-American String Quartet at the Los Angeles County Museum on May 21, 1948. Published by Peer-Music.

AMERICA: A VISION   *1953   Undetermined*
A composition by Mabel Bean which was orchestrated by Still. Published by WGSM.

LITTLE RED SCHOOLHOUSE   *1956   15 min.*

A. *Little Conqueror*

B. *Egyptian Princess*

Moderately

C. *Captain Kidd, Jr.*

Moderately

D. *Colleen Bawn*

Tenderly

E. *Petey*

This suite was adapted from a previous work entitled "Pages from a Mother's Diary." This piece is a humorous look at five children who attend "The Little Red Schoolhouse," and embodies the composer's deep love for children and his belief that innocence and youthful humor is the stuff of which brotherhood is made. Scored for orchestra or band, this suite consists of five sections: "Little Conqueror," "Egyptian Princess," "Captain Kidd, Jr.," "Colleen Bawn", and "Petey." In this version, it was first performed at Redlands University (California) on March 30, 1957, with Edward Tritt conducting. However, the earlier version, "Pages from a Mother's Diary," was first performed by the Santa Clara County Symphonette under Edward Azhderian on January 8, 1954. Of this performance, the San Jose *Mercury* wrote that, "it seemed marked by imaginative, energetic and impish qualities usually associated with the innocence, imagery and high spirits of childhood. The short movements are well contrasted and imbued with genuine sensitivity, charm, and creative inventiveness." The band arrangement was done by Bucky Steele. Published by Peer-Music.

Suite 1: *The East*

A. *On the Village Green*

B. *Berkshire Night*

C. *Manhattan Skyline*

Suite 2: *The South*

A. *Florida Night*

B. *Levee Land*

C. *A New Orleans Street*

249

Suite 3: *The Old West*

A. *Song of the Plainsmen*

Moderately

B. *Sioux Love Song*

Tenderly

C. *Tribal Dance*

Animated

Suite 4: *The Far West*

A. *The Plaza*

Daintily

B. *Sundown Land*

Slowly

C. *Navaho Country*

Lively

Suite 5: *A Mountain, a Memorial, and a Song*

A. *Grand Teton*

B. *Tomb of the Unknown Soldier*

C. *Song of the Rivermen*

This work consists of five suites for orchestra which depict life, scenery, and culture in various parts of the United States. The suites are:

Suite 1: *The East*--a) On the Village Green, b) Berkshire Night, c) Manhattan Skyline

Suite 2: *The South*--a) Florida Night, b) Levee Land, c) A New Orleans Street

Suite 3: *The Old West*--a) Song of the Plainsmen, b) Sioux Love Song, c) Tribal Dance

Suite 4: *The Far West*--a) The Plaza, b) Sundown Land, c) Navaho Country

Suite 5: *A Mountain, a Memorial, and a Song*--a) Grand Teton, b) Tomb of the Unknown Soldier, c) Song of the Rivermen

This work was premiered on November 18, 1990 by Jack Abell and the Rhodes Civic Orchestra, Memphis, Tennessee. "Florida Night" and "Grand Teton" were performed on March 31, 1960 in the Standard School Broadcast on the NBC Western Radio Network. The same radio program played "Levee Land" and "A New Orleans Street" on February 5th and 9th, 1959. "Berkshire Night" and "Tribal Dance" were programmed by the Rochester Civic Symphony in October 1964, under the direction of Paul White. The Beverly Hills Symphony Orchestra played "Tomb of the Unknown Soldier, "Grand Teton," and "A New Orleans Street" on February 19, 1962, with Herbert Weiskopf conducting. Dedicated to

Marjorie Lange, Miriam Matthews, Joseph Portanova, the Pasadena Inter-Racial Women's Club, and Helen Thompson. Excerpts from this piece are also available for chamber orchestra or band. The excerpts for band are, "Tomb of the Unknown Soldier," "A New Orleans Street," "Berkshire Night," "Tribal Dance," and "Grand Teton."

SERENADE   *1957*   *8 min.*

A. Principle Theme

B. Second Subject

This work for flute, harp, clarinet, and orchestra was originally inspired by Gregor Piatigorsky, who suggested that Still write something for 'cello. It was eventually transformed from a 'cello concerto into a work for Great Falls (Montana) High School which commissioned the piece. Later, the piece was reorchestrated for the Westchester String Symphony with George Berres. It is also arranged for string quintet, harp, flute, and clarinet. First performed on May 7, 1958 by the Great Falls High School Orchestra, under the direction of Paul Schull. Dedicated to Leroy and Ruth Brant.

SYMPHONY NO. 3   *1958*   *25 min.*

A. *Awakening*

B. *Prayer*

C. *Relaxation*

D. *Day's End and a New Beginning*

Subtitled "The Sunday Symphony," this piece was written to fill the void when the original *Symphony No. 3* became the *Fifth Symphony*, or "The Western Hemisphere." It is the composer's expression of daily worship. The symphony has four movements, describing a typical Sunday for the devout: a) Moderately: Awakening, b) Very slowly: Prayer, c) Gaily: Relaxation, and d) Resolutely: Day's End and a New Beginning. It was premiered on February 12, 1984 by Carlton Woods and the North Arkansas Symphony at Harrison, Arkansas. Dedicated to Christian Dupriez. Available through CFI.

SYMPHONY NO. 5   *1958*   *25 min.*

A. **Briskly**

B. **Slowly, and with utmost grace**

C. **Energetically**

D.

Subtitled "The Western Hemisphere," this was originally the *Third Symphony*, composed in 1945. However, the composer discarded the work and later revised it as the *Fifth*, and final, *Symphony*. It has four movements: a) Briskly -- the vigorous, life-sustaining forces of the Hemisphere, b) Slower, with utmost grace -- the natural beauties of the Hemisphere, c) Energetically -- the nervous energy of the Hemisphere, and d) Moderately -- the overshadowing spirit of kindness and justice in the Hemisphere. First performed by the Oberlin College Orchestra on November 9, 1970, in belated celebration of the composer's 75th birthday, with Robert Baustian conducting. Dedicated to Victoria Juarez Burke.

LEGEND *1959 Undetermined*

A work discarded by the composer for which only the conductor's score remains. Probably no performances of this piece were given.

PATTERNS *1960 15 min.*

A. *Magic Crystal*

B. *A Lone Teardrop*

C. *Rain Pearls*

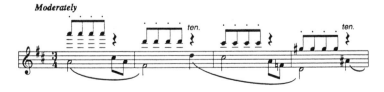

254

D. *Tranquil Cove*

E. *Moon-Gold*

An orchestral suite in five movements for reduced orchestra, described as "experimental music" by the composer. This piece is made up of five rhythmic designs based on five rhythmic themes, each one comprising a separate movement: "Magic Crystal," "A Lone Teardrop," "Rain Pearls," "Tranquil Cove," "Moon-Gold." Premiered on April 23, 1961 by Ernst Gebert and the Inglewood (California) Symphony Orchestra. The Hollywood *Citizen-News* described the piece as "a work of imaginative character and pervasive beauty, both in concept and execution. Each of its five movements was a different flight of fancy. Where so many modern composers attempt to overpower the listener with tonal force, Still has been content to intrigue him with delicate, tasteful utterance and the result was delightful. The orchestration, for a relatively small ensemble, was exquisite in its treatment of nuance and shading." Dedicated to Ernst Gebert and the Inglewood Symphony Orchestra.

THE PEACEFUL LAND   1960   9 min.

A.

B.

255

Written to honor the United Nations, this piece was selected from eighty-six other compositions to win the prize offered by the National Federation of Music Clubs and Aeolian Music Foundation in 1961 for a symphonic composition dedicated to the United Nations. First performed by Fabien Sevitsky and the University of Miami Symphony Orchestra on October 22, 1961. The Miami *Herald* said that the work "provided a less spectacular peak for listeners, mainly because it is so quiet, expressive, undramatic, genuine and non-showy a work." It is available for rental from Theodore Presser. It is scored for full orchestra.

PRELUDES   *1962*   *12 min.*

A.

B.

C.

D.

E.

An orchestral suite written for George Berres and the Westchester String Symphony. It is mainly, as Verna Arvey described it, an example of the composer's "inventive ability," rather than a thematic work. It has five movements: a) Moderately fast, b) Moderately slow, c) Delicately, d) Moderately, and e) Energetically. First performed by the Westchester String Symphony under the baton of George Berres in Los Angeles on May 26, 1968. This piece is also arranged for flute and piano or piano solo. Dedicated to Consuelo Pappy.

LOS ALNADOS DE ESPAÑA   *1962*   12 min.

A. *Prólogo y narracion*

Allegro moderato

B. *El Valle Escondido*

Lento

C. *Serenata*

Moderato

D. *Danza*

Allegretto

Spanish-Colonial life in the Western Hemisphere was the inspiration for this orchestral suite. The colonies were known as "Stepchildren of Spain," and yet their life was colorful and of a quality not to be found again. The suite, comprising four sections (a. "Prologo y narracion," b. "El Valle Escondido," c. "Serenata," d. "Danza") in a sense pays tribute to the composer's maternal grandfather, a Spaniard with holdings in Florida. It was first performed by Sheldon Bair and the Susquehanna Symphony Orchestra on October 29, 1994. It is scored for full orchestra and dedicated to the memory of Clarence Cameron White.

THRENODY: IN MEMORY OF JAN SIBELIUS *1965*   *4 min.*

An orchestral requiem written at the request of Fabien Sevitzky for the Sibelius Memorial Concert. Premiered on March 14, 1965 by the University of Miami Symphony Orchestra, conducted by Maestro Sevitsky, this piece won immediate approval from audience and critics. In 1966 it was broadcast over Finnish National Radio. It is scored for full orchestra.

CHOREOGRAPHIC PRELUDE   *1970*   *5 min.*

A suite for string orchestra which expresses the composer's interest in dance. This piece employs percussion motifs and dance rhythms so characteristic of primitive dance ceremonials. First performed on January 25, 1970 at the Los Angeles County Museum Concert, Exposition Park, California, with the composer conducting.

MINIATURE OVERTURE   *1965*   *2 min.*

One of five pieces written to honor Fabien Sevitzky and the inception of the Greater Miami Philharmonic Orchestra. First performed on October 17, 1965 by the Greater Miami Philharmonic Orchestra, Fabien Sevitzky conducting. It is scored for full orchestra.

WORKS FOR ORCHESTRA
WITH SOLOISTS OR CHORUS

JUNGLE DRUMS   *Early 1920's*   *Undetermined*
An early work for chorus and orchestra by Still and Phil Boutelse. Only the piano-conductor sketch remains.

LIFT EVERY VOICE AND SING   *Early 1920's*   *Undetermined*
A piece by J. Rosamond Johnson, arranged by Still for voices, strings, piano, and flute.

PROMISED LAND   *Early 1920's*   *Undetermined*
A sacred cantata by Frederick Martens, with music by Still. Only a sketch remains in the composer's journal.

SPIRITUALS: A MEDLEY   *Early 1920's*   *Undetermined*
Possibly written in 1927, this piece may have been the final version of either "The Devotion of a People" or "From the Heart of a Believer," or both. It is based on orchestral arrangements of several Negro spirituals and was discarded by the composer.

LEVEE LAND   *1925*   *10 min.*

Levee Land is not to be confused with "Levee Land" from the second suite of *The American Scene*. This piece is scored for two violins, woodwinds, banjo, piano, percussion, and soprano solo. It was premiered at the International Composers' Guild concert in New York's Aeolian Hall, with Florence Mills as soloist and Eugene Goossens conducting, on January 24, 1926. *The Musical Courier* said that, "these works are so good, healthy, sane--such good musical fooling--that they place this Negro composer on a high plane in the super-jazz now in vogue." The New York *World* noted "Curious and elemental were these songs by this brilliant young Negro composer, plaintive in part, blue, crooning and sparkling with humor, and Miss Mills gave them a perfect interpretation." This was one of the first efforts William Grant Still made toward a symphonic treatment of jazz motifs. The composer also wrote the words for these songs.

KAINTUCK' 1935 13 min.

Written for, and dedicated to, Verna Arvey, this piece is scored for piano and orchestra. It was first performed on two pianos at a Los Angeles Pro Musica concert on October 28, 1935, with Verna Arvey as soloist. The Hollywood *Citizen-News* described the piece as "ingratiating music," and "a work of attractive calibre, imbued with a langorous atmosphere properly typical of the Old South, while some passages were appropriately equine in suggestiveness." It was commissioned by the League of Composers.

SONG OF A CITY, RISING TIDE, VICTORY TIDE 1938 3 min.

A. *The City*

B. Choral Theme

This is a rousing symphonic work for chorus and orchestra, with a choral episode by Albert Stillman. Scored for SSATBB, SATB, TTBB, solo voice and piano, or band or chorus. Also known by the titles "Rising Tide" and "Victory Tide." The adaptation for orchestra, as the theme music for the New York World's Fair in 1939, was played continuously in the Perisphere for the duration of the Fair. The piece was written on a commission from the World's Fair Committee.

AND THEY LYNCHED HIM ON A TREE   *1940*   *19 min.*

Scored for two choruses, contralto soloist, narrator, and orchestra, this massive and moving piece tells of the lynching of a Negro as a result of mob violence, with a text by Katherine Garrison Chapin. Dedicated to Henry Allen Moe, it was written while the composer was on a Julius Rosenwald Foundation Fellowship. It was premiered at the Lewisohn Stadium in New York on June 24, 1940, under the direction of Artur Rodzinski, with the New York Philharmonic, the Schola Cantorum, and Louise Burge as contralto soloist. The New York *Times* stated that Still wrote "with utter simplicity and with deep feeling. He has used the orchestra to paint in the atmosphere . . . The music achieves its greatest eloquence in the pages devoted to the Negro men and women and especially to the solo sung by the boy's mother. Using themes that are akin to Spirituals, he gives her poignant, searching music."

PLAIN-CHANT FOR AMERICA   *1941*   *10 min.*

A.

B.

A work for orchestra, baritone soloist and organ, or chorus, orchestra and organ, with a text by Katherine Garrison Chapin. A patriotic work that was written for the Centennial of the New York Philharmonic Orchestra. It was first performed by Sir John Barbirolli and the Philharmonic Orchestra of New York, with Wilbur Evans as soloist, on October 23, 1941, to a standing ovation and critical approval. Dedicated to President and Mrs. Franklin D. Roosevelt. The composer wrote the choral version in the Sixties, and it was first performed by Werner Torkanowsky, the New Orleans Philharmonic-Symphony Orchestra and the Dillard

University Chorus on April 16, 1968. It was then described as being just as timely as when first conceived, and its patriotic theme even more appealing to listeners than at its inception.

THOSE WHO WAIT   *1942*   *10 min.*

Broth-ers, we are rea-dy for the world that is to come,

Written for chorus and orchestra, with bass and mezzo soloists, on a text by Verna Arvey. It deals with the race issue in a question-and-answer format, concluding that the post-war nation is ready for new human understanding. It was premiered by the Wisconsin Civic Symphony under Monte Perkins on November 29, 1992 at St. Mark's AME Church in Milwaukee, Wisconsin. Wallace Cheatham conducted the Nathaniel Dett Chorus, with Evelyn and Byron Jones as soloists. It is dedicated to Nimrod and Clara Allen.

WAILING WOMAN   *1946*   *10 min.*

This work is scored for full orchestra, mixed chorus and soprano soloist, on a text by Verna Arvey. It is an emotional response to a dance recital by a Jewish dancer interpreting the Psalms and an expression of the causes and sympathies which should unite Jews and Negroes. It was premiered on April 21, 1991 in Stephens Auditorium in Ames, Iowa. Kirk Smith conducted and Robert Molison directed the choir, assisted by the Iowa State University Orchestra and Chorus.

FROM A LOST CONTINENT   *1948*   *15 min.*

A. *Song of Worship*

I - to - a me u - la Co - de Ra - mo____

B. *Song for Dancers*

Go - de - la - bi   Te - wa - wa   Go - de - la - go___

C. *Song of Yearning*

So - lu - na Ti de Ron - di - mo,   Lo - wa ne.   Ro

D. *Song of Magic*

Do - wa can - i - le di - mo,   Lo - me San - e - di ya - ro,

Inspired by the composer's interest in the legend of the continent of Mu, which was purported to have sunk into the Pacific Ocean thousands of years ago, this is his concept of what the music on Mu may have sounded like. Words in the text were replaced by syllables to create the sense of a lost language. The piece has four parts: "Song of Worship," "Song for Dancers," "Song of Yearning," and "Song of Magic." First performed in its entirety with piano and chorus on May 22, 1953, by the Choral Guild of San Jose (California) under the direction of LeRoy V. Brant. First performed with orchestra and chorus over the I.N.R. (Flemish division) in Brussels on March 27, 1955. Dedicated to the Gordons of Berkeley.

THE LITTLE SONG THAT WANTED TO BE A SYMPHONY
1953   19 min.

A. Theme

B. Variation I--Indian

C. Variation V--Afro-American

Plaintively

D. Variation VI--Italian American

Animated

A children's story for orchestra, women's trio, and a narrator, this piece was written in order to impress upon children the need for brotherhood. Verna Arvey's text tells the story of a little song, only four notes long, which gives up his grand dream of becoming a symphony in order to help children from all over the world. The cultural idioms represented in the piece are: American Indian, Bayou dwellers, Oriental, Latin-American, Afro-American, Italian-American, Big City Youth, and Mountain Folk. It was first performed by Theodore Russell and the Jackson (Mississippi) Symphony Orchestra on February 15, 1955. Published by CFI.

A PSALM FOR THE LIVING   *1954*   *10 min.*

A. Theme 1

Moderately slow

Our Fath - er,   Who art   on earth   Hal - low - ed be Thy   name——

B. Theme 2

It is Thy   hand——   That builds our   brid - ges,   Our fac' - tries

Scored for chorus and piano or chorus and orchestra, this piece is an expression of the composer's belief that God is not dormant, but works actively in our lives. It is based on a text by Verna Arvey and dedicated to the composer's mother-in-law, Dr. Bessie Arvey. The choral parts (S.A.T.B.) are available for sale from Bourne, but the orchestral parts for reduced orchestra are available only on a rental basis.

A. *Pastorale*

Wood - land path - ways stretched a - head,___ Nev - er end - ing.___

B. *Romance*

My heart was search - ing for some - one yet un - known.

C. *Lullaby*

Sleep,___ my child, Trust - ing heart!___ You will

wake with the first faint com - ing of dawn!_____

D. *Paean*

March on - ward,___ World___ Ju - bi - lant! Sing to the glad day

of your vic - to - ry,

A song cycle for soprano and orchestra, with a text by Verna Arvey, which was commissioned by the Southside Conference Educational Fund for Mattiwilda Dobbs. The piece describes a woman's passage from girlhood to motherhood and eventually to a love of all mankind, and it has four parts: a) "Pastorale" (carefree youngster), b) "Romance" (love of a mate), c) "Lullaby" (love of a child), and d) "Paean" (awareness of brotherhood and love of all mankind). The work is dedicated to the memory of the composer's son-in-law, Larry Headlee, who died in a submarine accident in 1970.

ENNANGA *1958*   *15 min.*

A.

B.

C.

A harp suite for harp and orchestra, harp and piano, or harp string quartet. The word "Ennanga" is the name of an African harp. This suite has three movements and was inspired by African themes, though the themes actually used are original. It was first performed at the Westside Jewish Community Center in Los Angeles on October 12, 1958 with Lois Adele Craft on the harp and Verna Arvey at the piano. Lois Craft, to whom the piece is dedicated, said of it: "For me, the three movements speak of the development of life in the primitive world. In the first movement, with its percussive wildness, the listener gets a glimpse of the danger and rhythm of the jungle, the snakes and tigers and dense, dark undergrowth. The second movement is more spiritual, bringing into view the green beauty of ferns and grasses, the calm and peaceful water. The final segment brings out the magnificence of the environment, and the joy." It was reviewed as being "pleasantly melodic and, in feeling, related to the Negro Spiritual. The content has drive and manages to sound convincing."

A. *Prologue*

B. *Evocation*

We greet— the dawn - ing day! We hail— the ris - ing sun!

C. *Interlude*

D. *Call to Battle*

Spears a - loft, we rush in - to war, un - a - fraid!

E. *Interlude*

F. *Judgment*

Hear they come— the stran - gers want - ing our gold and our land!

G. *Interlude*

H. *Elegy*

A work for bass-baritone soloist and orchestra which describes the glory and fall of the Aztec Empire, with a text by Verna Arvey. It was written at the specific request of Jerome Hines, who later caused the composer much sadness when he rejected the work. The sections are: "Prologue" (spoken), "Evocation" (sung), "Interlude" (spoken), "Call to Battle" (sung), "Interlude" (spoken), "Judgment" (spoken), "Interlude" (spoken), and "Elegy" (sung). The world premiere of this piece took place on April 22, 1990 in the Holy Family Church in Grand Forks, North Dakota. It was performed by the Grand Forks Symphony under the direction of John Deal, with Herbert V.R.P. Jones as soloist.

CHRISTMAS IN THE WESTERN WORLD (LAS PASCUAS)
1967   20 min.

For voices and string orchestra, or string quartet and piano, or simply for voices and piano. Nine of the songs in this compilation are adapted from authentic Christmas folk tunes from various countries in the Western Hemisphere, while the tenth, the climactic one, is an original William Grant Still song with text by Verna Arvey. Titles of the individual sections are: "A Maiden was Adoring God, the Lord", "Ven, Niño Divino", "Aguinaldo," "Jesous Ahatonhia," "Tell Me, Shepherdess," "De Virgin Mary Had a Baby Boy," "Los Reyes Magos," "La Piñata," "Glad Christmas Bells," and "Sing, Shout, Tell the Story!" No record was made of this piece's first performance after publication by Peer-Music, but it has become a holiday favorite over the years.

WORKS FOR BAND

FANFARE FOR THE 99th FIGHTER SQUADRON   *1945*   *1 min.*

Scored for wind instruments, this short musical tribute was premiered by Leopold Stokowski and the Los Angeles Philharmonic Orchestra in the Hollywood Bowl on July 22, 1945.

FROM THE DELTA   *1945*   *8 min.*

A. *Work Song*

B. *Spiritual*

C. *Dance*

Scored for full band and for symphonic band (the first movement is also scored for orchestra), this suite has three segments: "Work Song," "Spiritual," and "Dance."   First performed on June 17, 1947 by Richard Franko Goldman and the Goldman Band at the Central Park Mall Concert

270

in New York City. The composer said, "This is the first time that I have tried to express in music the romance of the Delta country in my native state of Mississippi."

TO YOU, AMERICA! *1951* *11 min.*

A.

B.

This piece was commissioned by the United States Military Academy for the Sesquicentennial Celebration at West Point and is dedicated to Col. Francis E. Resta and the USMA Band, for whom it was written. First performed on February 17, 1952 by the United States Military Academy Band at West Point, the composer conducting. That same year it was awarded the Freedoms Foundation Award in Valley Forge, Pennsylvania. In describing the piece, the composer said, "Musically speaking, it is a development of a single theme, energetic at the beginning and progressing to a majestic, chorale-like Finale, pointing to a glorious national destiny." Published by Peer-Music.

FOLK SUITE FOR BAND *1963* *8 min.*

A.

B.

C.

An arrangement of four Negro Spirituals for symphonic band: "Get On Board, Little Children," "Deep River," "The Old Ark's a Moverin," and "Sinner, Please Don't Let This Harvest Pass." First performed by the Los Angeles Bureau of Music Symphonic Band at MacArthur Park, Los Angeles on August 18, 1963, Dale Eymann conducting. Published by Bourne.

STRING QUARTET MUSIC

LYRIC STRING QUARTET   *1960*   *9 min.*

A quartet in three movements which was later discarded by the composer, as he felt it was inadequate. The movements are: a) Moderately (the sentimental one), b) Moderately slow (the quiet one--based on an Inca melody), c) Moderately fast (the jovial one). An arrangement of this piece is available for four saxophones, done by Rudy Volkmann. Dedicated to the composer's friend, Joachim Chassman.

LITTLE FOLK SUITES #1-5 from the WESTERN HEMISPHERE

1968   17 min.

Composed for string quartet. Each of the five suite comprises arrangements of two folk songs of the Americas:

Suite #1
a. Salangadou (U.S.A., Creole)
b. El Capotin (U.S.A., Early California)
Suite #2
a. El Nido (Argentina)
b. Sweet Betsy from Pike (U.S.A.)
Suite #3
a. Aurore Pradere and Tant Sirop est Doux (U.S.A. and Martinique)
b. Wade in the Water (U.S.A.)
Suite #4
a. Los Indios and Yaravi (Brazil; Peru)
b. The Crawdad Song (U.S.A.)
Suite #5
a. Tutu Maramba (Brazil)
b. La Varsoviana (U.S.A., Spanish Colonial)

These suites are available from William Grant Still Music.

MIXED CHAMBER WORKS

FOUR INDIGENOUS PORTRAITS   *1956*   *10 min.*

A. *North American Negro*

B. *South American Negro*

C. *South American Indian*

D. *North American Indian*

A chamber suite for flute and string quartet, consisting of four sections: a) North American Negro (an original theme in the style of a Spiritual), b) South American Negro (based on Brazilian Negro themes), c) South American Indian (based on Peruvian and Brazilian themes), and d) North American Indian (an original theme in the style of American Indian folk music). This piece was eventually discarded by the composer as inadequate.

A LOOK AT JAZZ   *1922?   Undetermined*
An early work, this is an arrangement of jazz works for piano, guitar, strings, woodwinds, banjo, and percussion, also called "Songs: A Medley."

SONGS: A MEDLEY   *1927?   Undetermined*
Eight songs arranged for strings, piano, saxophones, clarinet, trumpet, drums, guitar, and banjo. The songs are: "Song of the Rivermen," "Slave Chant," "Oh! Dem Golden Slippers," "I'm Goin' Where Nobody Knows My Name," "Medley of Ain't Misbehavin' and Sweet Georgia Brown," "Some of These Days," "Love Will Find a Way," and "St. Louis Blues."

GET ON BOARD   *1927?   Undetermined*
An arrangement of the popular spiritual for flute, oboe, bassoon, piano, and string quartet.

MINIATURES   *1948   12 min.*
A suite for flute, oboe, and piano (a bassoon part by Fred Thayer is also available from WGSM). It is based on folk tunes of the Western Hemisphere and consists of five parts, entitled: a) I Ride An Old Paint (U.S.A.), b) Adolorido (Mexico), c) Jesus Is A Rock In A Weary Land (U.S.A.), d) Yaravi (Peru), and e) Frog Went A Courtin' (U.S.A.). Dedicated to Sir John and Lady Barbirolli. Published by the Oxford University Press.

SENTIMENTAL SONG   *1953   9 min.*
A work for chamber orchestra, discovered in the composer's papers after his death, for 1-1-2-0, 2-1-2-0, harp, celesta and strings.

FOLK SUITE #1   *1962   9 min.*
A chamber suite for flute, piano and string quartet, this is the first of four suites made up of adaptations of folk songs from various cultures. The three segments in this suite are: a) Bambalele (Brazil), b) Sometimes I Feel Like A Motherless Child (U.S.A.), and c) Two Hebraic Songs (Israel). This work is published by Peer-Music in New York.

FOLK SUITE #2   *1962   9 min.*
A chamber suite for flute, clarinet, 'cello, and piano, this is the second of the four Folk Suites, each made up of adaptations of folk songs from various cultures. The sections of this suite are: a) El Zapatero (U.S.A., Early California), b) Mo'le (Peru), c) Mom'zelle Zizi (U.S.A.,Louisiana),

and d) Peruvian Melody (Inca). This work is available from William Grant Still Music.

FOLK SUITE #3 *1962* *5 min.*

A chamber suite for flute, oboe, bassoon, and piano. This piece is the third of four suites made of arrangements of various folk songs from the Americas. The three segments of this suite are: a) An Inca Dance (Peru), b) An Inca Song (Peru), and c) Bow and Arrow Dance Song (U.S.A., Santo Domingo Pueblo, New Mexico). This piece is distributed by William Grant Still Music.

FOLK SUITE #4 *1962* *5.5 min.*

A chamber suite for flute, clarinet, 'cello, and piano, this is the fourth, and final, of the Folk Suites, each comprising adaptations of folk songs from the Western Hemisphere. The sections of this suite are: a) El Monigote (Venezuela), b) Anda Buscando de Rosa en Rosa (Mexico), c) Tayeras (Brazil). This work is published by William Grant Still Music.

VIGNETTES *1962* *11.5 min*

A suite for oboe, bassoon, and piano. Composed for Lady Evelyn Barbirolli, this piece has five sections, each representing folk idioms in the United States and South America. The five sections are: a) Winnebago Moccasin Game (U.S.A., Wisconsin), b) Carmela (U.S.A., Early California), c) Peruvian Melody (South America), d) Clinch Mountain (U.S.A., Southern Mountain Region), and e) Garde Piti Mulet La (also known as M'sieu Banjo; U.S.A., Louisiana).

LITTLE FOLK SUITE from the WESTERN HEMISPHERE
1968 *2.5 min.*

For brass quintet, this suite contains two sections: a) Where Shall I Be When the Great Trumpet Sounds? (U.S.A.) and b) En Roulant Ma Boule (French Canadian).

WORKS FOR SOLO
INSTRUMENTS AND PIANO

SUITE FOR VIOLIN AND PIANO   *1943*   *15 min.*

A. *African Dancer*

B. *Mother and Child*

C. *Gamin'*

Each movement in the three movements in this composition was inspired by the artwork of a Negro artist: "African Dancer" (the first movement) by Richard Barthe's dancing figure; "Mother and Child" by Sargent Johnson's touching portrait; and "Gamin'" by Augusta Savage's mischievous boy. It was first performed by Louis Kaufman, to whom it is dedicated, in Boston on March 15, 1944 and in New York's Town Hall on March 18, 1944, when it was said that "the music assumed the character of the subjects and was an adroit and interesting contribution to modern compositions." Also scored for orchestra. This suite has become one of the composer's most beloved works.

INCANTATION AND DANCE   *1945*   *5 min.*

This piece for oboe and piano was developed after a suggestion by Loyd Rathbun, principal oboist of the Los Angeles Philharmonic Orchestra, that the composer write something for the oboe. It was first performed by Rathbun and has been widely played since. It is dedicated to Betty and Loyd Rathbun and is published by CFI.

PASTORELA   *1946*   *11 min.*

A.

B.

C.

This piece for violin and piano was composed after a suggestion by Louis Kaufman that Still should write a "poem" for violin. The composer described this piece as "a tone picture of a California landscape, peaceful but exciting, arousing feelings of languor in some of its aspects and of animation in others, presenting an overall effect of unity in its variety." Premiered by Louis Kaufman in Town Hall, New York City on March 14, 1947. This work has also been scored for violin and orchestra and is dedicated to Samuel Marti.

CARMELA   *1949?*   *Undetermined*
A work in the Spanish-American idiom for violin or viola and piano, written for Louis Kaufman. An orchestral setting by Dr. Marshall Fine is also available.

A lyric work written for classical saxophone as a romantic instrument, this is one of Still's most popular pieces. It is dedicated to Sigurd Rascher, and was written at his request. It was originally intended as the first movement of a suite. However, the other movements were never completed. It is published by Bourne, and the arrangement for trombone by Douglas Yeo is available from the International Music Catalog. Orchestral parts are available from WGSM.

WORKS FOR PIANO

THREE VISIONS   *1935*   *11 min.*

A. *Dark Horsemen*

B. *Summerland*

C. *Radiant Pinnacle*

A work for piano in three parts: "Dark Horsemen," "Summerland," and "Radiant Pinnacle." These pieces have been widely played and were probably first performed by Verna Arvey in Los Angeles in 1936. Arrangements of "Summerland" are also available for small and full orchestras, for two pianos, for violin and piano, for chamber group, and for organ (arranged by Edouard Nies-Berger).

QUIT DAT FOOL'NISH   *1938*   *2 min.*

A short, humorous piece, dedicated to the composer's mischievous dog, Shep. There is no record of the first performance, but it was probably premiered by Verna Arvey in Los Angeles. There are also arrangements for orchestra, for saxophone and piano, for flute and piano, and for chamber group.

SWANEE RIVER   1939   4 min.

An arrangement of the popular song for piano, written for the book *29 Modern Piano Interpretations of "Swanee River,"* published by Robbins. A choral arrangement of this piece was made by Dana Paul Perna for Bardic Editions in Scotland.

SEVEN TRACERIES   1939   17 min.

A. *Cloud Cradles*

B. *Mystic Pool*

C. *Muted Laughter*

D. *Out of the Silence*

281

E. *Woven Silver*

F. *Wailing Dawn*

G. *A Bit of Wit*

A piano suite fashioned after seven tone poems: a) "Cloud Cradles" (dedicated to Helen and Allan), b) "Mystic Pool" (dedicated to Josephine Harreld), c) "Muted Laughter" (dedicated to Jessie, Marge, Adrian, and Charles), d) "Out of the Silence" (dedicated to William Duncan Allen), e) "Woven Silver" (dedicated to Kay Swift), f) "Wailing Dawn" (dedicated to Militza and James), and g) "A Bit of Wit" (dedicated to Florence and James). Verna Arvey described this work as "abstractions bearing the imprint of mysticism . . . Each has the delicacy of a rare print; each is a mood from another world expressed with an almost Oriental subtlety. Each is based on the simplest of motifs, developed to the extent of its own possibilities. The individual titles for the compositions were suggested to the composer by the music--the music did not arise from the titles." "Out of the Silence" has been arranged for harp, flute, piano and strings, and for string quintet and piano. Published by WGSM.

A. *Phantom Chapel*

B. *Fairy Knoll*

Scored for piano solo or for reduced orchestra, this suite has two parts: "Phantom Chapel" and "Fairy Knoll." It was first performed in its entirety on November 29, 1946 by the St. Louis Symphony Orchestra under the baton of Vladimir Golschmann. The St. Louis *Globe-Democrat* commented, "What is not a commonplace in concerts is great music by a Negro composer . . . So simple, so sincere, so colorful. So dramatic in its texture of tone!" "Phantom Chapel" is dedicated to Dolores Calvin and "Fairy Knoll" is dedicated to Phillippa Schuyler. The orchestral version is rented by MCA, while the piano music is distributed by WGSM.

MARIONETTE   *1946*   *1 min.*

A short sketch for piano written to be included in the book *U.S.A. 1946*, published by Belwin. Dedicated to Adelaide and Kenneth Winstead. Now published by MCA.

A. *Camel*

Moderately slow

B. *Bear*

Moderately slow

C. *Horse*

Moderately fast

D. *Lamb*

Playfully

E. *Elephant*

Ponderously

A suite of five short sketches for young pianists. Each piece describes a different animal: "Camel," "Bear," "Horse," "Lamb," and "Elephant." Included in the book *Music For Early Childhood*, published by Silver-Burdett, for the New Music Horizons School textbook series.

RING PLAY *1962*   *1 min.*

A teaching piece for young pianists, written for the Bernice Frost book *Twentieth Century Piano Music, Book IIB*, published by J. Fischer. Now published by WGSM.

PRELUDE *1971*   *6 min.*

A piano work written for the *New Scribner Music Library, IV*, edited by Howard Hanson for Charles Scribner's Sons, 1972. Now available from WGSM.

WORKS FOR ORGAN

REVERIE   *1962*   *3 min.*

A short organ piece written for the American Guild of Organists' *Prelude Book*, published by Avant Music. First performed on March 12, 1962 by Robert Pritchard at the Pasadena (California) Presbyterian Church. Now published by Western International Music in Colorado.

ELEGY   *1963*   *3 min.*

An organ work written for the West Coast Chapters of the American Guild of Organists. Published by WGSM.

286

WORKS FOR ACCORDIAN

ARIA   *1960*   *5 min.*

Commissioned by the American Accordionists' Association in 1959, this piece was inspired by the composer's friendship with Sidney B. Dawson and Myron Floren, both accordionists. He developed a great respect for the accordian as a classical instrument of great potential and virtuosity. He enlisted the aid of these two men to study the instrument and write for it with credibility. The analysis of the piece is as follows: a) Theme I, b) Theme II (extended by development), c) Theme III, d) A Codetta (in place of a transition), e) Theme II (strongly contrasted and extended by development), f) Re-transition, g) Theme I, h) Coda. First performed by Myron Floren at a Town Hall Recital, New York City on May 15, 1960.

LILT   *1960*   *4 min.*

A second work for accordian written right after the "Aria," also at the urging of the American Accordianists' Association and the AAA Director, Elsie Bennett. This piece is not technically difficult, as it was intended to be a "teaching piece."

WORKS FOR VOICE
OR VOICES AND PIANO

NO MATTER WHAT YOU DO   *1916*   *Undetermined*
An early work for solo voice and piano, with lyrics by Still's first wife, Grace Bundy. It was eventually discarded by the composer, but is still available from Handy Bros.

GOOD NIGHT   *1917*   *5 min.*

A.

The lark is si-lent in his nest, the

B.

A piece for solo voice and piano, written while the composer was studying at Oberlin College, and based on a poem by Paul Laurence Dunbar. First performed by Revella Hughes at St. Mark's Hall in New York on October 30, 1921. The manuscript is lost, unless a search at Oberlin discovers it.

BROWN BABY   *1923*   *3 min.*

Do you sup - pose_____ I ev - er will know_____ Brown Ba - by

A popular song, with lyrics by Paul Henry, which the composer wrote under the pseudonym of Willy M. Grant, as he did not wish to be known for his popular music.

MEMPHIS MAN   *1923*   *3 min.*

Mem - phis   man___ the lov - in' - est man___ I   know___

___   Loves you like you   nev- er lov'd__ be - fore

A popular song, with lyrics by Paul Henry, written under the pseudonym of Willy M. Grant, as the composer wished to be remembered for his classical works only.

WINTER'S APPROACH   *1926*   3 min.

De   sun hit shine___ and de wind hit blow,___

A short song for soprano and piano, based on a poem by Paul Laurence Dunbar. Published by G. Schirmer in 1928, this piece is now available in the Schirmer Colletion, *Romantic American Art Songs*.

BREATH OF A ROSE   *1926*   *5 min.*

Love is like dew___ on li - lacs at dawn___

An original song for soprano and piano, this lovely piece is based on a poem by Langston Hughes. Published by G. Schirmer in 1928, the piece was included in Schirmer's *A New Anthology of American Songs* which was published in 1942, and, more recently, in Schirmer's *Romantic American Art Songs*.

TWELVE NEGRO SPIRITUALS   *1937*   *25 min.*

Two volumes of Negro spirituals arranged for solo voice and piano. The twelve songs are:

a. I Got a Home in-a Dat Rock
b. All God's Chillun Got Shoes
c. Camp Meetin'
d. Didn't My Lord Deliver Daniel?
e. Good News

f. Great Day
g. Gwinter Sing All Along De Way
h. Keep Me F'om Sinkin' Down
i. Lis'en to de Lam's
j. Lawd, I Wants To Be a Christian
k. Mah Lawd Says He's Goin' to Rain Down Fiah
l. Peter, Go Ring Dem Bells

These songs were originally published by Handy Brothers in 1937, along with twelve stories by Ruby Berkeley Goodwin, and they are still available from Handy Bros.

KEEP ME FROM SINKIN' DOWN   *1937*   *5 min.*

An arrangement of a Negro spiritual for SATB and piano. (A solo version of this piece is included in the *Twelve Negro Spirituals*, published by Handy Bros.)

EV'RY TIME I FEEL THE SPIRIT   *1938*   *2 min.*

An arrangement of a traditional Negro spiritual for solo voice and piano. Published by Galaxy.

CARIBBEAN MELODIES   *1941*   *60 min.*

A collection of songs from the Caribbean Islands for solo voices, chorus, piano, and percussion, which were arranged by Still for Zora Neale Hurston. The islands represented are Jamaica, New Providence, Cat Island, Fox Hill, Eleuthera, Abaco, and Haiti. The songs included are:

a. Hand A' Bowl
b. Baintown
c. Two Banana
d. Woman Sweeter Than Man?
e. Peas and Rice
f. Bellamina
g. Mama, I Saw a Sailboat
h. Ah, La Sa Wu!
i. Evalina
j. Doo Ma
k. Hela Grand Pere
l. Going to My Old Home
m. Mister Brown
n. Ten Poun' Ten
o. Do An' Nannie
p. Eh, Bi Nango
q. Carry Him Along

The concluding song, "Carry Him Along," was published separately by Oliver Ditson in octavo form for SATB and is now distributed by Theodore Presser. The remaining songs are also available from Presser.

HERE'S ONE   *1941*   *4 min.*

One of Still's most popular vocal works, this is an arrangement of a Negro spiritual for solo voice and piano. Versions of this piece are also available for voice and string quartet, violin and piano, and chorus. The choral version is published by Presser.

BAYOU HOME   *1944*   *3 min.*

For solo voice and piano, text by Verna Arvey.

THE VOICE OF THE LORD   *1945*   *5 min.*

A setting of the 29th Psalm, "Mizmor Ledovid," or "The Voice of the Lord," for tenor, chorus, and organ. It was premiered at the Park Avenue Synagogue in New York City on May 10, 1946 for the Sabbath Eve service, by the Cantor David J. Putterman and choir. It was published in octavo edition in 1946 by Witmar, then reprinted in a collection of religious works entitled *Synagogue Music by Contemporary Composers* (1951, G. Schirmer). Dedicated to Dr. Edwin R. Embree, it is now available from WGSM.

SONGS OF SEPARATION   *1946*   *12 min.*

A. *Idolatry*

B. *Poeme*

C. *Parted*

She wrapped her soul in a lace of lies with a prime de-ceit to

D. *If You Should Go*

Love leave me like the light, the gent-ly pass-ing day;

E. *I Am A Black Pierrot*

I am a black pi-er-rot:___ She did not love me, so

A set of art songs for voice and piano based on the poems of five Negro poets, each one dealing with estranged love: the poems are "Idolatry" (Arna Bontemps), "Poéme" (Philippe-Thoby Marcelin), "Parted" (Paul Laurence Dunbar), "If You Should Go (Countee Cullen), and "I Am A Black Pierrot" (Langston Hughes). First performed by Herta Glaz on February 19, 1946 on the "Concert Time" program over the ABC Network, with no reviews. Later, on May 18, 1970, Marilyn Tucker in the San Francisco *Chronicle* described the pieces as "art songs rich with the freedoms of beautiful melody, dramatic force and lyric intensity." There are also versions of this work for voice and orchestra or voice and string quartet. Dedicated to Frieta Shaw, Hannah Bierhoff, Edyth and Eugene Pearson, Joyce Hansen, and Muriel Rahn.

MISSISSIPPI   *1948*   *3 min.*

Might - y name,— Mis - sis - sip - pi,—

This work for voices and piano was written for Mark Warnow and the United States Army's "Sound Off" program in the American Broadcasting Network. Originally titled "Mississippi March," this is a march-like piece

292

with lyrics by Verna Arvey. Premiered on the "Sound Off" program over the ABC Radio Network on July 26, 1948 (a U.S. Army broadcast).

SIPPING CIDER THROUGH A STRAW   *1940/50's?*   *Undetermined*
A humorous traditional song arranged for SATB and piano.

ARKANSAS   *1940/50's?*   *Undetermined*

A song for solo voice and piano, with a text by Verna Arvey, honoring the composer's home state.

LITTLE DAVID, PLAY ON YOUR HARP *1940/50's?*   *Undetermined*
An arrangement of the popular spiritual for SATB and piano, written in honor of the composer's maternal grandmother, Anne Fambro, for whom it was a favorite.

STEAL AWAY TO JESUS   *1940/50's?*   *Undetermined*
An arrangement of the traditional Negro spiritual for SAT, with soprano and piano soloists.

WERE YOU THERE?   *1940/50's?*   *Undetermined*
An arrangement of the popular Negro spiritual for SATB, or solo voice, and piano.

LAMENT   *1950*   *3 min.*

An original song for women's trio and piano, based on a text by Verna Arvey. Published in Silver Burdett's book, *American Music Horizons*, edited by McConathy, Morgan, and others in 1951. This volume was part of the *New Music Horizons Series*.

UP THERE _____ _1950_ _____ _2 min._

One of these days I'm gon-na climb a high moun-tain!

An original song for solo voice and piano, with a text by Verna Arvey. It was written for the school text, *World Music Horizons*, edited by McConathy, Morgan for Silver Burdett in 1951. This text is part of the *New Music Horizons Series*. The theme of the piece encourages young people to harbor "dreams of a lofty future."

SINNER, PLEASE DON'T LET THIS HARVEST PASS

_1950_ _____ _3 min._

A graceful arrangement of a Negro spiritual which was originally published in the textbook, *Let Music Ring*, edited by Peter W. Dykema and distributed by the California State Department of Education. It is written for acapella choir (SATB).

SONG FOR THE VALIANT _____ _1952_ _____ _3 min._

Martially

Firm 'gainst the odds stand I_____ Strong 'gainst the on-

A companion to *Song for the Lonely*, this piece speaks of the composer's success in overcoming obstacles through his faith in God. An original song, scored for orchestra and solo voice or voice and piano, with a text by Verna Arvey. Dedicated to Jerome Hines.

MEN OF THE ARMY _____ _1952_ _____ _2 min._

First_____ in war, first_____ in glo - ry;_____

A tribute to the United States Army for solo voice and piano.

SONG FOR THE LONELY   *1953*   *4 min.*

Rain-drops,— fresh from the mist, dis-turb the still-ness of my thoughts

An original song for voice and piano, with a text by Verna Arvey, also arranged for reduced orchestra and high or low voice. This song is an expression of the composer's deep sorrow over his inability to get his music performed or published, and the "long-lost dream" mentioned in the song refers to his dream of having his operas widely performed. This piece is dedicated to, and was first performed by, Marie Powers, who sang the role of Azelia in his opera, *Troubled Island.*

GRIEF   *1953*   *3 min.*

Weep-ing an-gel with pin-ions trail-ing And head bowed low in your hands

An original art song for solo voice and piano, based on a text by LeRoy V. Brant. First published by the Oliver Ditson Company, and later included in *An Anthology of Art Songs by Black American Composers*, edited by Willis Patterson in 1977, which was published by Edward B. Marks Music Corp. Now included in G. Schirmer's *Romantic American Art Songs.*

I FEEL LIKE MY TIME AIN'T LONG   *1956*   *3 min.*
An ethereal, atmospheric arrangement of the traditional Negro spiritual for SATB and piano. It is available from Theodore Presser.

IS THERE ANYBODY HERE?   *1956*   *3 min.*
An arrangement of the lively Negro spiritual for SATB and piano. It is sold by Theodore Presser.

CITADEL   *1956*   *2 min.*

Love can lace leaves to-geth-er and make them proof a-gainst the world,

A work for voice and piano or voice and chamber ensemble, this piece was eventually discarded by the composer, but resurrected by WGSM. It is based on a poem by Virginia Brasier Perlee.

FROM THE HEARTS OF WOMEN *1959* *9 min.*

A. *Little Mother*

B. *Midtide*

C. *Coquette*

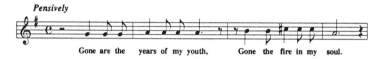

D. *Bereft*

A song cycle for voice and piano, this is the composer's tribute to women, and each section deals with a different aspect of the feminine personality. It has four parts with text by Verna Arvey: "Little Mother" (a child sings to her doll), "Midtide" (a women reaches middle age), "Coquette" (a young girl flirts), "Bereft" (a mother at the bedside of her dying son). First performed by Pearl Whitelow and an instrumental ensemble at a Los Angeles County Museum concert on February 19, 1962.

THREE RHYTHMIC SPIRITUALS *1961* *9 min.*
Arrangements of three popular Negro spirituals for chorus (SATB) and piano: "Lord, I Looked Down the Road," "Hard Trials," and "Holy Spirit,

Don't You Leave Me." Also scored for reduced orchestra and solo voice. These works are published by Bourne, with orchestral parts sold by WGSM.

ALL THAT I AM   *1965*   *2 min.*

All that I am, all I ev- er can be I owe to You, Lord, for You have mold- ed me.

An original hymn for SATB (with orchestration by Ray Anthony Delia) expressing the composer's belief in and his gratitude to God. First performed by the cast of *Minette Fontaine*, at the closing of the first performance of that opera on October 22, 1984. Text by Verna Arvey. Now published by Cambria Publications, and distributed by WGSM.

YOUR WORLD   *1968*   *3 min.*

Your world_ is as big as you make it I know_ for I used to a- bide

This piece, for solo voice and piano, is a setting of a poem by Georgia Douglas Johnson. It was written for a textbook called *The Magic of Music, VI*, edited by Walters, Wersen, and others (1971, Ginn and Co.). It is now available from WGSM.

GOD'S GOIN' TO SET THIS WORLD ON FIRE   *1968*   *1 min.*
An arrangement of a traditional Negro spiritual for solo voice and piano. Published by Holt, Rinehart, and Winston in the educational textbook, *Exploring Music, VII*, edited by Beth Landis.

HIKING SONG
Masters and information on the song have been lost.

FOUR OCTAVO SONGS   *1971*   *10 min.*

A. *Toward Distant Shores*

A man in life con - fronts the sea and prays, "Oh Lord, How vast Thy hand."

Four songs arranged for SATB and piano, three of which are traditional Negro spirituals and one of which ("Toward Distant Shores") is based on a poem by Judith Anne Still, the composer's daughter. The titles of the songs are: "Ev'ry Time I Feel The Spirit," "The Blind Man," "Toward Distant Shores," and "Where Shall I Be?" Available in octavo form from Gemini Press.

MINORITIES AND MAJORITIES   *1971*   *Undetermined*

A work for SATB, mixed voices, and piano, which expresses the need for racial understanding, and celebrates the common cause of minorities in the nation. With a text by Verna Arvey, it was originally part of the "Four Octavo Songs." First published in the ABC Choral Art Series, this piece was not reprinted by Gemini Press. It is now available from WGSM.

MY BROTHER AMERICAN   *1971*   *2 min.*

A piece written for the seventh grade music text called *Sound, Beat and Feeling* (1972, American Book Co.), edited by Choate, Kaplan, and Standifer. This book was part of the *New Dimensions in Music Series* for the public schools. The lyrics, by Verna Arvey, emphasize the need for brotherhood among all people.

RISING TIDE   *1939*   *Undetermined*
For chorus. Also known as "Victory Tide." See the listing under "Song of a City" in the orchestral works section with added vocalists.

WE SANG OUR SONGS   *1971*   *3 min.*

This work for SATB and piano was commissioned by the Fisk Jubilee
Singers to celebrate the Fisk University Centennial on October 6, 1971.
The lyrics, by Verna Arvey, pay tribute to the Negroes who broke barriers
of color in the post-Civil War era.

SONG OF THE HUNTER <u>1968</u> <u>1 min.</u>

An original song for solo voice and piano, with a text by Verna Arvey,
written for the textbook *Exploring Music (The Junior Book)*, edited by
Beth Landis for Holt, Rinehart, and Winston. Rights to the piece were
later returned to the composer.

NOTATIONS

♦ Full Orchestra, with some exceptions, means: Strings, 3 flutes (interchangeable with piccolo), 2 oboes, English Horn, 2 clarinets, bass clarinet, 2 bassoons, 4 horns, 3 trumpets, 3 trombones, tuba, timpani, percussion, harp, and celesta.

♦ Reduced Orchestra, generally speaking, means that the woodwinds and brasses are in parts.

Manuscripts noted as missing or which William Grant Still Music does not have, may be on file in the Library of Congress.

PUBLISHERS

American Music Edition, Publishers - 263 E. 7th Street, New York, NY 10009, or, see **Theodore Presser**.

Belwin-Mills Publishing Corp. - 25 Deshon Drive, Melville, NY 11746. Belwin-Mills is owned by Columbia Pictures in Hialeah, FL, but, for rentals, contact **Theodore Presser**.

Bourne Co., Inc. - 5 W. 37th Street, 6th Floor, New York, NY 10018, (212) 391-4300.

Cambria Publishing - P. O. Box 374, Lomita, CA 90717, (310) 831-1322.

CFI or **Carl Fischer, Inc.** - 62 Cooper Square, New York, NY 10003. (They also operate for the **Eastman School of Music, ESM**.) Call (212) 777-0900, Serious Music Division only.

E. C. Schirmer Music Co. - 138 Ipswich Street, Boston, MA 02215.

Gemini Press, Inc. - Pilgrim Press, Box 390, Otis, MA 01253.

Ginn & Co. - 191 Spring Street, Lexington, MA 02173.

G. Schirmer, Inc. - 225 Park Avenue, South, New York, NY 10003, (212) 254-2100.

Hal Leonard Publishing Corp. - 7777 W. Bluemond Road, Milwaukee, WI 53213, (414) 774-3630. Contact Supervisor, Concert Music Division.

Handy Brothers Music Co. - 1697 Broadway, Room 407, New York, NY 10019.

Holt, Rinehart & Winston - 383 Madison Avenue, New York, NY 10017.

IMC, International Music Catalog - 5 W. 37th Street, New York, NY 10018.

John Church, Theodore Presser, Oliver Ditson - 1 Presser Place, Bryn Mawr, PA 19010, (215) 525-3636. (To obtain orchestral works, contact the Rental Department Manager.)

Marks, Edward B. Marks Music Corp. - See **Hal Leonard** or **Theodore Presser**, or **Belwin-Mills**, (414) 774-3630.

MCA Music Publishing - 1755 Broadway, 8th Floor, New York, NY 10019.

Oliver Ditson - See **John Church**.

Oxford University Press - 2001 Evans Road, Cary, NC 27513, *or* 200 Madison Avenue, New York, NY 10016, (212) 679-7300.

PMC, Peer-Music Co. (Formerly **Southern Music**) - 810 - 7th Avenue, New York, NY 10019, (212) 265-3910. Ask for the Concert Music Division or contact their selling agent, **Theodore Presser**.

Presser, Theodore Presser Co. - See **John Church**.

Robbins Music Corp. (Now **Columbia Pictures Publications**) - 15800 N.W. 48th Avenue, P. O. Box 4340, Hialeah, FL 33014, (305) 620-1500.

Scribners, Charles Scribner's Sons, MacMillan - 866 - 3rd Avenue, New York, NY 10022, (212) 702-2000.

Silver Burdett - 250 James Street, Morristown, NJ 07960, (201) 285-7700.

SMC, Southern Music - P. O. Box 329, San Antonio, TX 78292, (512) 226-8167.

Theodore Presser Co. - See John Church.

WIM, Western International Music, Inc. - 3707 - 65th Avenue, Greeley, CO 80634-9626, (303) 330-6901.

WGSM, William Grant Still Music - 4 South San Francisco, Suite 422, Flagstaff, AZ 86001-5737, (520) 526-9355.

XI

RECORDINGS IN THE WILLIAM GRANT STILL COLLECTION

WILLIAM GRANT STILL
List of Recordings

1940-1941 Scherzo from the AFRO-AMERICAN SYMPHONY, recorded by Howard Hanson and the Eastman-Rochester Symphony Orchestra for Victor Records, #2059-B.

1940-1941 Excerpts from the SEVEN TRACERIES, recorded by Verna Arvey, pianist, for Co-Art Records, #5037A and #5037B.

1941 The Blues from LENOX AVENUE , recorded by Artie Shaw and his orchestra for Victor Records, #27411A and #27411B.

1942 The Flirtation from LENOX AVENUE, played by the Hancock Ensemble under the direction of Loren Powell and issued by the Hancock Foundation at USC, #395.

1942 AND THEY LYNCHED HIM ON A TREE, live broadcast with Leopold Stokowski conducting, a cassette tape issued by the Leopold Stokowski Society, 106 E. Curtis Street, Mount Vernon, OH 43050. #CA11LSSA.

1944 Scherzo from the AFRO-AMERICAN SYMPHONY, recorded by Leopold Stokowski and the All-American Orchestra for Columbia Records, #11992-D.

1948 HERE'S ONE and the Blues from LENOX AVENUE, recorded by Louis Kaufman (violinist) and Annette Kaufman (pianist) in an American album for Vox, #667-A.

1948 Work Song from FROM THE DELTA, recorded by Morton Gould and his symphonic band for Columbia Records, #4519-M.

1950 HERE'S ONE and the Blues from LENOX AVENUE, recorded by Louis Kaufman (violinist) and Annette Kaufman (pianist), was reissued by Concert Hall Records as "Contemporary American Violin Music," #H-1640 and #CHS 1140.

1952 The AFRO-AMERICAN SYMPHONY, recorded by Karl Krueger and the Vienna Opera Orchestra for New Records, Inc. #NRLP105.

1952	Excerpts from the SEVEN TRACERIES, LENOX AVENUE and THREE VISIONS, played by Gordon Manley, pianist, and distributed by Belwin-Mills Publishing Corporation.
1952	TO YOU, AMERICA! recorded by Lt. Col. Francis E. Resta and the West Point Symphonic Band and included in the recordings of the Pittsburgh International Contemporary Music Festival, made by ASCAP for non-commercial use by educational institutions, #CB177.
1959	A tape of the FOURTH SYMPHONY (Autochthonous) available from the National Association of Educational Broadcasters to educators only. Taken from a 1959 UNESCO concert in Denver, the composer conducting. WGSM can make copies.
1960	Suite from the ballet SAHDJI, recorded by Howard Hanson with the Eastman Rochester Orchestra and the Eastman School Chorus for Mercury Records, #MG50257B.
1963	HERE'S ONE, recorded by Bill Mann (tenor) and Paul Mickelson (organist) for Word Records, Inc., #W-3061 LP.
1964(?)	HERE'S ONE, recorded by Robert McFerrin, baritone, for Riverside Records, #812.
1965	The AFRO-AMERICAN SYMPHONY, recorded by Karl Krueger and the Royal Philharmonic Orchestra of London in an album called "Music in America," #MIA-118, released by the Society for the Preservation of the American Musical Heritage.
1965	The AFRO-AMERICAN SYMPHONY, as recorded by Karl Krueger and reissued by the Library of Congress on CD or cassette, #CD-106 or CA-106, sold by WGSM.
1968	GOD'S GOIN' TO SET THIS WORLD ON FIRE, recorded on a demonstration record to go with the Exploring Music Junior Book, published by Holt, Rinehart and Winston, 1968, 383 Madison Avenue, New York, NY 10017.
1970	FESTIVE OVERTURE, recorded by Arthur Bennett Lipkin and the Royal Philharmonic Orchestra of London, LP #CRI-SD259, Composers' Recordings, Inc. Cassette tapes were also available until 1993.
1970	SONGS OF SEPARATION, recorded by Cynthia Bedford and the Oakland Youth Symphony Orchestra in an album called "The Black

305

Composer in America," #DC7107, Desto Records, CMS Records, Inc. Conducted by Robert Hughes.

1970   THREE VISIONS, played by Natalie Hinderas (pianist) on an album called "Music by Black Composers," #DC7102-3, issued by Desto Records. Later reissued by Composers Recordings, Inc. and available from WGSM.

1971   FROM THE BLACK BELT and DARKER AMERICA, recorded by Siegfried Landau and the Westchester Symphony Orchestra on an LP called "The Contemporary Composer in the U.S.A.," #TV-S34546, Turnabout Records.

1971   Excerpts from Suite #3 from THE AMERICAN SCENE (THE OLD WEST), recorded by the All-State Group of the National Music Camp at Interlochen. Excerpts recorded were "Song of the Plainsmen" and "Sioux Love Song."

1971-72   ENNANGA, recorded by Lois Adele Craft (harpist), Annette Kaufman (pianist), and the Kaufman string quartet; SONGS OF SEPARATION and SONG FOR THE LONELY recorded by Claudine Carlson accompanied by Georgia Akst; DANZAS DE PANAMA recorded by Louis Kaufman, George Berres, Alex Neiman and Terry King; SUITE FOR VIOLIN, PASTORELA, SUMMERLAND, Blues from LENOX AVENUE, CARMELA and HERE'S ONE, all recorded by Louis Kaufman (violinist) and Annette Kaufman (pianist). First issued on LPs, #ORS7152 and #7278, later available on a double cassette, #633, from Orion Records. The string works were later reissued on #WGSM1001.

1972   PLAIN-CHANT FOR AMERICA, recorded by the Paine College Choirs, Augusta, GA, live performance, April 16, 1972, Century Records (#40598).

1972   WE SANG OUR SONGS, as done by the Fisk Jubilee Singers at their 43rd Annual Festival, on an LP called "Eye of the Storm."

1972   The SONGS OF SEPARATION from the Orion Recording of Claudine Carlson, and the SEVEN TRACERIES, a new recording, issued by Music and Arts, P.O. Box 771, Berkeley, CA 94701. Both recordings are CDs. Write for details.

1972(?)   The Blues from LENOX AVENUE, recorded by Verna Arvey (pianist) for an educational kit with two LPs, or cassettes, filmstrips, teacher's guide and visual aids. The kit is called "Pathways to Music: From Jazz to Rock." The WGS Scherzo from the AFRO-

AMERICAN SYMPHONY is presented in a similar kit called "American Composers." Both kits are from Keyboard Publications, P.O. Box 622, Belmont, MA 02178.

1974   The AFRO-AMERICAN SYMPHONY and two arias from HIGHWAY 1, U.S.A., done by the London Symphony Orchestra, Paul Freeman conducting, for Columbia Records, #M32782, the "Black Composers Series," Vol. 2. The series is now available from WGSM.

1974   The ballet SAHDJI, recorded by Paul Freeman and the London Symphony Orchestra, with the Morgan State Choir, for the "Black Composers Series," Columbia #M33433, Vol. 7. The series is now available from WGSM.

1974(?)   LAWD I WANTS TO BE A CHRISTIAN, recorded by John Patton in "Black Spirituals and Art Songs," a Narthex Recording, Minneapolis, MN.

1976   Arrangements by William Grant Still for Paul Whiteman were included in an album called "Happy Feet," recorded by the New England Conservatory Jazz Repertory Orchestra and Gunther Schuller, conductor, on a Golden Crest Record, #CRSQ31043.

1977   AFTER YOU'VE GONE, arranged by Still, on a Publisher's Central Bureau-LP, prepared by the Whiteman Archive at Williams College, MA.

1977   Excerpts from the THREE VISIONS and SEVEN TRACERIES are executed by Ruth Norman in an anthology of American Black Music, Opus One, #39, available from Opus One, Box 604, Greenville, ME 04441.

1978   SEVEN TRACERIES, performed by Frances Walker (pianist) for Orion Records, #ORS78305/306.

1981   GRIEF, recorded by Susan Matthews for the University of Michigan, is also sold in the two-LP set called "Art Songs by Black American Composers," #SM0015. Available from WGSM.

1982   The Blues from LENOX AVENUE , recorded by Artie Shaw and his orchestra and reissued by RCA Records, Bluebird Label #AMX2/AXK2-5572, from Vol. IV, "The Complete Artie Shaw," obtainable from RCA, 1133 Avenue of the Americas, New York, NY 10036. (Time-Life LPs issued in 1983.)

307

1982	The piano works KAINTUCK', QUIT DAT FOOL'NISH, BELLS, THREE VISIONS, recorded by Richard Fields for Orion Records, #ORS82442.
1983	LENOX AVENUE, an excerpt from LA GUIABLESSE, and a portion of Still's G-MINOR SYMPHONY, recorded on an LP called "William Grant Still Conducts William Grant Still" by Glendale Records, and now sold as LPs or cassettes by WGSM, #GL8011 or #CAGL8011.
1983?	THREE VISIONS, recorded by Felipe Hall on an LP called "Black American Piano Music," #SM93144, available from Da Camera Schallplaten Records, 10 bis 12 Lameystrasse, Germany, Mannheim.
1984	The THIRD SYMPHONY, excerpts from the FOLK SUITES, ROMANCE and some SPIRITUALS are included in an LP done by the North Arkansas Symphony Orchestra. Both cassettes and LPs are sold by WGSM, #NASO1001 or #CANA1001.
1985	SUITE FOR VIOLIN AND PIANO, plus works by others such as Amy Beach, performed by Mary Louise Boehm and friends in the Center for American Music Inaugural Concert, on a pantheon recording, #CA-PFN2231, cassette tapes.
1986	MINIATURES FOR FLUTE, OBOE AND PIANO, featuring Peter Christ on Crystal Records Recital Series, #S321, obtainable from Crystal Records, Inc., 2235 Willida Lane, Sedro Woolley, WA 98284. Also available on CD, #CD-321.
1986(?)	The Blues from LENOX AVENUE and HERE'S ONE recorded by Louis Kaufman, on an album called "The Kaufman Legacy," (Masters of the Bow), Vol. 2, #MB1032, available from James Lesley Creighton, Discopaedia, c/o Recordings Archive, Edward Johnson Music Library, University of Toronto, 80 Queen's Park Crescent, Toronto, Ontario M5S1A1, Canada.
1986(?)	FRENESI, GLOOMY SUNDAY and ADIOS, MARIQUITA LINDA, Still's arrangements for Artie Shaw, recorded as part of the "Cream" Series, also MARINELLA, DON'T FALL ASLEEP, CHANTEZ-LES BAS, #CD-9779, Pavilion Records, Sussex, England.
1988	The major PIANO WORKS of William Grant Still, recorded by Albert Dominguez on "William Grant Still: Piano Music," and issued by WGSM on LP or tape, #WGSM1002 or #CASM1002.

1988	The major works for STRINGS, KEYBOARD and HARP, taken from the Orion LPs done by Louis and Annette Kaufman, #WGSM1001, entitled "William Grant Still: Strings, Keyboard and Harp," by WGSM. Cassettes available as #CASM1001.
1989	Representative choral, solo vocal and piano works, including excerpts from CHRISTMAS IN THE WESTERN WORLD, on a cassette tape #WGSM1003; recorded by the WGSPAS youth group of the NANM, entitled "William Grant Still: Voices and Piano," and sold by WGSM.
1990	Chamber and vocal works, recorded by Videmus for New World Records, including the SUITE FOR VIOLIN AND PIANO, SONGS OF SEPARATION, INCANTATION AND DANCE, HERE'S ONE, SUMMERLAND, CITADEL, SONG FOR THE LONELY, OUT OF THE SILENCE, ENNANGA, and LIFT EVERY VOICE AND SING. Available on CD only, #80399-2, under the title, "Works by William Grant Still," from New World Records, 701-7th Avenue, New York, NY 10036, (212) 302-0460.
1990(?)	The AFRO-AMERICAN SYMPHONY, SAHDJI, and two arias from HIGHWAY 1, USA, are included in the "Black Composers Series" reissued by the College Music Society and sold by WGSM, #P9-19424.
1991	ENNANGA and a part of the DANZAS DE PANAMA, on #CD638, Music and Arts Programs of America, entitled "Louis Kaufman, Violin." Write to Music and Arts, P.O. Box 771, Berkeley, CA 94701.
1991	LENOX AVENUE, PASTORELA, SUMMERLAND, HERE'S ONE, CARMELA, part of the DANZAS DE PANAMA, SONG FOR THE LONELY, SONGS OF SEPARATION, SUITE FOR VIOLIN AND ORCHESTRA, an archival CD presenting old recordings by the CBS Symphony, on the Standard Hour, and Louis Kaufman, and produced by Bay Cities, #BCD1033.
1991	BLUES for violin and piano, performed by Louis Kaufman on a Bay Cities CD, #BCD1019.
1991	BELLS, SEVEN TRACERIES, BLUES, SWANEE RIVER, PRELUDES, SUMMERLAND, AFRICA, all for piano, played by Denver Oldham, on KOCH-CD3-7084-2H1, available from KOCH, 2 Tri-Harbor Court, Port Washington, NY 11050-4617.

1992   SAHDJI, as recorded by Howard Hanson and the Eastman-Rochester Orchestra, reissued on a CD by Mercury Recordings, #CD-434324-2, Polygram Recordings, Phillips Classics, 825-8th Avenue, New York, NY 10019, (212) 333-8317.

1992   THREE VISIONS and SEVEN TRACERIES, as done by Monica Gaylord on a Music and Arts CD called "Black Piano," #CD-737, available from Music and Arts, P. O. Box 771, Berkeley, CA 94701, (510) 525-4583.

1993   The AFRO-AMERICAN SYMPHONY, as done by Neemi Jarvi and the Detroit Symphony, a best-selling Chandos CD #CD9154, available from KOCH International, 2 Tri-Harbor Court, Port Washington, NY 11050-4617.

1993   LA GUIABLESSE, DANZAS DE PANAMA, QUIT DAT FOOL'NISH and SUMMERLAND, performed by the Berlin Symphony and Alexa Still on KOCH #CD3-7154-2, sold by KOCH, 2 Tri-Harbor Court, Port Washington, NY 11050-4617.

1993   THREE VISIONS, as performed by pianist Althea Waites on a recording from Cambria Recordings, #1097, called "Black Diamonds." Available on CD or cassette, from Cambria Recordings, P. O. Box 374, Lomita, CA 90717.

1994   SYMPHONY #3, FESTIVE OVERTURE, ROMANCE and excerpts from the FOLK SUITES and SPIRITUALS, as performed by the North Arkansas Symphony, on CD and cassette, Cambria Records, sold by WGSM.

1989-1994 TROUBLED ISLAND, MINETTE FONTAINE, BAYOU LEGEND, and HIGHWAY 1, USA, live performances of four operas by William Grant Still and Verna Arvey, in four beautiful tape sets, issued by Demand Performance and sold without profit for non-commercial purposes by WGSM, as #TI3001, #MF3002, #BL3003, and #H13004.

1994   HERE'S ONE for chorus, as done by the Northern Arizona University Chorale, on the CD "Songs of Innocence," #CD-NACM09. Only a few copies available from WGSM, but WGSM sells tapes of ALL THAT I AM and HERE'S ONE together.

1994   SYMPHONY IN G-MINOR, Still's "Symphony #2," as recorded by Neemi Jarvi and the Detroit Symphony, a Chandos CD #CD-CHN9226, available from KOCH International, 2 Tri-Harbor Court, Port Washington, NY 11050-4617.

1994   SUMMERLAND, QUIT DAT FOOL'NISH, PASTORELA, FOLK SUITE #1, SUITE FOR VIOLIN AND PIANO, PRELUDE, HERE'S ONE, IF YOU SHOULD GO, SONG FOR THE LONELY, BAYOU HOME, performed by Alexa Still (flute) and the New Zealand String Quartet. A KOCH CD #3-7192-2H1.

1994   SEVEN TRACERIES, performed by Richard Crosby on a CD entitled "An American Portrait." Produced by Richard Crosby, RAC-001.

1994   ROMANCE for saxophone and piano, performed by Lawrence Gwodz on a CD entitled "An American Tribute to Sigurd Rascher." A Crystal Records CD, #CD652.

1994   FROM THE DELTA, FOLK SUITE, & LITTLE RED SCHOOLHOUSE for band, as performed by the Northern Arizona University Wind Symphony, conducted by Dr. Patricia Hoy. From a CD entitled "From The Delta," #NAUWS001.

1994   MINIATURES, FOLK SUITES #2, #3, AND #4, INCANTATION & DANCE, QUIT DAT FOOL'NISH, SUMMERLAND, ROMANCE, VIGNETTES, AND GET ON BOARD, as performed by the Sierra Winds, on a Cambria CD, #CD-1084.

1995   THE AMERICAN SCENE: THE SOUTHWEST, THE FAR WEST, THE EAST, FROM THE HEARTS OF WOMEN, MOTHER & CHILD, THE CITADEL, PHANTOM CHAPEL, GOLDEN DAYS, & SERENADE, performed by the Manhattan Chamber Orchestra, Newport Classic, #NPD85596.

XII

BIBLIOGRAPHY

CREDITS

A. GENERAL BIBLIOGRAPHY FOR THE CHAPTER BY PAUL HAROLD SLATTERY

Apel, Willi. *The Harvard Dictionary of Music*. Cambridge, Massachusetts: The Harvard University Press, 1944.

Arvey, Verna. *William Grant Still: Studies of Contemporary American Composers*. New York: J. Fischer & Bro., 1939. Includes an Introduction by John Tasker Howard.

Arvey, Verna. *Choreographic Music: Music for the Dance*. New York: E.P. Dutton & Co., Inc., 1941.

ASCAP Biographical Dictionary. New York: 1948, 1952, 1966.

Austin, William W. *Music in the Twentieth Century*. New York: W. W. Norton & Co., 1966.

Bagar, Robert and Louis Biancolli. *The Concert Companion*. New York: McGraw-Hill Book Company, Inc., 1947.

Baker's Biographical Dictionary of Musicians. New York: G. Schirmer, 1940.

Baldwin, Lillian. *A Listener's Anthology of Music, Vol. II*. New York: Silver Burdett Company, 1948.

Bardolph, Richard. *The Negro Vanguard*. New York: Rinehart & Company, Inc., 1959.

Barlow, Harold and Sam Morgenstern. *A Dictionary of Musical Themes*. New York: Crown Publishers, 1948.

Bauer, Marion. *Twentieth Century Music*. New York: G. P. Putnam's Sons, 1933.

Beaumont, Cyril W. *Complete Book of Ballets*. New York: G. P. Putnam's Sons, 1938.

Bergman, Peter M. and Mort N. *The Chronological History of the Negro in America*. New York: A Mentor book, published by the New American Library, 1969.

Block, Maxine. *Current Biography*. New York: The H. W. Wilson Company, 1941.

Blom, Eric. *Grove's Dictionary of Music and Musicians, Vol. VIII*. New York: St. Martin's Press, Inc., 1962.

Blume, Frederick. *Die Musik in Geschichte und Gegenwart, Vol. II*. Kassel: Barenreiter-Verlag, 1949.

Boyden, David D. *The History and Literature of Music: 1750 to the Present*. Berkeley, California: University Extension Press, 1959.

Brawley, Benjamin. *The Negro Genius*. New York: Dodd, Mead and Company, 1937.

Bull, Storm. *Index to Biographies of Contemporary Composers*. New York: The Scarecrow Press, Inc., 1964.

Butcher, Margaret Just. *The Negro in American Culture*. New York: Alfred A. Knopf, 1956.

Carpenter, Paul S. *Music, An Art and a Business*. Norman, Oklahoma: University of Oklahoma Press, 1949.

Chase, Gilbert. *America's Music from the Pilgrims to the Present*. New York: McGraw-Hill Book Company, Inc., 1955.

Colee, Nema Weathersby. *Mississippi Music and Musicians*. Magnolia, Mississippi: Mississippi Federation of Music Clubs, 1949.

Collier, Paul. *A History of Modern Music*. Cleveland, Ohio: The World Publishing Company, 1955.

314

Cowell, Henry. *American Composers on American Music.* Palo Alto, California: Stanford University Press, 1933.

Cuney Hare, Maud. *Negro Musicians and Their Music.* Washington, D. C.: The Associated Publishers, Inc., 1936.

Deakin, Irving. *Ballet Profile.* New York: Dodge Publishing Company, 1936.

de Lerma, Dominique-René. *Black Music in Our Culture.* Ohio: Kent State University Press, 1970.

Dizionario Ricordi della musica e dei musicisti. Milano, Italia: Ricordi, 1959.

Embree, Edwin R. *American Negroes, A Handbook.* New York: The John Day Company, 1942.

Embree, Edwin R. *Thirteen Against the Odds.* New York: The Viking Press, 1944.

Engle, Donald. L. *Collier's Encyclopedia, Vol. XVIII.* New York: P. F. Collier and Son, 1955.

Ewen, David. *American Composers Today.* New York: H. W. Wilson Company, 1949

Ewen, David. *The Complete Book of 20th Century Music*, Revised edition. Englewood Cliffs, New Jersey: Prentice-Hall, Inc., 1959.

Ewen, David. *Composers of Today.* New York: The H. W. Wilson Company, 1934.

Ferguson, Blanche E. *Countee Cullen and the Negro Renaissance.* New York: Dodd, Mead and Company, 1966.

Franklin, John Hope. *From Slavery to Freedom.* New York: Random House Vintage Books, 1969.

Goss, Madeleine. *Modern Music Makers*. New York: E. P. Dutton & Co., Inc., 1952.

Grabbe, Paul. *The Story of Orchestral Music and Its Times*. New York: Grosset & Dunlap, 1942.

Guzman, Jessie Parkhurst. *1952 Negro Yearbook*. New York: William H. Wise & Company, Inc., for Tuskegee Institute.

Handy, W. C. *Father of the Blues*. New York: The Macmillan Company, 1941.

Hansen, Peter S. *An Introduction to Twentieth Century Music*. Boston: Allyn and Bason, Inc., 1961.

Howard, John Tasker. *Our Contemporary Composers*. New York: Thomas Y. Crowell Company, 1942.

Howard, John Tasker and James Lyons. *This Modern Music*. New York: Thomas Y. Crowell Company, 1942.

Hughes, Langston and Milton Meltzer. *Black Magic, A Pictorial History of the Negro in American Entertainment*. Englewood Cliffs, New Jersey: Prentice-Hall, 1967.

Hughes, Langston. *Famous Negro Music Makers*. New York: Dodd, Mead and Company, 1955.

Jacobs, Arthur. *A New Dictionary of Music*. Chicago: Aldine Publishing Company, 1962.

Kaufmann, Helen L. *From Jehovah to Jazz: Music in America from Psalmody to the Present Day*. New York: Dodd, Mead and Company, 1937.

Kaufmann, Helen L. *The Story of One Hundred Great Composers*. New York: Grosset and Dunlap, 1943.

Kaufmann, Schima. *Everybody's Music.* New York: Thomas Y. Crowell Company, 1938.

Locke, Alain. *The Negro and His Music.* Bronze booklet No. 2, Washington, D.C.: The Associates in Negro Folk Education, 1936.

Landis, Beth and Lara Hoggard. *Exploring Music, the Junior book.* New York: Holt, Rinehart & Winston, 1968.

Larson, Clotye M. *Marriage Across the Color Line.* Chicago: Johnson Publishing Company and New York: Lancer Books. Copyright 1945 and 1965.

Machlis, Joseph. *Introduction to Contemporary Music.* New York: W. W. Norton and Company, 1961.

Marrocco, W. Thomas and Arthur C. Edwards. *Music in the United States.* Dubuque, Iowa: William C. Brown, publisher, 1968.

McKinney, Howard D. *Music and Man.* New York: American Book Company, 1956.

Miller, Hugh M. *History of Music* (in the College Outline series). New York: Barnes & Noble, Inc., 1947, 1953.

Mize, J.T.H. *Who is Who in Music?* Chicago, 1951.

Mueller, John T. H. *The American Symphony Orchestra, a Social History of Musical Taste.* Indiana University Press, 1951.

Noble, Peter. *The Negro in Films.* London: British Yearbooks Ltd. 30, Cornhill, E. C. 3.

Oderigo, Nestor R. Ortiz. *Panorama de la Music Afroamericana.* Buenos Aires: Editorial Claridad, 1944.

Oderigo, Nestor R. Ortiz. *Rostros de Bronce.* Argentina: Compania General Fabril Editora, 1965.

Osgood, Henry O. *So This is Jazz*. Boston: Little, Brown and Company, 1926.

Parry, Hubert H. *The Evolution of the Art of Music*. New York: D. Appleton and Company, 1923.

Posell, Elsa Z. *American Composers*. Boston: Houghton Mifflin Company, 1963.

Quarles, Benjamin. *The Negro in the Making of America*. New York: MacMillan Company, Collier Books, 1964.

Read, Gardner. *Thesaurus of Orchestral Devices*. London: Sir Issac Pitman & Sons, Ltd., 1953.

Reis, Claire R. *American Composers, A Catalogue*. New York: The United States section of the International Society for Contemporary Music, 1932.

Reis, Claire R. *Composers in America*. New York: The Macmillan Company, 1938, revised 1947.

Reis, Claire R. *Composers, Conductors and Critics*. New York: Oxford University Press, 1955.

Richardson, Ben. *Great American Negroes*. New York: Thomas Y. Crowell Company, 1945.

Roach, Hildred. *Black American Music: Past and Present*. Boston: Crescendo Publishing Company, 1973.

Rosenfeld, Paul. *An Hour With American Music*. Philadelphia: J. B. Lippincott Company, 1929.

Ross, David J., Jr. *Great Negroes Past and Present*. Chicago: Afro-Am Publishing Company, Inc., 1963.

Rossi, Nick and Robert Choate. *Music of Our Time*. Boston: Crescendo Publishing Company, 1969.

318

Rugg, Harold. *An Introduction to Problems of American Culture.* Boston: Ginn and Company, 1931.

Sandved, Kjell Bloch. *The World of Music.* London: The Waverly Book Co., Ltd., 1965. Norwegian version: *Musikkens Verden.* Oslo: 1951. Also published by Abradale Press in New York in extended form, as a four-volume illustrated encyclopedia.

Salazar, Adolpho. *Music in Our Time.* New York: W. W. Norton Company, 1946.

Sargeant, Winthrop. *Jazz Hot and Hybrid.* New York: Arrow Editions, 1938.

Scholes, Percy A. *The Oxford Companion to Music.* London: Oxford University Press, 1938.

Schuller, Gunther. *Early Jazz: Its Roots and Musical Development.* New York: Oxford University Press, 1968.

Southern, Eileen. *The Music of Black Americans: A History.* New York: W. W. Norton and Company, Inc., 1971.

Southern, Eileen. *Readings in Black American Music.* New York: W. W. Norton and Company, Inc., 1971.

Spaeth, Sigmund. *A Guide to Great Orchestral Music.* New York: Random House, Modern Library, 1943.

Spaeth, Sigmund. *A History of Popular Music in America.* New York: Random House Press, 1948.

Stearns, Marshall. *The Story of Jazz.* New York: The Oxford University Press, 1956.

Thompson, Oscar. *The International Cyclopedia of Music and Musicians.* New York: Dodd, Mead and Company, 1952.

Ulrich, Homer and Paul A. Pisk. *A History of Music and Musical Style*. New York: Harcourt, Brace and World, Inc., 1963.

Waters, Ethel. *His Eye Is On the Sparrow*. New York: Doubleday, 1951.

Watson, Jack M. and Corinne. *A Concise Dictionary of Music*. New York: Dodd, Mead and Company, 1965.

Watters, Lorrain and Louis G. Wersen, William C. Hartshorn, L. Eileen McMillan, Alice Gallup, Frederick Beckman. *The Magic of Music: Book 6*. Boston, Massachusetts: Ginn and Company, 1968.

Woodson, Carter G. and Charles H. Wesley. *The Story of the Negro Retold*. Washington, D. C.: Associated Publishers, 1935.

Who's Who in America. All editions since 1942. Chicago: The A. M. Marquis Company.

Unpublished Material

Simpson, Ralph Ricardo. *William Grant Still--The Man and His Music*. Ph. D. dissertation, Michigan State University, 1964.

Slattery, Paul Harold. *A Comparative Study of the First and Fourth Symphonies of William Grant Still*. Masters' Thesis, San Jose College, 1969.

Still, Judith Anne. *A Voice High-Sounding*. A collection of essays dealing the life and work of William Grant Still, 1980's.

Thompson, Leon Everette. *The Music of William Grant Still*. Ph. D. dissertation, University of Southern California, 1966.

Books Consulted For Definitions Only

Cook, Deryck. *The Language of Music*. London: Oxford University Press, 1959.

320

Dallin, Leon. *Techniques of Twentieth Century Composition*. Dubuque, Iowa: William C. Brown Company, 1957.

Forte, Allen. *Contemporary Tone Structures*. New York: Bureau of Publications, Teachers' College, Columbia University, 1955.

Jones, George Thaddeus. *Music Composition*. Evanston, Illinois: Summy-Birchard Company, 1963.

Meyer, Leonard B. *Emotion and Meaning in Music*. Chicago: The University of Chicago Press, 1956.

Ratner, Leonard G. *Music: The Listener's Art*. San Francisco: McGraw-Hill Book Company, 1966.

Sessions, Roger. *The Musical Experience of Composer, Performer, Listener*. New York: Atheneum Press, 1965.

B. BY WILLIAM GRANT STILL

"An Afro-American Composer's Point Of View," *American Composers on American Music*, edited by Henry Cowell, 1933.

"The Art of Musical Creation," *The Mystic Light* (Rosicrucian Magazine), July 1936.

"The American Composer," *The Baton*, March 1937.

"Are Negro Composers Handicapped?" *The Baton*, November 1937.

"For Finer Negro Music," *Opportunity*, May 1939.

"A Negro Symphony Orchestra," *Opportunity*, September 1939.

"A Recorded Conversation," *Co-Art Turntable*. Beverly Hills, CA, August 1942.

"The Negro And His Music," *War Worker*. Los Angeles, CA, October, 1943. This was the text of a speech delivered at UCLA for a seminar dealing with Music and the War. It was also printed in the book, *Writers' Congress*, published by the University of California and the Hollywood Writers' Mobilization.

"The Men Behind American Music," *The Crisis*, January 1944.

"How Do We Stand In Hollywood?" *Opportunity*, Spring 1945.

"Politics In Music," *Opera, Concert and Symphony*, August 1947.

"American Music and the Well-Timed Sneer," *Opera, Concert and Symphony*, May 1948.

"A Symphony of Dark Voices," *Opera, Concert and Symphony*, May 1947.

"Can Music Make A Career?" *Negro Digest*, December 1948.

"Music, A Vital Factor in America's Racial Problems," *Australian Musical News*, November 1, 1948. This was reprinted in the *Oberlin Alumni Magazine*, March 1950.

"The Composer Needs Determination and Faith," *Etude*, January 1949.

"The Structure of Music," *Etude*, March 1950.

"La Musica de Mi Raza," *Musica,* Bogota, Columbia. *Vol. I.*

"Fifty Years of Progress in Music," *Pittsburgh Courier*, November 11, 1950. This was reprinted in Denmark as "Negrene i Amerikansk Musik," *Dansk Musiktidsskrift.* Copenhagen, 1951.

"Toward A Broader American Culture," Convention address to the American Symphony Orchestra League. Printed in the *American Symphony Orchestra League Newsletter* Vol. 6, No. 1; reprinted in the *Southwestern Composers' Journal* 1955-56, Vol. 1, No. 2.

"The History And Future Of Black American Music Studies: Practices And Potentials," Condensed from the speech delivered at Indiana University's Seminar on Black Music, June 21, 1969. Printed in the *Music Bulletin of Lincoln University*, PA for August 4, 1969, Vol. II, No. 4.

"The Negro Musician In America," *Music Educators' Journal*, January 1970.

"A Composer's Viewpoint," chapter by William Grant Still in *Black Music In Our Culture* by Dominique-René de Lerma. Ohio: Kent State University Press, 1970.

C. BY WILLIAM GRANT STILL (In Collaboration With Verna Arvey)

"Negro Music In The Americas," *Revue Internationale de Musique*, Bruxelles: May-June 1938.

"Does Interracial Marriage Succeed?" *The Negro Digest*, April 1945.

"The King Is Dead--Long Live The King!" New York Stadium Concerts Review, June 25, 1945.

"Serious Music: New Field For The Negro," *Variety*, January 1, 1955.

"Modern Composers Have Lost Their Audience: Why?" *Australian Musical News*, July 1956. Reprinted in the *Music Journal 1966 Annual* under the title, "The Lost Audience For New Music."

"Our American Musical Resources," *Showcase* (Music Clubs Magazine), Fall 1961.

"My Arkansas Boyhood," *Arkansas Historical Quarterly*, Autumn 1967.

"Answer To A Questionnaire," *Arts and Society*, published by University Extension: University of Wisconsin, 1968. Issue dedicated to the Arts in the Black Revolution.

D. ABOUT WILLIAM GRANT STILL

Arvey, Verna. "The Ballets of William Grant Still," *The New Challenge: A Literary Quarterly*, Fall 1937. This was later included in the book, *Choreographic Music*, published by Dutton in 1941.

William Grant Still photographs, *Flash!*, November 15, 1938.

Arvey, Verna. "Is There A Place For Negroes In Classical Music?" *Upbeat*, January 1939.

Arvey, Verna. "William Grant Still: Creative Aspects Of His Work," *Dillard University Arts Quarterly*, January-March 1938.

Arvey, Verna. "Studies In Contemporary American Music: William Grant Still." New York: J. Fischer & Bro., 1939.

Arvey, Verna. "William Grant Still, Creator Of Indigenous American Music," *Chesterian* (London), May-June 1939.

Arvey, Verna. "William Grant Still, American Composer," *Co-Art Turntable* (Beverly Hills), February 1942.

Jones, Isabel Morse. "Meet The Composer: William Grant Still," by Isabel Morse Jones, *Musical America*, December 25, 1944. This was reprinted in *The Negro Digest*, May 1945, under the title of "From Tin Pan Alley To Opera."

Cook, J. Douglas. "Visits To The Homes Of Famous Composers, No. 3: William Grant Still," *Opera, Concert, and Symphony*, November 1946.

Arvey, Verna. "Still Opera Points The Way," *Music Forum and Digest*, August 1949.

Matthews, Miriam. "Phylon Profile XXIII: William Grant Still, Composer," *Phylon*, Georgia: Atlanta University, Second Quarter 1951.

Kennan, Clara B. "Native Of Little Rock Is Widely Celebrated Negro Composer," *Arkansas Gazette*, August 5, 1951.

Fleming, John. "Composer Proves There's No Color Line In Music World," *Arkansas Gazette*, August 9, 1953.

"Classified Chronological Catalogue Of Works By The United States Composer, William Grant Still," *Boletin Interamericano de Musica*, November 1959, Washington, D.C.; Pan American Union: This was later reprinted in Volume 5 of *Compositores de America*, also published by the Pan American Union.

Arvey, Verna. "With His Roots In The Soil," *International Musician*, July 1963.

Seidenbaum, Art. "Harmony Aim Of Negro Composer," *Los Angeles Times*, September 7, 1963.

Greene, Patterson. "Bridging A Musical Gap," *Los Angeles Herald-Examiner*, September 8, 1963.

Lippey, Joyce and Walden E. Muns. "William Grant Still," *Music Journal*, November 1963.

Robinson, Louie. "38 Years Of Serious Music," *Ebony Magazine*, February 1964.

Hudgins, Mary D. "An Outstanding Arkansas Composer, William Grant Still," *Arkansas Historical Quarterly*, Winter 1965.

Nelson, Boris. "William Grant Still: 50 Years Of Music," *Toledo* (Ohio) *Blade*, May 2, 1965.

Doernberg, Jerry. "Musical Premiere Due At E. L. A.," San Gabriel Valley edition of the *Los Angeles Times*, May 13, 1965.

Hudgins, Mary D. "William Grant Still, The Dean Of Negro Composers," *Arkansas Gazette*, January 30, 1966.

Monson, Karen. "Still Has Lived Through Musical Changes," *Los Angeles Herald-Examiner*, January 24, 1970.

Butler, Henry. "Still Is Grateful For Tin Pan Alley Days," *Indianapolis News*, March 6, 1970.

Rossi, Nick and Robert A. Choate. *Music Of Our Time*: A Chapter, Crescendo Publishing Company, 1969.

Ewen, David. *Composers Since 1900*, H. W. Wilson Company, 1969.

ABOUT THE CONTRIBUTORS

VERNA ARVEY (Mrs. William Grant Still)

Pianist, journalist, largely for publications devoted to music and the dance. Author of the book, *Choreographic Music*, published in the early forties by Dutton. Also librettist for most of William Grant Still's operas and later vocal works. Born February 16, 1910 in Los Angeles, California, and died November 22, 1987.

DONALD DORR

As Artistic Director of Opera/South (Jackson, Mississippi) and Baton Rouge Opera, Donald Dorr produced three Still operas--two of them, *A Bayou Legend* and *Minette Fontaine*, world premieres. In 1987 his article, "Chosen Image: The Afro-American Vision in the Operas of William Grant Still," originally appearing in *Opera Quarterly*, won an ASCAP-Deems Taylor award.

DR. ROBERT BARTLETT HAAS

Editor of the first edition of this volume and Director of the Department of Arts and Humanities, University Extension, UCLA, Dr. Haas has been active in several phases of the arts in California. He has numerous and unusual publications--translations from the German on Kurt Schwitters, and books and articles about Psychodrama, pioneer California photographers, textiles and the visual arts. His book, *A Primer for the Gradual Understanding of Gertrude Stein*, has been published by the Black Sparrow Press. His first acquaintance with the music of William Grant Still was made during his high school years in Stockton, California--an interest which he has maintained until today. After his retirement from his position at UCLA, Dr. Haas went to live in Europe and became the author of *Muybridge Man in Motion*, the story of the invention of motion pictures, published by the UCLA Press.

DR. FREDERICK D. HALL

Composer, instrumentalist, conductor, music educator, and one of the most distinguished figures in Afro-American music. Born December 14, 1898 in Atlanta, Georgia and educated in American universities as well as in the Royal College of Music in London, he was director of music in several colleges in the South, especially Dillard University in New Orleans. He was a member of the American Guild of Organists and a fellow of the Royal Anthropological Institution in recognition of his studies of the African origins of some American Negro music. He died early in 1983.

DR. HOWARD HANSON

Dean of American composers, also conductor and leading music educator in the United States. First and still strongest sponsor of serious American music through his now-famous American Composers' Concerts at the Eastman School of Music, which he directed until his retirement. Born October 28, 1896 in Wahoo, Nebraska, died in 1981.

CELESTE ANNE HEADLEE

The fourth grandchild of William Grant Still and Verna Arvey, she was born on December 30, 1969. The only grandchild to become a musician, she learned to play the oboe and saxophone, and studied voice and theater at Idyllwild Academy of the Arts and at Northern Arizona University, where she graduated with honors. She has held lead female roles in productions such as *Man of La Mancha* and *Nunsense* and has been praised for her charisma and talent.

LISA HEADLEE-HUFFMAN

Born on June 18, 1964 as the oldest granddaughter of William Grant Still and Verna Arvey. She received a Bachelor of Arts degree in Communications from the University of the Pacific, graduating Magna Cum Laude, and recently worked as Training Specialist for Pacific

Mutual Life Insurance Company in Newport Beach, California. She is the mother of the composers' two great-grandchildren and wife of Ronald Huffman, who also assisted with preparation of this manuscript.

DR. ANNETTE KAUFMAN

The pianist-wife of Louis Kaufman has been his accompanist in concerts in North America, South America and Europe, and his associate in research. Her teachers were James Friskin in New York City and Madame Jeanne Blancard, assistant to Alfred Cortot, at the Ecole Normale in Paris, France. She was awarded an Honorary Doctorate of Music on May 27, 1985 at Oberlin College. Since her husband's death, she is busy preparing his memoirs for publication.

DR. LOUIS KAUFMAN

The *New York Times* has called him a "violinists' violinist and a musicians' musician." He has appeared as soloist with many of the major symphony orchestras and has received the Naumburg Award and the Loeb Prize in New York City for performances, the "Grand Prix du Disque" in France for his recording of Vivaldi's "Four Seasons" concerti and a Citation from the Los Angeles Chapter of the National Association of American Composers and Conductors for his recordings and performances of works by Samuel Barber, Robert Russell Bennett, Aaron Copland, Everett Helm, Quincy Porter, Walter Piston, Robert McBride, and William Grant Still. His recordings range from the first 12 concertos written by Guiseppe Torelli and 36 concerti of Antonio Vivaldi to contemporary works by Toch, Milhaud, Copland, Bennett, and Still. He was awarded an Honorary Doctorate of Music on May 27, 1985 at Oberlin College. He died in February of 1994.

DR. JEAN MATTHEW

Jean Matthew holds three doctorates, one at Florida State University (1972), and she has taught at George Washington University, Norfolk State University, and at Northern Arizona University. As a clinical

329

psychologist, she has served as Acting Deputy Warden at Arizona State Prison, in Winslow, Arizona. At present, she teaches at Coconino Community College, in Flagstaff, Arizona. Her many publications include articles and books on the use of music as a communication vehicle, workbooks such as *Thinking And Feeling: A Tool For Change* (Virginia State Department of Corrections), and *You Are The Future*, a multi-media presentation for Columbia University and West Point. Her work in musicology and psychology has been recognized by a "Personalities of the South" award, a "Noteworthy Americans" award, and a "Sword of Honor" award from Sigma Alpha Iota.

MIRIAM MATTHEWS

California's first Afro-American librarian with professional training, Miriam Matthews holds degrees from the University of California at Berkeley and the University of Chicago. Her distinguished career as a librarian with the Los Angeles Public Library from 1927 to 1960 included four posts as Branch Librarian and one as Regional Librarian supervising twelve branch libraries. While she was an active member of the American Library Association and the California Library Association she gave speeches at a number of conventions, served a four-year term as councilor of the national body and as chairperson of the California Intellectual Freedom Committee. Among her current commitments are membership on the Los Angeles City Historical Society Board of Directors, NAACP Legal Defense and Educational Fund Executive Committee, El Pueblo Park Association Board of Trustees, Friends of the Los Angeles City Archives Board, Community Health Association Executive Board, Historian for the Dunbar Museum and Sojourner Truth Industrial Club. Mayor Tom Bradley presented her with a citation in 1981 for her contributions to the City of Los Angeles, especially during the City's Bicentennial celebration.

CHARLES WHITE MC GEHEE

Direct descendant of slave-owners in Mississippi, whose plantation was near the birthplace of William Grant Still, Sr., Reverend McGehee was a prolific writer, orator, and civil rights activist. Born 1914 in Summit,

Mississippi, he received his theological education at Tufts University Theological School and Harvard Divinity School. He founded the Unitarian Universalist Church in Jacksonville, Florida, was President of the Northeast Florida Human Relations Council, and served on the boards of the Jacksonville NAACP and Tree Hill Nature Center. After his retirement, he became a columnist and newspaper editor in Mentone, Alabama, where he died in June 1993. His widow, Jean, wrote to Judith Anne Still after his death, "He was always proud of his friendship with your father--he cherished it (October 25, 1993)."

DR. CAROLYN L. QUIN

Currently serves as the Chair of the Department of Music at Winthrop University in Rock Hill, South Carolina. She was formerly an Associate Professor of Music and Chair of the Division of Liberal Studies at Lane College in Jackson, Tennessee, and the Executive Director of the Jackson (TN) Symphony Orchestra. Dr. Quin is a harpsichordist and frequent performer of chamber music. She has served as co-chair of the Chamber Music Panel and as a member of the Overview Panel for the National Endowment for the Arts. As an active member of the CMS Southern Chapter, she serves as board member for musicology. Dr. Quin received her doctorate at the University of Kentucky with a dissertation on Fanny Mendelssohn Hensel. An active researcher and presenter of papers on Afro-American music for the last ten years, Dr. Quin taught a graduate course in "The Music of Black Americans" at the University of Kentucky in 1992.

ANNE KEY SIMPSON

Anne Simpson, musicologist and pianist, was Staff Accompanist for the School of Music at the University of Southwestern Louisiana in Lafayette, Louisiana from 1965-1986. She is the author of approximately thirty published articles and reviews in music journals and newspapers, and of biographies on Harry T. Burleigh, Arthur Farwell, Ernest J. Gaines, and Nathaniel Dett. Simpson holds degrees in piano performance and musicology from Texas Women's University, and has been an adjucator for the National Guild of Piano Teachers.

PAUL H. SLATTERY

Instrumental music instructor in the public schools of Jackson and of Cupertino, California. He was born in San Francisco, California on April 5, 1927 and attended St. Anselm's Tamalpais High School, and College of Marin. He received his A.B. and B.M. from the College of the Pacific (now University of the Pacific) and his M.A. from San Jose State College in 1969. A portion of his Master's Thesis is used in this publication. His present activities include choir directing and community service.

JUDITH ANNE STILL

After becoming a member of Phi Beta Kappa and graduating with high honors from the University of Southern California, Judith Anne Still received her M.A. degree and secondary teaching credentials from California State University at Fullerton. She then pursued varied careers as an instructor of college English, correspondent for a noted actress of the stage and screen, founder of the Larry Headlee Scholarship Fund (named for her deceased geologist husband who pioneered in mini-submarine operations), and freelance writer. Her many published works have received several awards, including a Washington Educational Press Award, an American Legion Award, and a Freedoms Foundation Award. One of her early articles was read into the Congressional Record. She is also the mother of four now-grown children and the manager of William Grant Still Music.

DR. WILLIAM GRANT STILL

Often called the Dean of American Negro composers, he was born May 11, 1895 in Woodville, Mississippi. His career has spanned more than half a century in serious and commercial American music. Self-taught in orchestration, he was an innovator in that field for radio, and was a pioneer in elevating the Negro musical idiom to symphonic status. In the area of human relations he was also outstanding, becoming the first Negro to conduct a white radio orchestra in New York, first to write a symphony which was performed, first to have an opera produced by a major opera company in the United States, first to conduct a major symphony

332

orchestra in the United States (1936) and first to conduct a major symphony orchestra in the Deep South (1955). His compositions, in many different media, place him among the top composers of serious music in America. He died on December 3, 1978.

DR. GRANT DELBERT VENERABLE II

This Southern California-born scientist completed his undergraduate training at UCLA and his Ph.D. degree in physical chemistry at the University of Chicago. Cited in *Who's Who in the West*, he is recognized in the international scientific community from California to the Soviet Union for his oil paintings on chemical structure. He has served on chemistry, education, and humanities faculties of the California Polytechnic State University, San Luis Obispo and at the University of California, Santa Cruz. His National Endowment for the Humanities Faculty Fellowship at Michigan State University led eventually to a second career in the Silicon Valley Industry. He is also an accomplished musician, most recently as organist-in-residence at First Congregational Church of Sonoma, California. He is a member of the American Chemical Society, serves on the Board of the California Alliance for Arts Education, and now directs the Department of Afro-American Studies at San Francisco State University.

333

ACKNOWLEDGMENTS

For the issuance of this 100th anniversary edition, we lovingly and gratefully acknowledge the untiring encouragement of Joan Palevsky, our friend and scholarly advisor.

We gratefully thank the following publishers for permission to reprint their articles: *An Afro-American Composer's Viewpoint*, American Composers on American Music: Stanford University Press: 1933. *Still Opera Points The Way*, Music Forum and Digest: August 1949. *Phylon Profile, XXIII: William Grant Still--Composer*, XII, June 1951. *Modern Composers Have Lost Their Audience: Why?*, Australian Musical News: July 1956. *Horizons Unlimited*, A lecture delivered at UCLA: November 21, 1957. *With His Roots In The Soil*, The International Musician: July 1963. *My Arkansas Boyhood*, The Arkansas Historical Quarterly: Autumn 1967. *Memo For Musicologists*, Music Journal: November, 1969. *A Composer's Viewpoint*, From the Dominique-Rene deLerma book, "Black Music in our Culture": Ohio, Kent State University Press: 1970. Text of a speech delivered at the 1969 Indiana University Seminar on Black Music. *Chosen Image: The Afro-American Vision in the Operas of William Grant Still*, The Opera Quarterly, 4, Summer 1986.

Musical Examples: Engraved by Kathleen Mayne.

Typing of the manuscript: Lisa Headlee-Huffman, Ronald Huffman, and Patricia Bedimol. Mary Reichling assisted Anne Simpson in proofing her contribution.

Photographs: From the collection of Mr. & Mrs. William Grant Still.

Cover Artist: Ira Liss.

XIII

INDEX

INDEX

344

347

349

351

University of California at Los Angeles, 208, 211, 327, 333
University of Chicago, 206, 330, 333
University of Miami, 19, 47, 157, 230, Illus. section
University of Miami Symphony Orchestra, 19, 256, 258
University of Southern California, 6, 197, 199, 332
University of the Pacific, 328, 332
Unknown Brahms, The, 24
Up There, 294
U. S. A., 1946, 283
Uusi Suomi, 195

V

Valley of Echoes from *From the Journal*, 233
Van Doren, Mark, 94
Van Grove, Isaac, 151
Van Hoesen, Karl, 225
Van Vechten, Carl, 25, 30, 41, 45, Illus. section
Varèse, Edgar, 5, 14, 16, 54-55, 73-74, 81, 174, 181, 193, 231-232, 234
Varèse, Louise, 159
Venerable, Grant Delbert, II, 205-209, 207, 333
Ven, Niño Divino from *Christmas in the Western World*, 269
Verdi, Giuseppe, 56, 147
Victory Tide, 152, 194, 261, 298
Vignettes, 19, 276
Vivaldi, Antonio, 329
Vodery, Will, 22, 69

Voice of America, The, 30, 158
Voice of the Lord, The, 44, 291
Volkmann, Rudy, 273
Von Jones, Louia, 69
Voorhees, Don, 5, 193, 228

W

Wade in the Water from *Little Folk Suites #1-5 from the Western Hemisphere*, 169, 273
Wagenaar, Bernard, 198
Wagner, Richard, 48, 56, 86, 153 156, 159-160
Wailing Dawn from *Seven Traceries*, 89, 176, 282
Wailing Woman, v, 44, 263
Waldo, Elisabeth, 164, 247
Waldo Latin-American String Quartette, 247
Waltz from *The Prince and the Mermaid*, 230
Warm Gravy, 97
Warnow, Mark, 292
Warrior, The, 152
Washington, Martha, 207
Watkins, Clifford, Dr., 228
Weber, Carl Maria von, 159-160
Webster, Noah, 61
Weede, Robert, 26, 28, 155
Weiskopf, Herbert, 251
Were You There?, 293
Werlein, Philip, 95
We Sang Our Songs, 298-299
West Point, 6, 271, 330
Westchester String Symphony, 252, 257
Western Hemisphere, See *Symphony #5*

DATE DUE

JUN 18 '01 F			
MAR 07 2001			
GAYLORD			PRINTED IN U.S.A.